Introducing
American Folk Music

KIP LORNELL
Smithsonian Institution

WCB Brown &
Benchmark
P U B L I S H E R S

Madison, Wisconsin • Indianapolis, Indiana
Melbourne, Australia • Oxford, England

Book Team

Publisher *Rosemary Bradley*
Acquisitions Editor *Chris Freitag*
Senior Developmental Editor *Deborah Daniel Reinbold*
Production Coordinator *Kay Driscoll*
Associate Marketing Manager *Kirk Moen*
Copywriter *Jennifer Smith*

Brown & Benchmark
PUBLISHERS

President and Chief Executive Officer *Thomas E. Doran*
Vice President of Production and Business Development *Vickie Putman*
Vice President of Sales and Marketing *Bob McLaughlin*
Director of Marketing *John Finn*

Times Mirror
Higher Education Group

Chairman and Chief Executive Officer *G. Franklin Lewis*
Executive Vice President and Chief Operations Officer *James H. Higby*
President of Manufacturing and Senior Vice President *Roger Meyer*
Senior Vice President and Chief Financial Officer *Robert Chesterman*

Cover design by Kay D. Fulton

Cover photo by permission of Michael Ochs Archives/Venice, CA

A Times Mirror Company

Library of Congress Catalog Card Number: 91–77817

ISBN 0–697–13383–4

Printed in the United States of America by Wm. C. Brown Communications, Inc.,
2460 Kerper Boulevard, Dubuque, IA 52001

10 9 8 7 6 5 4 3 2

Contents

9

The Folk Revivals 187

10

*The Folk Roots of
ContemporaryPopular
Music 219*

11

*Fieldwork in Postmodern
America 235*

Musical Selections

Preface and Acknowledgments

This book is for the student possessing a lively interest in our distinctly American vernacular culture and music. For the instructor, this text is designed in such a way that all the topics can be covered in one term and still allow instructors to focus on or go into greater detail on a topic of particular interest to themselves or the students. Specifically, *Introducing American Folk Music* examines folk and closely related grass roots music—such as gospel, Western swing, and folk rock—that developed in the United States. Its bias towards the evolution of the folk music of English-speaking people from the early nineteenth century to the present is firm but balanced by its inclusion of ''ethnic'' traditions as well as Native American and folk based music. The book covers a wide variety of topics from the unique Cajun music of Louisiana and Hawaiian hulas to the more familiar blues and gospel music. Jazz and rock, two important forms of twentieth-century American vernacular music that drew a large portion of their original strength and inspiration from folk music, are mentioned throughout the text, but they largely remain outside of our scope.

American folk music, however, retains its close ties to popular trends. Rock, as well as other forms of popular music, often display direct links to this heritage. Go-Go (a type of urban black popular music pioneered in Washington, D.C., in the early 1980s) is performed in clubs patronized almost exclusively by younger African Americans. One of the top Go-Go bands, Experience Unlimited, always begins its show with a ''call and response'' (antiphony) interlude between the band members and audience. Antiphony has graced black American music since slavery, and its contemporary use recalls prayer and church services, railroad gandy dancers (track layers), and blues singers. Without these earlier folk expressions, Go-Go would not exist.

Bill Monroe at a bluegrass festival circa 1967.
Ralph Rinzler.

Folk based styles, some of which have crossed into popular culture, form the entire book. The folk roots of contemporary African American popular music are explored in the final chapter.

The influence of traditional music moves through space as well as over time. In the first two decades of the twentieth century, black migrants carried their love of blues and gospel northward during the ''Great Migration,'' as they fled from both Southern racism and its impoverishing working conditions. The interest in Western swing remains quite strong in California despite its Texas roots. This is due to the westward movement of ''Dust Bowl'' residents who looked towards its fertile valleys during the 1930s and 1940s. A strong affinity for bluegrass developed among blue- and white-collar workers in Ohio and Michigan who abandoned the South for industrial jobs in the 1940s and 1950s. Be it food, colloquial expressions, or music, we Americans always carry our folk culture with us.

My own approach to this subject is interdisciplinary, drawing from the ideas of scholars in ethnomusicology, cultural geography, anthropology, history, and folklore. Although the emphasis of this book is on our musical and historical culture, it also defines several basic musical concepts in order to discuss some fundamental aspects of the music itself. Performances by a variety of musicians drawn from the extensive Smithsonian/Folkways catalogue constitute the audio package that accompanies ***Introducing American Folk Music.*** The inquisitive reader may wish to delve further into the subject by exploring the resources described in the annotated bibliography (Books), discography (Audio), and visual tools (Videos) that close each chapter.

This book surveys the entire field, supplementing the textbook written by Jean Ferris, *America's Musical Landscape,* as well as the sweeping scholarly surveys by Gilbert Chase, *America's Music,* and Daniel Kingman, *American Music: A Panorama.* Its chapters are divided into discrete sections about blues, ballads, cowboy songs, spirituals, and so forth. *Introducing American Folk Music* builds upon the important writings of Bruce Bastin, Harlan Daniels, Arthur Kyle Davis, Serge Denisoff, David Evans, Robert Winslow Gordon, Archie Green, Alan and John Lomax, Bill Malone, Paul Oliver, Neil Rosenberg, Tony Russell, Dorothy Scarborough, Dick Spottswood, Charles K. Wolfe, and dozens of other scholars and enthusiasts. These individuals scoured the juke joints, churches, prisons, bunkhouses, mountains, and cities across the United States in order to write about and record America's ballads, cowboy tunes, bluegrass, blues, and work songs. To this corpus I add my own idiosyncratic vision, a perspective based on my research, field recording, and writing about black folk music, gospel singing, and hillbilly artists, which began in 1969.

I would like to thank the following people and institutions for their help in making this book possible. First of all, I wish to acknowledge the assistance of the Smithsonian Institution, which awarded me the postdoctoral fellowship during which much of this book was written. Tony Seeger, curator of the Folkways Collection of the Smithsonian Institution, served as my advisor during this period. Nick Spitzer, John Hasse, Ralph Rinzler, and Martin Williams of the Smithsonian Institution encouraged this project from its outset and helped bring it to fruition. Also the staff of the Blue Ridge Institute of Ferrum College, most notably Vaughan Webb and Roddy Moore, whose encouragement and wise counsel is always appreciated. Special thanks to Jim Griffith of the Southwest Folklore Center of the University of Arizona, Phil Martin of the Wisconsin Folk Museum for his many helpful suggestions in the Scandinavian American section, and Bill Vaughan of George Mason University, each of whom helped with maps or photographs. Others who contributed in a variety of ways are Bruce Bastin, Andy Cahan, Sam Charters, Joe Hickerson, Kim Gandy, Peter B. Lowry, Ted Mealor, Mike Seeger, Jared Snyder, Nick Spitzer, Mark Tucker, and Charles K. Wolfe. I would like to thank the following people for their expertise in reviewing the manuscript: Alan A. Luhring (University of Colorado—Boulder), Ron Pen (University of Kentucky), and Dick Weissman (University of Colorado—Denver).

I need to especially acknowledge the encouragement of five outstanding mentors—David Evans (Memphis State University), Frank Keetz (Bethlehem Central Senior High School), Wallace and Betty Jane Lornell (a.k.a. Ace and Beagle), and Daniel Patterson (University of North Carolina at Chapel Hill). They motivated me to follow my muse by exploring American vernacular musical history and to challenge conventional educational wisdom. I would not have even attempted to write this book were it not for all of the important American musicians who touched me over the years—David Byrne, John

Coltrane, Jimi Hendrix, Robert Johnson, Thelonious Monk, Bill Monroe, Charlie Poole, Cole Porter, Sonny Rollins, Sonny Boy Williamson, and many others. Their music has been a constant source of inspiration. My best wishes and thanks also to the entire Brown and Benchmark team for their patience and understanding from beginning to end.

Eleanor Roosevelt at the 1933 Whitetop (Virginia) Folk Festival. *Southern Historical collection, CB #3926, Wilson Library, University of NC–Chapel Hill, Chapel Hill, NC 27599–3926.*

Introduction to Early Folk Music: Southern and Black

Distinctly American music began to emerge almost as soon as the first Europeans and Africans arrived in the New World. Both the European settlers and African slaves brought instruments and musical traditions with them. The Europeans contributed fiddles and pianos, while Africans brought the knowledge of making and performing upon banjolike instruments with them. By the nineteenth century, these three instruments were played by black and white Americans, but often in very different ways. White settlers brought their ballads, transplanted Africans contributed the concept of call and response. While the races may have remained legally separate, there was no way to legislate the strict segregation of musical ideas and instruments. Contemporary American folk music draws from this common background.

The states east of the Mississippi River dominated our country into the early part of the nineteenth century. Outside of New England, the Middle Atlantic states became the first extensively settled section of the United States. Scotch, Irish, and German pioneers settled in the mountains and valleys of the Blue Ridge and Appalachians, far from the port cities and slowly growing cities on the Piedmont. Face-to-face communication among these settlers, particularly those who chose the hills and mountains, was the norm. Many people remained illiterate or obtained little formal education. Travel along the rutted, unpaved roads proved difficult at best and impossible during the worst of times; physical, and sometimes spiritual, isolation was the norm. As the United States emerged from the shadow of British domination, new hybrids began to emerge. The seeds of syncretization had been planted, and the beginnings of Anglo-American folk music could be heard in the first few decades of the nineteenth century.

Outside of the major cities, this was a rural, insular world populated by neighbors and family that one knew almost always from birth until death. Paved roads were unknown, telephones didn't exist, and electricity came to many with "rural electrification" programs of the New Deal 1930s. Musical activity was an important means of entertainment at home, at homes of neighbors, and in church. The fact of isolation combined with slowly developing American idioms insured that we would be blessed with regional differences in folk music. Not only did we have French-speaking citizens in Louisiana and northern New England in 1800, the physical separation of Maine lumbermen from Kentucky River roustabouts led to unique regional differences. The tripart levelers of musical regionalism (phonograph records, radios, and television) lay in the future, poised to forever alter our modern world.

The folk music of English-speaking white Americans is a complex, complicated topic involving a variety of vocal and instrumental traditions. The eighteenth and early nineteenth-century musical styles largely followed the lead of their counterparts from the British Isles, in part because of the ongoing domination by England of the United States. Churchgoers sang Wesley's hymns, ballads of British origin entertained folks at home, and the old-world fiddle tunes provided dance music on Saturday night.

Our knowledge of early folk music is almost entirely derived from a crazy quilt of primary and secondary printed sources: newspaper and magazine articles, diaries, travel accounts, and fiction. Fascinated by slavery and black people, literate people often wrote of everyday black life. Until the 1820s, some writers occasionally noted aspects of African survivals such as drumming, singing, and dancing. However, most writers seemed more interested in the contemporary black folk music that surrounded them. Visual evidence, especially paintings of blacks performing music, also suggests the widespread development of black American music. Unfortunately, few blacks wrote accounts of their own music until after the Civil War, a true loss to American music history but not a surprising one given the trying conditions under which slaves lived.

Early African American folk music resulted from the synthesis of African music, which often arrived by way of the Caribbean Basin, and European music, creating a richly unique blend. Our interest is in the traditional music that developed out of this cultural clash. Because the cruel legacy of slavery did not include literacy or formal musical education for most blacks, early African American styles were handed down in a traditional manner. The majority of the early slaves came to the United States from West Africa, thousands of square miles ranging from beautiful beaches to large expanses of flat, hot savannahs. Seventeenth-century West Africa was a huge multi-cultural region ruled by a loose mixture of tribes and clans.

Its musics were just as diverse, though religious and public ceremonies, rites of passage, and other types of functions most often called for music-making. Because of these inherent links between music and everyday life, the contemporary West African musics were difficult to separate from the societies themselves. Most private and public rituals called for music as part of the event, hence much of this music was functional. From formal court ceremonies to the songs chanted by pole-wielding boatmen, music was an integral part of these societies.

Drums of varying sizes and shapes were the primary instruments of West Africans. Often played in ensembles of two or more, drummers sometimes used the palm of their hands or sticks to beat out the complex rhythms. Fingertips created yet more complicated rhythms, and drum ensembles played patterns that crossed meter, pitting duple against triple time. Master drummers of the highest skill were valuable members of any clan or tribe because they added so much to the rituals. Some of these drummers, in fact, held great status among their peers and were viewed as specialists. Because percussion was so integral to West African musical culture, younger men—this was the domain of males—aspired to achieve higher status through drumming.

Like their African ancestors, black Americans incorporated music into their everyday experience. This was difficult because of the conditions of slavery, in which slave owners attempted to control all vestiges of culture. Nonetheless, black Americans did maintain customs and rituals utilizing music. They sang and drummed at Virginia funerals as late as the second decade of the 1800s. Secondary accounts suggest that blacks appropriated the Dutch "Pinkster Day" celebrations, a day free from work during which banjos, wild dancing, and drumming lasted for many hours.

Precisely how quickly African music was acculturated in the United States is difficult to ascertain. The legal sanctions against African culture—dancing, drumming, language, etc.—were in place before the dawn of the eighteenth century, but to measure the degree to which these actually affected the culture itself is not easy. Because of reports of drumming and African religious practices, it appears that acculturation in the West Indies took much longer. The sheer number of slaves imported to the southern United States indicates that this pattern of gradual acculturation was true in the South. Except for South Carolina, where for a short period the number of slaves actually exceeded the white population, Africans brought to the South soon learned of European culture. The South was also home to most of the slowly maturing black American music. It also spawned most of the unique forms of American folk music—such as blues, gospel, Cajun, and hillbilly—that have received the greatest worldwide attention.

A gathering of folk musicians in central Virginia circa 1936. *Southern Historical Collection, CB #3926, Wilson Library, University of NC–Chapel Hill, Chapel Hill, NC 27599–3926.*

Beginnings

Thanksgiving in Franklin County, Virginia, marks a period of transition. By late November most of the leaves on the trees are carpeting the gentle knolls of the Blue Ridge Mountains, leaving the landscape bleak and quiet. The high school football season is but a memory, and reports of the upcoming basketball campaign have begun to appear in local newspapers. People are just starting to think about Christmas plans, while the deer, bear, and squirrels prepare for their annual winter struggle.

Thanksgiving Day in 1987 dawned cloudy and the temperatures remained unusually warm. I was among a half-dozen people gathered for homemade bread, pumpkin pie, roasted chestnuts, mashed potatoes, and turkey. Before supper we lolled casually on the front porch; the seventy-degree temperature invited us to sit outside in order to swap stories and sing. Joni Mitchell, Suzanne Vega, America, and Bob Dylan numbers were popular, but Neil Young and John Prine were the two most requested singer/songwriters that evening.

Just as the yearning words and simple chord progressions of an early Neil Young composition, ''Sugar Mountain,'' settled into the air, Rusty's eyes lit up as he picked up his guitar. He sang a ditty that began: ''Last night when I got home, drunk as I could be. Saw another car parked, where my car ought to be.'' When he finished, I asked Rusty where he had picked up this song. ''From an old drunk at a fiddlers convention in Union Grove, North Carolina. I thought it was fun, so I learned it,'' came his instant reply. After musing for a few seconds, Rusty launched into John Prine's ''Paradise'' and the rest of us joined him in singing the chorus about the long-gone, nostalgic days of Prine's Muhlenberg County, Kentucky, youth.

During the course of daily living, we rarely intellectualize the differences between the elements of **traditional** and **popular culture** in our lives. Nor do we necessarily make the distinction between what is old and new. Most of us casually throw these elements into a cultural brew without thinking about it. Many self-taught musicians are like Rusty, who learns his songs from commercial phonograph records, friends, the radio, sheet music, and other musicians. ''Our Goodman,'' the eighteenth-century British ballad that Rusty casually learned from an anonymous musician, and his well-studied version of ''Muhlenberg County'' represent the range of the acoustic music that he enjoys. And both songs reflect Rusty's proclivity for folk and **popular music.**

The traditional styles discussed in this book result from the hybridization that keeps traditional American music in constant evolution. Its lyrics have never been frozen into immutable texts with fixed melodies. Diversity within established aesthetic boundaries is an important key to these musical forms. Traditional songs and the instruments that frequently accompany them are combined in a variety of contexts. The very human sound of a harmonica, for instance, can be heard accompanying the clogging of a Franco-American dancer in northern Vermont, as the heavily amplified lead instrument of a southside Chicago blues band, or integrated into a small Louisiana Cajun string band. Moreover, ''Our Goodman'' was recorded in the 1920s by Coley Jones, a black Texas singer, and the famous Georgia hillbilly fiddler Earl

Johnson long before Rusty heard it performed in Union Grove in the middle 1980s. Its text has also been ''collected'' by folklorists and English professors across the country.

In the twentieth century, music, which once thrived through face-to-face transmission, ''travels'' quite rapidly because CD players, radio, television, jukeboxes, phonographs, tape players, and literacy now reach into every corner of the United States. Scholars have suggested that the **mass media** will eventually obliterate today's racial, ethnic, regional, and traditional styles of American music, which clearly stem from their eighteenth- and nineteenth-century roots. This may eventually come to pass, but not anytime soon. The fact remains that the multilayered interaction fostered by the mass media inevitably enriches and expands our musical vocabulary.

Music in Our Daily Lives

Our senses are daily bombarded by music that we hear on the television, in elevators, and at the local shopping mall. Even on the highways, many cars come fully equipped with a radio, cassette machine or, CD player. When we attend church or a concert, we are exposed to live performances of music. Whether one prefers Beethoven's compositions to the extended jazz works of Duke Ellington or the guitar artistry of Andrés Segovia to Kentucky picker Merle Travis, at least we agree that these people are musical composers or performers. Some might argue that the popular ''heavy metal'' groups of the 1970s and 1980s, such as Led Zeppelin, KISS, Poison, Anthrax, or AC/DC, made devilish noise and not music. Are rap and hip-hop merely highly rhythmic, percussive, vocalizing or music? Others take the stance that opera stars, twentieth-century legends like Beverly Sills or Luciano Pavarotti, stand on stage in ludicrous costumes and bellow loudly but that it's not **really** singing. I believe that during our objective moments, each of these detractors would accept the fact that all of these artists are engaged in making music.

''Music is a healing force in the universe'' was the spiritual sentiment sometimes chanted during the late 1960s performances of jazz saxophonist Pharaoh Sanders. This premise was set forth during the close of a decade of exceptional turmoil and change in the United States and much of the rest of the world. We had struggled through the early stages of the civil rights movement and the dawning of the age of feminism (two ongoing struggles), riots that had blackened many major cities in the United States, and students' protests of the unpopular war in Vietnam. Today Sander's cry might sound naive, but his thoughts of love and peace directly reflected the hopefulness of its Aquarian age. The concept that music truly is a spiritual force binding us together is quite interesting and bears closer scrutiny. However, is music a truly universal language? The easy initial response is yes, music is found across the entire world and in each society.

Despite the differences that cut across cultural lines, music **is** a part of each human society. But these differences in interpretation, presentation, and meaning are precisely what make the study of music so vitally interesting.

The Grand Canyon Cowboy Band on the south rim of the canyon, August 1984. While working as cowboys and packers for Fred Harvey in the 1930s, 1940s, and 1950s, these men made extra pay by entertaining tourists in the canyonside hotels and on pack trips into the canyon itself.
Jim Griffith Photo, courtesy of the Southwest Folklore Center.

Individual concepts of music are inherently tied to one's culture. Just as some cultures cannot easily accept snails, grasshoppers, and cow intestines as food, other cultures cannot conceive of the work of avant-garde composer Philip Glass, Ron McCroby's improvised jazz whistling, or the blues guitar of Muddy Waters as music. Because this book focuses upon music in the United States, our task is less controversial, though far from simple. What is music depends on the group, and today our country of 250 million people is becoming increasingly **multicultural.**

Dictionary definitions of music are not particularly helpful because they tend to overlook the difficulties inherent in describing the complexities of this phenomenon. Typically, they use phrases like ''the ability to pleasantly combine vocal or instrumental sounds'' or ''tones which incorporate varying melody, harmony, timbre, and a structured form to create an emotionally complete composition.'' Although music is clearly an aural phenomenon, it cannot be defined in terms of sound alone. You must remember that music is also a culturally based phenomenon that varies greatly over time and our own geographical landscape. Consequently, our definition of music comes from a slightly different perspective:

Music is any complex of vocal or instrumental sound that is organized in a manner agreed upon by members of a particular racial, **ethnic,** or regional group.

But how do we learn about music, music history, and emerging trends? The electronic media, our parents' and friends' tastes, and magazines are among the forces that help shape musical conceptions and interests in the United States. So do our teachers and academic institutions. Most scholars affiliated with the academy look towards the notated music of western Europe for their role model. Historical **musicologists** largely concern themselves with the German, French, and Italian music created by educated white males between 1500 and 1900, from Palestrina, Gluck, Bach, Mozart, and Beethoven to Wagner. They created marvelous music, and this grand body of choral works, symphonies, operas, and so forth contains hundreds of important artistic works invaluable to Western culture. But what about the music, which includes most of the music performed across the world, that falls outside of these parameters?

Ethnomusicologists, folklorists, and other interdisciplinary scholars are usually the ones that investigate the rest of music across the world: African ''highlife,'' the tangos of Argentina, India's ragas, and American bluegrass. The list is most impressive and seemingly inexhaustible. These allied fields are also vitally interested in music as culture; consequently, an ethnomusicologist studies music as one aspect of culture. Much of their work involves placing music in the context of human activity. Ethnomusicologists often receive training in anthropology, folklore, history, sociology, and linguistics in addition to music. Given their strongly contrasting interests and preparation, it is not surprising that musicologists and ethnomusicologists not only study different types of music but often understand and treat music differently.

In order to illustrate some of these contrasting perceptions about the nature of music, let us briefly step outside the U. S. border into the heart of Africa. Ethnomusicologist Alan Merriam points out that for the Basongye people, who live near the Congo River, music emanates only from human beings. Therefore birds cannot ''sing'' nor can electronic instruments produce music. The Basongye are uncertain about whistling. If whistling is used to signal during a hunt, then it is not music; however, the whistling that accompanies dancing is accepted as music. Closer to home, it is interesting to note that the traditional Navaho language has no word for music or musical instruments. The languages of many Native Americans generally lack a word to describe overall musical activity, though the Blackfoot's word for dance describes a religious activity that encompasses ceremony, dance, and music. The Blackfoot also have a word that can be translated as ''song,'' but this excludes any instrumental music without words. It is clear that once we look outside of our own culture, definitions of what is music become more problematic.

Defining American Folk Music

Defining folk music in our **postmodern** world is not an easy task. In the nineteenth century, the United States was a less hectic, rural, and agrarian society, but today we can immediately view the latest news about the use of robots in Japanese automobile factories. Furthermore, prior to modernization the United States did not support such a strong and extensive popular music industry nor very many academically trained composers. The ways in which music is performed, sold, and disseminated in the late twentieth century has become extremely complex, blurring the easy attributes that one could have previously made about folk music. Despite these complicating factors, our focus in this book is upon ''music with strong regional ties or a racial/ethnic identity and direct links with its past.''

In order to expand upon this simple definition, consider these six general characteristics of folk music:

1. *It is music that varies greatly over space but relatively little over time.* A cowboy song such as ''When the Work's All Done This Fall,'' for example, has been sung in Wyoming for many decades, and in this context its lyrics about ranch/cattle work are timeless. However, its message is rather abstract to a Polish American autoworker on a Flint, Michigan, assembly line who might prefer the sounds of a local polka band. Innovations, however minor, tend to occur slowly because the forms of folk music are largely determined by a conservative musical culture.

2. *Folk music emanates from a specific, identifiable community, such as coal miners, Louisiana Cajuns, or Native Americans.* Such communities are found throughout the United States, and they are associated by way of their occupation, ethnic identity, or physical proximity. These folk communities also share some of the characteristics of **folk culture** (speech patterns, **foodways,** etc.) that are described later in this chapter. Folk music often retains well-established associations with functional activities within the **community**—work, religious ceremonies, or dance.

3. *The authorship or origins of folk songs and tunes are generally unknown.* We rarely know who writes folk music. The authorship of tunes such as ''Soldier's Joy'' or ''Old Molly Hare'' is unknown and almost certain to remain that way. A specific song can sometimes be attributed to one region or folk community. For example, ''Pony Blues,'' ''Walking Blues,'' and ''Rollin' and Tumblin''' clearly emanate from the Mississippi Delta blues tradition. However, the precise originator of any folk song is generally anonymous.

4. *Folk songs are usually disseminated by word of mouth, aurally, or through informal apprenticeships within a community.* Folk music is learned within a community by people who grow up in or join that community. The process does not entail formal lessons, as one would take at a conservatory. You learn the music that you grew up with, that others in the community play as part of worship, relaxation, or for dances. Today, folk music is also transmitted by way of mass communication, particularly through radio and recordings.

5. *Folk music is most often performed by nonprofessionals.* Specialists within folk communities often perform music, but only a very small percentage of them actually make their full-time living from music. The network of folk music performers consists primarily of unpaid or part-time musicians who play for others within their community. The distinctions between musicians and listeners is sometimes indistinct; for example, at a church during the performance of a lined-out hymn that involves the entire congregation.

6. *Short forms and predictable patterns are fundamental to folk music.* Most American folk music falls into repetitive paradigms that are generally familiar to members of the community. Blues, for instance, tends to follow the same harmonic model based on I, IV, and V chords; however, its form invites individual expression within these boundaries. Similarly, hula meles can be distinguished by the vocal qualities demonstrated by the singers. While the folk music itself is often complex, its general performance ''rules'' vary little from one presentation to the next.

It might help to also consider folk music in light of popular and **classical music.** We know that folk songs are not composed, ''art'' ballads championed by academic institutions, nor are they often heard in formal, sometimes highly subsidized, concerts. Unlike folk music, the work of popular tunesmiths enjoys fleeting, short-lived popularity, which fundamentally owes its dissemination to the mass media. Folk music tends to be overlooked by ''serious'' music scholars and sometimes used by the tradesmen of popular culture. Perhaps you can think of it as the forgotten music of America that reflects both our diverse heritage and our everyday lives. An appreciation for roots and a sense of tradition are very important in our dynamic society, which is becoming increasingly multicultural and complex.

''Folk'' and ''traditional'' are used interchangeably in *Introducing American Folk Music*. In the world of popular culture, however, ''traditional'' often carries a different meaning—it is used to describe something old or created in the past. In 1991 the National Association of Recorded Arts and Sciences (the folks who operate the Grammy Awards) added the category of ''Best Traditional Pop Vocal Performance.'' They were simply referring to popular songs written in a style that existed prior to the advent of rockabilly and rock 'n' roll in the middle 1950s. Perhaps the next Grammy category should be ''Best Traditional Classical Instrumental Performance'' to differentiate older classical musicians such as Christoph Gluck from a more modern figure such as Stravinsky. Maybe they should also distinguish between the ''traditional'' country music of Uncle Dave Macon and the ''contemporary'' sound of Emmylou Harris.

The modes of transmission—word of mouth, radio, CDs, etc.—underscore the ways in which alterations occur within these traditions and the subsequent creation of new movements. The twin processes of industrialization and urbanization have increased contact with other culture groups, which causes even greater **creolization.** This term generally refers to a cross-pollination between two or more different cultures, resulting in a unique hybrid that contains elements from both. Cajun and zydeco music in southwestern Louisiana are specfic examples of creolized American folk music. ''Ethnic and Native American Traditions'' discusses other examples of the varied forces that have accelerated changes in our folk music.

Cultural Geography and Traditions

Cultural geographers are the scholars who study the spatial variations in human culture: the differences in human culture from one place to another. Sports, politics, languages, and architecture are among the aspects of culture that have been studied by cultural geographers. Since about 1970, cultural geographers have focused some of their attention on music in the United States. Because the attributes of folk music include **regionalization** and **diffusion,** the study of American folk music clearly intersects with geography.

A **cultural region** is an area inhabited by people possessing one or more cultural traits in common. Cultural regions generally reflect multiple traits. Our Navaho cultural region in the Southwest is delineated by language, religion, foodways, and architecture, among other factors. Because culture is fluid, such regions do not have fixed borders. Vernacular culture regions are particularly important because they are perceived by their inhabitants to exist. ''Dixie,'' for example, is a regional term for some sections of the South that is both informed and restrained by its historical connotations.

Musical styles like ''Southern California beach music'' or ''Southern rock'' are often informally grouped by cultural regions. American folk music is quite often defined by region or community: ''Mississippi Delta blues,'' ''sea shanties,'' and ''the folk songs of Northwestern lumberjacks.'' Regional variation is one of the main attributes of American folk culture, and it helps to explain the differences in the music produced by members of a specific community.

Every cultural region in the United States evolved through communication and human contact. Cultural diffusion describes the spread of ideas, innovations, and attitudes across time and space. Prior to our postmodern era, most diffusion resulted from the relocation of human beings from one place to another and was communicated face-to-face. This communication then spread throughout the general population like the rippling waves of a rock thrown into a pond.

Today's ideas and innovations are equally likely to result from electronic discourse or the printed media. Although they once had stronger local or regional ties, radio and television now provide instantaneous contact with the entire world. Newspapers and magazines exchange information on a daily or weekly basis. It would be impossible to find an American folk musician in the 1990s untouched by these forces. Folk music is still widely disseminated through informal means, but records and the radio have both added a new dimension to this process.

In our pastoral vision, folk music emanates from homogeneous, static, rural communities, but the twentieth-century reality is of increased mobility and **electronic communication.** Nonetheless, these ties to a community are essential in any discussion of contemporary American folk music. Robertson Davies wrote a wonderful book, *What's Bred in the Bone,* which takes its title from an expression meaning that certain traits become culturally ingrained. We follow them almost unconsciously because they are part of our daily lives. Such ''breeding'' reflects **regionalism,** of course, but it implies something more subtle and possibly profound. These are the traditions and patterns inculcated by way of our immediate surroundings and our families. Highly respected twentieth-century American folk musicians—such as Muddy Waters (blues), Bill Monroe (bluegrass), or Roberta Martin (gospel)—remained intrinsically tied to the music they inherited. Some people deliberately and very willfully shed their past, renouncing family and community. This is a matter of conscious choice, sometimes born of necessity or survival. However, we cannot fully escape our pronounced familial influences.

Folk musicians usually come from families or small communities immersed in the music. For example, **Wade Ward,** who grew up in Galax, Virginia, came to embody many of its values and traits in his life and music. Older members of his immediate family played the fiddle and banjo, which Wade also embraced. In short, Wade Ward became a product not only of the Upland South but more specifically of the Grayson County/Blue Ridge community and his extended families. His music and lifestyle were bred in the bone, so to speak, rather than adopted in an arbitrary way. He came about his music as a natural consequence of his familial and regional heritage.

A clear distinction needs to be made between a folk musician such as Ward and those from outside of his community who learn to play folk music. Wade himself served as the mentor to dozens of musicians, including many younger people who grew up far from Grayson County, Virginia. The majority of these musicians learned from Wade Ward during the 1960s at folk festival workshops, through visiting his home, or by listening to his numerous recordings. Some of these musicians spent months living near Ward and learned to play his versions of fiddle and banjo tunes such as ''Fox Chase,'' ''Sally Anne,'' and others with great authority.

The aural differences between Ward's music and that of his students may be slight; however, the master's music is bred in the bone. Wade Ward's music reflects subtle, sometimes intangible, cultural and family attributes missing from his student's interpretations. Qualities tangential to the music itself (expressions that easily roll off of one's tongue, racial attitudes, stories about local musicians, even diet) encompass a lifestyle and breeding that one cannot learn by listening to Ward's recordings or even by living in Grayson County, Virginia, for several years. Think of his students as expatriates. No matter how well they learn to speak the (musical) language, they remain ''foreigners.'' People in this category may play folk music well, but they cannot be

Bred in the Bone

Wade Ward (top right) and the Bogtrotten Band in the late 1930s. *Library of Congress.*

M u s i c a l   E x a m p l e

Wade Ward (banjo) and Glen Smith (fiddle) played together for many years around Galax, Virginia. This piece, which is often performed for square dancing, displays Ward's virtuoso ''clawhammer'' banjo technique. ''Clawhammer'' refers to a style of brushing the banjo strings with the back of one's fingers on the downstroke; bluegrass musicians employ a three-finger ''roll'' on the upstroke that is accomplished with finger picks. This performance was recorded in the middle 1960s. [Folkways 3802]

Title ''Sally Goodin' ''
Performers Glen Smith—fiddle; Wade Ward—banjo
Instruments fiddle and banjo
Length 1:11
Notable Features

1. The lead melody is played on both the fiddle and banjo.
2. It is cast in a simple *ab* song form.
3. They perform this piece at a rapid tempo.
4. Note that neither instrument takes a ''solo'' break.
5. ''Sally Goodin''' is in a major tonality.

---

considered folk musicians. They have acquired an interest in folk music and have deliberately learned a style outside of their own. Such performers of folk music are often called **revivalists,** and their role will be discussed in a later chapter.

It is clear the importance of American folk music extends well beyond its immediate communities. Folk music has influenced the work of American composers such as Aaron Copland and Charles Ives as well as rock musicians on the order of the Rolling Stones, the Cowboy Junkies, the Allman Brothers Band, and R.E.M. Such musicians are not ''folk,'' but they sound closer to their folk roots because of their appreciation of Leadbelly, Robert Johnson, Uncle Dave Macon, Howlin' Wolf, Riley Puckett, and Patsy Montana. These earlier musicians grew up in a society closer to the ones found in idealized rural folk communities, albeit during four decades (1900–1940) of startling transitions.

In addition to describing the genres of traditional music, *Introducing American Folk Music* discusses the impact of the folk revivals and some of its personalities, such as Bob Dylan and Pete Seeger. I prefer Dick Weissman's term **folk based** to describe these professional and semiprofessional musicians with a strong interest in various types of traditional music (Sandberg and Weissman 1989). Folk based performers are an important part of the story because of their strong impact on our national consciousness and their commercialization of the more traditional styles.

Listening to American Folk Music

A formal background in music theory, ear-training, and harmony is not necessary to use this textbook. However, you will be required to listen carefully to the musical examples that illustrate this book. These basic skills are not difficult to obtain, though this is an active process that is critical in appreciating any kind of music. They can be applied to nearly any form of music from punk rock, Bill Monroe, and blues to hip-hop.

Pitch is a single tone or note, which is produced by vibrating air. Train whistles, voices, bird wings, and instruments each vibrate the air. When a single guitar or violin string is plucked, it produces a pitch. The faster the air vibrates, the higher the pitch; a slower rate of vibration causes a lower pitch. A sound with a definite pitch is called a tone.

If you sit at the keyboard of a piano, you see a pattern of white and black keys that are arranged in a series of pitches. The black keys have the same names as the white keys, except they are a half step higher (sharp) or a half step lower (flat) than the adjacent white key. The lower pitches are to your left, while the higher pitches can be heard as you strike the keys to your right. These pitches fall into three basic registers: low, middle, and high. Other instruments can be thought of in this way, also. For example, a piccolo falls into the high register, while a tuba is usually classified as a low-register instrument.

In our western European system, these tones are named A through G, with each of the seven different keys representing a different pitch. The notes on a piano are organized into systems that are usually referred to as scales. Some are a simple series of five notes, which constitute a pentatonic scale. Or they can be quite complicated, but we will basically refer to major and minor scales. The first and last names of the eight pitches in a scale have the same name, which is known as its tonic. For instance, a C-major scale begins and ends on C and you play only the white keys in between. An A-minor scale begins and ends on the tonic and you strike only the white keys, except that it sounds dissimilar. This is because the interval (the distance in pitch between two tones of a scale or melody) between the keys are arranged differently. A major scale is: whole, whole, half, whole, whole, whole, half. A minor scale is: whole, half, whole, whole, half, whole, whole.

When you combine tones vertically, they are heard simultaneously. Two simultaneous tones create an interval, but three or more simultaneous pitches are perceived as a chord. This system of chords is known as harmony and it forms the basis for our folk and popular music. Most traditional American music is built upon the movement from one chord to another in simple progressions. Their chords tend to be based on thirds, usually the first, third, and fifth degrees of the scale. In this book we will most often refer to the tonic chord (built upon the first tone of a scale), the subdominant chord (built on the fourth tone), and the dominant (built upon the fifth scale tone).

A series of individual tones makes up a melody. If a melody is derived from a series of close intervals, usually a second or whole step in a major scale, it is referred to as conjunctive. American folk songs tend to be conjunctive. However, tunes that contain larger intervals, more than a third, are disjunctive. You may think of a melody as a tune, but to make it interesting, the element of rhythm is added to the series of tones. Rhythm refers to the long and short patterns of duration, which can be simple or complex, regular or irregular. The rhythm generates an energy, an impulse that drives the music forward in interesting ways. A simple, regular pulse can be felt in the music used for marching or that sets our feet tapping. A complex, irregular beat characterizes much of traditional African American music.

Meter is what organizes the rhythm of music, just as it orders the reading of poetry. American folk music is almost always organized in measured beat patterns of duple (two) meter or triple (three) meter, which is usually easy to count. Think again of a march, which is in duple meter, and you can feel the two-beat rhythm: STRONG, weak; STRONG, weak. A waltz, on the other hand, has the distinct sense of ONE, two, three—ONE, two, three—ONE, two, three. Unaccompanied solo singing, such as a ''field holler,'' occasionally has a ''free'' feeling that wavers or sometimes shifts between duple and triple meter. Accents are heard in music, just as they are in language. You will notice that in the examples above, the first beat is accented. One way to create rhythmic interest is to accent beats unexpectedly. This is called syncopation and it is a fundamental rhythmic element of ragtime master Scott Joplin and the ''funk'' music of Bootsy Collins, Parliament Psychedelic, and George Clinton. A triple meter that is accented one, TWO, three—one, two, THREE—one, TWO, three illustrates the feel of syncopation.

Dynamics refers to the degree of loudness or softness of music. The less intense degree of energy used to produce a tone results in a soft sound. The greater the degree of energy, the louder the sound. ''Crescendo'' refers to a sound that gradually gets louder, while ''decrescendo'' means that the dynamic level is decreasing. American folk music usually doesn't contain extended works with dramatic changes in dynamics; such alterations are generally more subtle.

Timbre refers to the unique tonal quality that can be attributed to all voices and instruments. We can recognize our favorite singer, not only through their repertoire but because their voice has a distinctive timbre. Similar instruments, such as a string bass and a cello, may sound alike, but they are usually played in a different register and possess a related but particular timbre. Today's electronic synthesizers are able to reproduce the sound of a harmonica, clarinet, even a piano with uncanny accuracy. It is now possible to confuse the sound of instruments because of this technological advance, though a closer aural inspection usually reveals the difference.

Another important musical concept is texture, which refers to the density of sound. It is directly related to the number of musical lines sounding at a particular time during a musical performance. Music can be texturally rich and full at one extreme or spare and thin at the other. A monophonic texture means a single, unaccompanied melodic line, which can be sung or played on one or more instruments. When more than one melodic line is sounded simultaneously, a polyphonic texture is created. A melody that is in the foreground and supported by harmonic underpinning results in a homophonic texture. The majority of the music you will learn about in this book is homophonic.

All of our folk genres are cast into forms—the basic structure or shape of a piece of music. All types of music evolve and change, but repetition and contrast are the two keys to understanding form. Binary (two-part or *ab*) and ternary (three-part or *aba*) are the most common forms you will encounter in American folk music. The *a* refers to the first musical statement, while *b* presents a contrasting idea. If a second contrasting statement is made, it is known as the *c* section. Ballads are often performed in strophic form—the same music is used for each stanza. The most influential folk form to develop in the United States is the twelve-bar blues, which uses an *aab* verse form built upon the tonic, subdominant, and dominant chords. This form has greatly affected most types of twentieth-century American folk and popular music.

These basic elements can be applied to all of the musical examples that you will find in Introducing American Folk Music. Applying them to these examples will deepen your appreciation of the music, aside from its historical, cultural, and geographical importance. You can also think of them when you listen to other forms of music for your own relaxation or enjoyment.

Instruments

Many different instruments are utilized by musicians throughout the United States. The use of these instruments are rarely limited to one genre of music; violins/fiddles are heard in symphony orchestras, Ukrainian American bands, chamber music groups, bluegrass quintets, and rock bands. On the other hand, accordions are rarely heard in contemporary popular music. In folk music, the use of certain instruments depends partially on regional or ethnic background

A collage of homemade and unusual instruments, such as a washboard. *Library of Congress.*

as well as personal preference and family traditions. Some of them have surprisingly long histories that sometimes cross continents and many decades. Most of these instruments are acoustic models, although electrification and amplification have become increasingly common since World War II.

Accordion

The accordion is one instrument enjoying a late twentieth-century renaissance among folk musicians from the bayous of Louisiana directly northward to the Nebraska plains. ''Squeeze boxes'' were originally promoted by the waves of European immigrants, usually German, Irish, French and Italians, who commonly used this instrument. Because of its durability, volume, and portability, the accordion makes an ideal instrument for dance music.

Accordions are a European invention. It is a free reed instrument that uses a keyboard similar to that found on a piano. It has a range of up to five octaves. The smaller accordions are one-half to one-third in size, and their reeds are activated by depressing small buttons. Each button or key corresponds to a specific reed. Both types require the performer to squeeze the instrument, forcing air in and out of the bellows. The more versatile piano accordion is favored by ''polka'' musicians like Frankie Yankovich who are usually of northern European background. Marc Savoy, Ally Young, Freeman Fontenot, and other French Louisianans usually play the smaller accordions, which do not have a keyboard but are activated by depressing small buttons.

These modern accordions were developed in Germany and Austria in the 1820s and 1830s. They were particularly popular in France in the middle nineteenth century, which perhaps accounts for their widespread use among French-speaking Americans. Monarch and Hohner models have long been favored by Cajun musicians, though a younger generation (most notably Marc Savoy of Eunice, Louisiana) now makes a ''Cajun accordion.'' This model improves the timbre of the upper range and its bellows are easier to use.

Banjo

What began as an instrument brought to the United States by West African slaves has become closely identified with country music. As early as the late seventeenth century, banjolike instruments made from gourds and called banzas, bandores, or banjas were being played by New World slaves. Contemporary accounts of life in the Middle Atlantic states from around the time of the American Revolutionary War suggest that the banjo was the most common instrument used by slaves and freed blacks. The number of strings on early banjos varied from between three to eight, although by the 1820s these homemade instruments usually had four strings.

The size and shape of banjos began to be regularized by the middle of the nineteenth century. Joel Walker Sweeney and other minstrel show entertainers brought banjos to the attention of urban white Americans at about the same time that they began to be made commercially. Within thirty years, white musicians in the rural South and, to a far lesser degree the Northeast, had embraced the banjo as their own instrument. During Reconstruction the banjo gradually became more closely associated with Anglo-American music and began losing its African American identity.

Pre–Civil War banjo playing was often done with a downstroke of the thumb and back nail of the index or middle finger. This style is often called ''clawhammer'' or ''frailing.'' A new style of finger picking developed and gained rapid acceptance during the late nineteenth century, and it closely resembles the guitar picking upon which it was modeled. By 1900 many folk musicians were using this two-finger style, although in the 1940s the three-finger ''bluegrass roll'' began to gain wide favor.

Around the turn of the twentieth century, banjos flirted with popular acceptance. Transcriptions of light classical and popular music were marketed to the innumerable banjo, mandolin, and guitar orchestras that sprang up on college campuses and in cities across the United States. During the 1920s, commercially produced four-string tenor banjos were coming into vogue. They were preferred by the musicians who performed with popular dance and jazz bands. However, the five-string banjo made its comeback following World War II because of bluegrass, the folk revival, and its continued use in commercial country music.

Diddley-Bow

This one-string instrument is most often played by blacks born in the Deep South. Well into the twentieth century, musicians from the Mississippi Delta have fashioned diddley-bows as their first instrument. They take a single strand of wire or a guitar string and nail it to the wall of a house, which serves as a resonator. They raise either end away from the wall with a block of wood and use a slide or bottleneck to fret the diddley-bow. The picking is done with a finger, a guitar pick, a metal nail, or some other similar object.

Diddley-bows, which are almost always played by children, foreshadow the bottleneck guitar style. Both Muddy Waters and Big Joe Williams learned to play music on a diddley-bow. Rock 'n' roll pioneer Ellas McDaniel reversed the name of this instrument in order to use it as his pseudonym, Bo Diddley.

Dulcimer

The best known is the Appalachian, mountain, or lap dulcimer, which developed from the German zither that came with immigrants to Pennsylvania. Developed in the southern Appalachian mountains, they are narrow and usually between two and three feet long. Dulcimers date from the early nineteenth century, though the ''modern'' shape did not emerge for another one hundred years. Today's dulcimers have a full fretboard and four strings. The melody is played on the first string, with the other strings serving as drones. Dulcimers are usually placed across the performer's knee and plucked with the fingers of some type of pick. Dulcimers are used to accompany both dances and singing.

A hammered dulcimer is a different instrument. It is also a member of the zither family, but it is always played with small mallets that are hand-held in order to strike the sixty or so strings. Hammered dulcimers are in the form of a trapezoid that is between 2 1/2 and 4 feet in length, 1 to 2 feet in height, and 3 to 6 inches in depth. These instruments were introduced by English settlers sometime prior to 1700. Nineteenth Century dulcimers were made by both commercial and folk artisans. The tradition has remained largely in New England and upstate New York, although it diffused to Piedmont North Carolina and the Great Lakes region during the early twentieth century. Today's hammer dulcimer players are largely the product of a revival of interest that began in the late 1960s.

Fiddle

Violins and other closely related instruments, such as the viola, were first used by European musicians during the sixteenth century. The size and precise shape of fiddles, as they are called by American folk musicians, became standardized by the seventeenth century. With only a few minor alterations, violins look almost exactly like they did three hundred years ago. The highly skilled craftsmanship of early Italian makers like Stradivari and Guarneri has resulted in instruments the rich sound of which is hard to match today.

These instruments have been among the mainstays of European art music, and fiddles were among the first instruments to arrive in the New World. Not only were they popular, they were highly portable and versatile, too, for they could be used for performing music in all idioms. Within a few decades, Americans were making their own violins. Some people crafted their instruments with great skill and reverence for European craftsmanship. Others, particularly African Americans, were forced to use whatever materials and means they could muster.

Since the late eighteenth century, fiddles have perhaps been the most prominent folk instruments in the United States. Some Anglo-American fiddlers have repertoires that include up to four hundred tunes, some of them brought over from the British Isles. Genres such as early hillbilly and bluegrass feature fiddles as one of their principal lead instruments. Most of these fiddlers hold the instrument against their chin, though a minority of players nestle the instrument against their chest.

Guitar

Although they are now commonly associated with folk and rock music, the six-string guitar was developed in southern Europe in the late eighteenth century. It was regularly imported to the East Coast by 1800; the first American-made instruments did not appear until the 1830s. These early models were plucked by the fingers, smaller than contemporary acoustic guitars, and strung with gut or silk strings. The C. F. Martin Company became the first American company to manufacture guitars, and it was not until Reconstruction that they were joined by Ephiphone (1873), Harmony (1892), and Gibson (1894).

During the 1890s, steel-string guitars, which were commonly found in Central America, began to be mass produced in the United States. Both Montgomery Wards and Sears, Roebuck and Company sold mail-order guitars for under ten dollars. Within thirty years, the production of guitars had risen to approximately 150,000 annually. This same period witnessed two important innovations. Gibson's ''arch-top'' instruments, with their f-shaped sound hole

Note the unusual homemade fiddle held by the bearded man. His partner is playing a mandolin. *Southern Historical Collection, CB #3926, Wilson Library, University of NC–Chapel Hill, Chapel Hill, NC 27599–3926.*

and arched body, came into vogue during the 1920s. They gave some competition to the slightly softer Martin flattop models, which remained popular. A bit earlier, Hawaiian guitars and Dobro resonator guitars, both of which are primarily made from steel and are usually played with a slide or bottleneck, rather than finger-picked, became popular. They found a ready audience because of the volume they generated with little effort.

Gibson experimented with electronic pickups for guitars in the middle 1920s, but the first amplified guitars were not introduced for another ten years. These hollow-body models did not gain prominence until after World War II, however. Solid-body electric guitars, developed primarily by Leo Fender and Les Paul, became affixed to the scene by the middle 1950s.

Rather than eschew technology, today's folk musicians play both electric and acoustic instruments. Those who play electric guitars generally use hollow-body instruments, although many African American blues performers use the solid-body models. Since the 1950s, flattop acoustic models have been the instrument of choice among American folk musicians.

Harmonica

This is a free reed instrument of German descent that is related to the accordion. It was perfected by Christian Friedrich Ludwig Buschman about 1828, whose first successful prototype was successful because it was easy to play and to control its dynamics. The instrument slowly caught on in central Europe, where its manufacture constituted a cottage industry for several decades. By the 1860s, harmonicas caught the eye and imagination of Matthias Hohner. He spent several years making harmonicas by hand before he discovered a method to mass produce them. His annual output skyrocketed to almost a million harmonicas by 1885, and nearly two-thirds of these were exported to the United States. Today Hohner is still the predominant name in the manufacturing of harmonicas.

There are two types of harmonica: diatonic and chromatic. With the exception of a few ''Chicago-style'' blues musicians, folk harmonica players almost always use diatonic harps. These ten-hole instruments are tuned to a tonic chord, which is attained by alternating exhaling and inhaling. Chromatic harmonicas are larger and consist of twelve holes with a slide on one end. You depress the slide in order to attain the accidentals needed to complete a major scale. These instruments have a three-octave range.

Diatonic harmonicas are played by all types of American folk musicians. They are most important in the blues idiom, where they are one of its essential instruments. Early twentieth-century country musicians also used them to accompany singing or as a lead instrument in a small string band.

Mandolin

This stringed instrument came to the United States by way of Italian immigrants beginning in the late eighteenth century. It is small-bodied and features a double set of four strings, which causes it to ring out loudly. Mandolins are almost always played with a flat pick, permitting a tremolo effect.

For over one hundred years, it was used almost exclusively within the Italian community. The mandolin's popularity increased during the 1880s because of touring European string ensembles that featured it. By the turn of the century, it was not unusual to find mandolin orchestras or societies in small towns and colleges across America. Such groups played contemporary rags, marches, jigs, etc., that they learned from other musicians or from one of the many specialty periodicals that sprang up to serve these musicians. During this same period, hybrid instruments such as mandolas and mandocellos were developed but never gained widespread acceptance.

By World War I the craze had slowed down, supplanted by a craze for Hawaiian music and jazz. More folk musicians picked up the mandolin, and it could be heard on some of the string band recordings of the 1920s. During the 1930s, fraternal groups such as the Mainers and Bill and Earl Bolick (the Blue Sky Boys) were using it in tandem with the guitar. By the middle 1940s, Bill Monroe had made it the centerpiece of his first bluegrass band. Today mandolins are still primarily associated with bluegrass music, though country music and some rock groups have used them since the early 1980s.

Mouth Bow

This is a single-string instrument that is shaped like a bow for shooting an arrow. Most often found in Africa and South America, mouth bows are relatively rare in the United States. It resembles and sounds like a large Jew's harp and is played in similar fashion. A mouth bow's range and timbre are somewhat limited. It is played by resting the bow itself on one's slightly parted lips and then plucking the strings with the fingers. The pitches that it produces are raised or lowered by changing the tension of one's mouth as it grips the bow itself. Mouth bow playing is found in both black and white traditions.

Quills

These are a simple wind instrument, also known as panpipes, which are found across the entire world. They consist of between four and eight tubes of increasing length bundled together; the longer the tube, the lower the pitch. Quills are most often made by the person playing them, usually of cane. A tone is produced by blowing across the top of each pipe. Blowing across the top of a partially filled bottle of soda pop produces a similar effect.

Panpipes were played by the ancient Greeks, who called them syrinx. They were also found in fifth century China. Today panpipes are a folk instrument that is often heard from Burma eastward to western Latin America, especially in the mountainous sections of Peru and Ecuador. In the United States, they are only rarely found in twentieth-century American folk music, usually in the Deep South among African Americans.

Folk Culture in the United States

It is important to make the distinctions between the levels of culture that touch and shape our daily lives. As a college student, you are presently part of the elite academic world, which involves, among other things, attending lectures, library research, writing critical essays, performing scientific experiments, and

---

M u s i c a l   E x a m p l e

Joe Patterson lived in Ashford, Alabama, and Ralph Rinzler came upon him while researching Southern folk traditions for the Newport Foundation in 1964. This selection was recorded in May of 1964 at Patterson's home. It is a unique performance that combines playing with vocalizing. This is one of the very few examples of African American quill playing that has ever been made. [Previously Unissued]

Title Untitled
Performer Joe Patterson
Instruments percussion, quills, voice
Length 1:30
Notable Features

1. Patterson maintains a steady underlying duple meter with his homemade percussion instrument.
2. The quills have a limited range of about five notes.
3. A feeling of syncopation is established by the tension between the steady percussion and the quills' mixed rhythmic patterns.
4. This performance roughly follows an *ab* song form.

---

reading novels. At the same time, you also participate in popular culture by enjoying comic strips like ''Calvin and Hobbes,'' eating the occasional hamburger at a McDonald's restaurant, or listening to a top-selling music artist on the radio.

Simultaneously, we almost subconsciously participate in folk culture. These are the customs and traditions that we learn or assimilate from our family, members of the community, and our ethnic or racial group. Folk culture can be expressed in the way we celebrate our religious holidays, greet one another, or pronounce certain words. It is the ''traditional, unofficial, noninstitutional part of culture. It encompasses all knowledge, understandings, values, attitudes, assumptions, feelings, and beliefs transmitted . . . by word of mouth or by customary examples'' (Brunvand 1986, 4). Folk culture is circulated when people communicate. Allowing for the inevitable exceptions, this communication is almost always oral. For instance, the telling of a ghost story or an urban legend about a poodle in the microwave. But it can also be transmitted by example; I learned to make meatballs by watching my second-generation Swedish-American mother prepare scores of them for our annual Christmas smorgasbord.

Folklore (the ''items'' of folk culture) are usually grouped into three categories:

Oral Folklore   At its most basic level, an individual word or phrase may qualify as "folk speech." One example is the oft-used pronunciation of the word "chimblee" for "chimney" in southwestern Virginia. Because of their speech patterns and pronunciations, most any resident of "down east" Maine can be easily identified as soon as they open their mouth. At greater level of complexity are proverbs or proverbial sayings, such as "Red sky at night, sailor's delight." Finally, there are more complicated forms of **oral folklore** such as narratives (tall tales or cowboy recitations) and songs.

Customary Folklore   These often combine oral communication and example for their transmission. For instance, superstitions can be transmitted orally. When you were a youngster, perhaps your father warned you that black cats mean bad luck. Or it can be promulgated by example—catching the bride's flowers because it means you will be the next to marry. Children's jump rope games almost demand that one both move and speak properly to participate. Folk dance and drama provide two other examples of customary folklore.

Material Folklore   These are the tangible objects created by a craftsperson or by members of a community. For example, the seasonal icehouses found on lakes in the frigid North during the midwinter fishing season. Navaho blankets woven by Native Americans in the Southwest fall into this category, as do the traditional foods prepared by Greek Americans for Easter.

Significantly, we continue to distinguish the geographical origins of our fellow Americans based on speech patterns and expressions—for example, how we greet one another. "Howdy," a diminutive for "how do you do," is commonly heard in the South but rarely in Idaho. If one ordered a "frappe" (milk shake) in a restaurant outside of New England, you would no doubt be asked to explain your request. By the same token, the use of the Scandinavian

Senor Alejandro Gomez carving a Mexican American religious figure, a *Santos.*
Smithsonian Institute.

expletive ''Uff-daa!'' (a very ethnic/family-specific term) is generally greeted with blank looks in Phoenix, Arizona.

Food is perhaps the most common way by which people distinguish their geographic and cultural backgrounds. Hogjowls and greens can be found in Northern urban supermarkets largely patronized by black Americans, many with strong Southern ties. In New Mexico, ''eggs rancheros'' (an omelet with salsa sauce) is found on many menus, while grits are rarely found on the tables of the hearty residents of Michigan's Upper Peninsula. Restaurants in Rhode Island sometimes offer quail dishes in deference to their Portuguese and Portuguese American patrons. Wherever Swedes, Norwegians, or Danes have settled, you are likely to find lutefisk, a whitefish preserved in brine and noted for its distinctive smell.

While the United States is not yet a bland melting pot composed entirely of K-Marts, the CBS television network, and General Motors, homogenization increases each year. The ''modern'' era began early in the twentieth century, transforming America from our fundamentally rural agrarian society into a new age. Today we live in a postmodern United States linked by instantaneous communication, interstate highways, and informed by almost universal public education. These factors help to make us more alike one another in our speech, foodways, music, and other basic aspects of culture. **MTV** similarly informs viewers from Portland, Maine, to Portland, Oregon, with identical news, videos, and commercials.

Regional and ethnic variations remain important keys to understanding twentieth-century American folk music because they clearly display great variety across the country. The music of a Norwegian American polka band in Wisconsin is, for example, easily distinguished from a north Georgia country string band. Think also of the differences between the music of two neighboring churches in Washington, D.C. Performances of ''Amazing Grace'' by an African American Primitive Baptist congregation and an Anglo-American Methodist choir present a study in strongly contrasting musical cultures. America's melting pot still steams with a warm and rich brew of Cajun music from Louisiana and southeastern Texas, German and Scandinavian polka music in the upper Midwest, and sacred-harp singing in Georgia and Alabama. The regional differences found in American music remain strong. They have been reinforced by a recent resurgence of interest in ethnic traditions and racial roots, which is illustrated in everything from T-shirts (''Coonass and Proud,'' worn boldly by Louisiana Cajuns) to children's names such as Sven, Bubba, Zelodious, or Paco.

This book focuses upon the traditional music that has developed in the United States between the eighteenth century and today. American folk music exists alongside popular and elite music, and often interacts with these other levels of musical culture. Folk music is rarely heard over the radio or seen on television today; nonetheless thousands of folk-music recordings are available and folk festivals of every size and description abound in the United States. In full-service music stores across the country, the bins of CDs and cassettes

Chief Charles Taylor of the White Cloud Hunter tribe, dressed for the 1984 Mardi Gras in New Orleans (1984).
Nick Spitzer.

include categories such as ''Cajun,'' ''bluegrass,'' ''zydeco,'' ''blues,'' and other grass roots forms of American music.

The periodic revivals of interest in our heritage and ethnicity often express themselves musically. This occurred most dramatically during the ''folk revival'' of the early 1960s, when many people discovered blues and hillbilly music. Popular musicians such as Neil Young, Bob Dylan, Roger McGuinn, John Lennon, and Janis Joplin drew from the wellspring of folk music to help create the music of the ''British Invasion,'' San Francisco's ''psychedelic rock,'' and folk rock. In a more contemporary vein, hip-hop's use of poetic, simple, often obscene, rhymes stems directly from the African American tradition of toasts and the dozens (an insult game often played by males). The chanted/sung lyrics also have strong roots in the sermons performed in many black Baptist churches. The use of syncopation in the bass lines and drum patterns follows a tradition that relates back to early jazz, ragtime, and ultimately to West African drumming.

Final Thoughts

Even though America's distinctive regional and ethnic characteristics remain strong, the differences are slowly dissipating. The rapid changes in American music illustrate this process. Before the era of instant electronic communication (television, radio, telephones, and computers), improved long-distance transportation, and literacy for the masses, people spoke face-to-face. Most folk music was also transmitted directly from neighbor to neighbor or from a mother to her daughter or nephew. Because this music was passed along orally/aurally, most types of American folk music remained within small groups, relatively narrow geographic regions, or small communities. Today's students of American folk music stand on a fulcrum, glancing back towards our antecedents, while on the other side are more contemporary developments brought on by increased acculturation.

Key Figures and Terms

classical music
community
creolization
cultural region
diffusion
electronic communication
ethnic
ethnomusicologist
folk based
folk culture
foodways
MTV
mass media
multicultural
musicologist
oral folklore
popular culture
popular music
postmodern
regionalism
revivalists
traditional
Wade Ward

Audio

Anthology of American Folk Music. Folkways 2951/3. These three (two-record) sets cover almost every important style of American folk music and are taken from recordings originally issued from the 1920s through the 1940s.

Folk Music in America. Library of Congress. Dick Spottswood compiled these fifteen carefully annotated, broad-ranging anthologies designed as a Bicentennial tribute to the breadth of American folk music.

Folk Music U.S.A. Folkways 4530. A two-record compilation that provides a solid sampling of Anglo- and African American, as well as Hispanic traditions.

Roots of American Music. Arhoolie 2001/2. This double album is a fine cross section of black and white folk music from across the United States.

Books

Bohlman, Philip. 1988. *The Study of Folk Music in the Modern World*. Bloomington: Indiana University Press. A scholarly and thoughtful approach to the problems of defining folk music in our postmodern world.

Brunvand, Jan. 1986. *The Study of American Folklore*. New York: Norton. A solid introduction to folklore and folk life, including a good section on music.

Carney, George O., ed. 1987. *The Sounds of People and Places: Readings in the Geography of American Folk and Popular Music*. Lanham, Md.: University Press of America. A series of essays about the geographical implications of American folk and popular music.

Chase, Gilbert. 1987. *America's Music From Pilgrims to the Present*. Urbana: University of Illinois Press. The third edition of this magnum opus contains substantial chapters on minstrelsy, ragtime, blues, and other germane topics.

Davies, Robertson. 1985. *What's Bred in the Bone*. New York: Viking.

Hitchcock, Wiley, and Stanley Sadie, eds. 1986. *The New Grove Dictionary of American Music*. New York: Macmillan. The four-volume reference set contains hundreds of well-written entries related to American folk music.

Kingman, Daniel. 1990. *American Music: A Panorama*. New York: Schirmer. This book surveys the spectrum of American music, including a good survey of folk styles.

Miller, Terry. 1987. *Folk Music in America: A Reference Guide*. New York: Garland. Miller provides an invaluable handbook to articles, books, and other studies of American grass roots music.

Nettl, Bruno. 1965. *An Introduction to Folk Music of the United States*. Englewood Cliffs, N.J.: Prentice-Hall. A rather dated, but still valuable survey, which is due for revision.

Oliver, Paul, Max Harrison, and William Bolcolm. 1986. *The New Grove Gospel, Blues and Jazz with Spirituals and Ragtime*. New York: W. W. Norton. A handy and accurate guide to these important forms of black American music.

Sandberg, Larry, and Dick Weissman. 1989. *The Folk Music Sourcebook*. 2d ed. New York: Da Capo Press. With sections titled ''Listening,'' ''Learning,'' ''Playing,'' and ''Hanging Out,'' this book covers nearly everything in contemporary American folk music.

Wilgus, D. K. 1959. *Anglo-American Folk Song Scholarship Since 1898*. New Brunswick, N.J.: Rutgers University Press. An excellent and exhaustive study of folk-song scholarship through the late 1950s.

An important note about audio and video material Many of the video and audio products listed in this book can be found in full-service retail stores. Most of them, however, will have to be special ordered through video and audio stores, or they can be purchased through mail-order outlets. The two best sources for both audio and video material are listed below. They have *very* comprehensive catalogues and many years in the mail-order business:

Roots and Rhythm
6921 Stockton Avenue
El Cerrito, California 94530
510–525–1494 (phone)
510–525–2904 (fax)

Round-Up Records
P.O. Box 154
North Cambridge, Massachusetts 02140
617–661–6308 (phone inquiries)
800–443–4727 (phone orders)

Mass Media

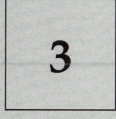

The **commercialization** and popularization of American folk music have taken many paths over the decades. Nineteenth-century folk music relied most heavily upon **aural transmission.** By the middle 1800s, however, shape-note hymnals and ballad "chapbooks" emerged as two early examples of the confluence of the printed media, commerce, and traditional music. This trend became more pronounced in the late nineteenth century and reached a new level of importance with the development of the electronic media in the early twentieth century.

All types of folk music have gained commercial attention, but very rarely have they become truly popular. The commercialization of American folk music has tended to focus upon established, small groups of consumers already familiar with the traditions. Cajun music, for example, enjoys commercial popularity in Louisiana and southeastern Texas. It can be heard on the radio (and sometimes seen on local television stations) and has been recorded by major and local record labels. But its appeal largely remains within the area settled by the Acadians in the eighteenth century. Probably because of the language barrier (many Cajuns still speak a creolized, heavily accented French) and its propensity to perform easygoing two-steps and waltzes, this music has never come into the popular American mainstream. A similar situation exists for Norwegian American folk music in the northern Midwest and Native American music in selected reservations across the United States. There remains a small but well-defined commercial market for traditional and folk based music within several regions of the United States.

We've also discovered that music and musical styles migrate across regional boundaries, both due to human movement and the influence of the electronic media. Although cowboy music and its 1930s counterpart, Western swing, originated on the lone prairies, their impact was not confined to the plains. The musicians of the Blue Ridge Mountains were deeply impressed by the Sons of the Pioneers, Roy Rogers, and Bob Wills. This did not occur because of the movement back east of musicians from Oklahoma and Texas; rather, easterners heard this music over their radios and on their phonographs and were captivated by Western music's genuine appeal and its intrinsic nostalgia. In the Midwest, groups such as the Modern Mountaineers (Missouri) and the Prairie Ramblers (Illinois and Kentucky) worked in a style closely allied with Western swing. This chapter discusses several ways in which the electronic mass media and popular culture have interacted with folk music.

Minstrel and Medicine Shows

By the 1840s, black performance practices were well enough known across the United States to lampoon in **minstrel shows,** the first distinctly American form of popular entertainment. Minstrel shows represent the country's first major exploitation of folk culture through their presentation of black music and entertainment on the popular stage. An amalgamation of racial stereotypes and elements of actual black American vernacular culture, the minstrel stage brought a vision of Southern plantation life to audiences throughout the country.

Early minstrels rarely featured African American performers; rather, they embraced white entertainers sporting blackened faces and playing their own interpretations of African American music. This **blackface** tradition provided Anglo-American performers with a mask of safety, removing them from the daily reality of the life that they portrayed. "Blacking up" became a staple vernacular entertainment, appearing later in medicine shows and the twentieth-century **vaudeville** stage.

Blackface white performers singing, rendering sermons, and telling stories in "Negro" dialect first gained prominence shortly after 1800. Within thirty years, popular white performers such as George Washington Dixon, J. W. Sweeney, and Thomas Rice captivated audiences with their interpretations of emerging black culture. Their models were both British and African American. The tunes they sang often followed well-known Irish and Scottish melodies while the lyrics relied upon images from American lore of the black man as a shuffling comic dandy, such as in songs like "Zip Coon" and **"Jump Jim Crow."** Thomas Rice popularized "Jump Jim Crow" in the late 1820s, taking it to the stages of America and to Europe by the middle 1830s. Some songs that we think of as "folk" and that are often performed by traditional musicians, like "Oh, Dem Golden Slippers," were actually composed by professional musicians touring on the minstrel circuit.

New York City is the birthplace of the minstrel show; it also served as its lexus during the classic period—1840 through 1870. Sometime in the early 1840s, blackface entertainers joined together on the same stage to delight white audiences with their songs and stories about Sambo and other octoroons. Minstrel shows were actually born when small bands of blackface interpreters added a theatrical element to their acts. Short skits about Southern black culture featuring stock black characters merely reinforced stereotypical views for urban audiences eager to learn more about the curious "Ethiopians" of the South. This combination of oral traditions and visual lampoons proved irresistible, and audiences flocked to hear this new entertainment form. For the first time, on the stage at least, Americans paid to look at a reflection of themselves and of the development of their own vernacular culture.

The Virginia Minstrels—as Bill Whitlock, Dick Pelham, Dan Emmett, and Frank Brower billed themselves in early 1843—became the first group to popularize their format. Complete with ragged costumes, Negro dialects, and the curious gait of the Southern colored people, the Virginia Minstrels literally set the stage for America's first unique form of popular entertainment. By 1850 minstrels were seen across the United States, and through the beginning of the Civil War, Anglo-American performers dominated the minstrel stage.

The significance of minstrel shows extends beyond the appropriation of black culture by whites, a pattern that will repeat itself many times in this book. When people flocked to the minstrel stage, they reaffirmed America's slow emergence from the domination of European culture. Minstrels presented a distorted vision of America's common people: illiterate but hardworking African Americans who toiled in the fields, frolicked to the sounds of banjos, and then shuffled off to church on Sunday to sing spirituals. It also acknowledged our country's agrarian roots, particularly for Northern audiences who themselves labored in urban settings very unlike the laconic southerners portrayed in minstrels. Despite the oftentimes crude images and presentation, minstrel shows helped to prepare northerners for their eventual glimpses of the ''real life'' of Southern blacks.

Many northerners, and even some southerners, got their first taste of black folk music through minstrel shows. The highly rhythmic and often lightly syncopated minstrel songs clearly prepared audiences across the country for the ragtime, blues, and jazz styles that began emerging in the early 1890s. But minstrel shows also introduced music that ultimately filtered back to become a part of the folk musicians' repertoire; ''Turkey in the Straw'' and ''Buffalo Gals'' are two fine examples of fiddle tunes that were introduced by traveling minstrels. Popular songs that have become part of the American consciousness, such as James Bland's ''Carry Me Back to Old Virginny,'' were often originally disseminated by way of minstrels and sheet music publication. Ironically, the unofficial anthem of the South, ''Dixie,'' betrays its minstrel origins.

Traveling medicine shows proved to be another source of steady income for black and white musicians alike. From the 1870s into the era of rock 'n' roll, these shows crisscrossed the United States. They were similar to minstrel shows in some respects, but instead of charging admission, they sold medicine, salves, and tonics. While minstrels sold themselves as purveyors of Southern black plantation life, medicine shows often played up the Indian theme with their sales of herbal and medicinal products. Medicine shows traveled under names both eye-catching and grandiose: the Great Mac Ian's Mastodon Medicine Company, the Jack Roach Indian Medicine Show, the Kickapoo Indian Medicine Company, and Dr. Lou Turner's Shaker Medicine Company. Most were operated by alleged doctors who promoted their shows as clean, medically sound, and family oriented. The shows themselves abounded with entertainment: theatrical performances, magicians, ventriloquists, contortionists, trapeze artists, blackfaced comedians, jugglers, and of course the pitches of the doctors themselves. Important American popular singers/entertainers such as Billy Golden and William Hughes worked medicine shows. Naturally, the door was also open to black folk musicians with a sense of adventure.

Black singers found employment as songsters with other types of road shows, too. The nineteenth-century traveling troupes expanded to include tent shows by the turn of the century. The mobile equivalent of vaudeville, tent shows provided audiences with a variety of entertainment for one modest admission fee. Often touring in conjunction with carnivals or as an adjunct to carnivals, tent shows of the teens featured some of the singers who went on to be the recording blues stars of the 1920s. One show in particular, the F. S. Wolcott Carnival, toured with a lineup of future impact artists: Bessie Smith, Ethel Waters, Butterbeans and Susie, Ida Cox, and Ma Rainey.

A wall in Alabama in the middle 1930s holds posters for two forms of entertainment. *Library of Congress.*

In addition to offering black musicians steady employment, these shows brought various types of music to audiences across the South. Because of traveling shows, rural folks were exposed not only to the familiar minstrel and ragtime songs but to the ballads and popular songs of the day. You can be certain that the posters announcing the arrival of a traveling show and the advance work of the buskers (entertainers who arrived in advance of the show in order to advertise it) had an easy time drawing a large opening-night crowd.

At the beginning of the twentieth century, most blacks still lived in the South; however, many others were new arrivals to the urban North. The "Great Migration" north began after the turn of the century. In the years following the close of World War I, hundreds of thousands of African Americans caught the Dixie Flyer and other trains to New York, Toledo, Chicago, Buffalo, Detroit, Milwaukee, Philadelphia, Minneapolis, and Hartford. They were searching for a new life away from the South, the Ku Klux Klan, humid and oppressive summers, and limited job opportunities.

The migrating black population did not leave their traditions behind; **down home** ways moved northward, too. This diffusion is also illustrated by Southern foodways. Barbecue restaurants and rib joints quickly appeared and proliferated along the streets of Northern "black bottoms." Moreover, the availability of collard greens and pigs' feet in grocery stores illustrates these

Blues on Record

changes. Southern cuisine was celebrated in song as well as in stomachs, perhaps most notably by Bessie Smith in ''Gimme a Pigfoot (And a Bottle of Beer).'' Such songs signified not only the relationship between food and music but a strong link with ''down home.''

These early commercial blues and jazz performers shared another trait, their choice of ''royal'' names. This flush era of commercial success provided opportunities for local and regional performers to tour and record, some of whom wished to aggrandize their status. Bessie Smith and Ma Rainey were billed as the ''Empress'' and ''Queen'' of the blues, respectively; they were sometimes accompanied by the likes of New Orleans-born trumpeter ''King'' Oliver. Such self-importance betrays their commercial orientation towards the stage and the promotion it requires, but also the importance they placed on their pride as a well-recognized member ''of the race'' and as a purveyor of black music in a racist, segregated society. African American gospel groups often promoted a similar image through names such as the Royal Crown Quartet (Hampton Roads, Virginia), the Five Kings of Harmony (Birmingham, Alabama), and the Majestic Soft Singers (Memphis, Tennessee).

''Country'' blues was the first down home style documented by the record companies as they explored ways to expand their **race** series and sell product. Ed Andrews, recorded by OKeh in Atlanta in April 1924, became the first country blues artist to record. His performance of ''Time Ain't Gonna Make Me Stay'' and ''Barrel House Blues'' typifies the Southeastern blues artists: a relaxed vocal accompanied by a nicely syncopated ragtime-styled guitar. This music appealed not only to Northern immigrants but also to Southern record buyers. Many record buyers came to local furniture stores (where both phonographs and records were sold) to purchase the latest discs, or they checked the newspaper advertisements to see about the most recent Paramount, Columbia, and Victor releases. In addition to news and gossip, each weekly issue of the *Amsterdam News* (New York City), *Chicago Defender,* or the *Norfolk Journal and Guide* (Virginia) contained advertisements for the newest country blues releases by Blind Lemon Jefferson, ''Daddy'' Stovepipe, Frank Stokes, and Lonnie Johnson.

Beginning in the 1920s and continuing for approximately thirty years, blues simultaneously functioned as folk and popular music within the black community. One key to understanding this process is cultural integration, which points out that ''folk groups'' retain their unique character while remaining part of the larger popular culture. This relationship has resulted in an ongoing dialogue: an interchange in which ideas and innovations move back and forth between folk and popular culture. The result is an integration or coexistence of the two. This is a natural synthesis in a world united by instant communication and easy interregional movement. The ''ideal'' isolated folk community or folk group no longer exists in the United States today. Nearly everyone is touched by the news, editorials, information, and music brought to us by radio and television . . . and has been for decades.

"Daddy" Stovepipe in the Gennett Studio. Richmond, Indiana, in 1924.
Kip Lornell.

Before the 1920s, blues was primarily a folk music propelled by the oral tradition. W. C. Handy and a handful of others had published sheet music in the mid-teens that furthered interest in the tradition, but the folk blues remained the province of African American performers. The media's sudden explosion intruded into the lives of many people, interesting them in new musical styles. Inside the black community, an even greater appetite developed for blues, its inherent popularity enhanced by the attention it received. The status of blues changed because this down home folk music that people previously associated with the South, beer gardens, and ''black-bottom'' dancing, quickly became commercial property. People from Kennebunkport to San Jose could now order recordings of down home and vaudeville blues performances without ever seeing these performers in person. The absolute need for personal contact with black folk musicians was obliterated.

One by-product of the increasing popularity of blues during the 1920s was the standardization of the form. Early blues were of varying lengths and did not always follow the same scheme of rhyming in the lyrics. Again, some of the more down home musicians adhered to their musical sensibilities, which had developed over years of playing. Musicians such as Sam Collins, Joe Callicot, or Bo-Weevil Jackson were so heavily steeped in early twentieth-century rural black vernacular music that they paid little attention to popular trends. They continued to play songs with eleven or thirteen bars, wordless moans, and to markedly speed up during the course of their performances—sometimes as much as 20 percent. By the middle 1920s, the blues form—twelve bars, *aab* verse form—had been standardized, especially through the recordings of the classic female blues singers, who almost always adhered to this format. This standardization can largely be attributed to the growing professionalization of blues and, in the case of female vaudeville blues performers, the need for a larger ensemble to follow a more predictable song form.

Innovations occurred more quickly as a result of these alterations in dissemination. The single-string solo work of the innovative, popular black blues guitarist Lonnie Johnson's numerous OKeh recordings touched musicians and listeners alike. Johnson's music influenced his black recording contemporaries, including such obscure blues musicians as Gene Campbell and George Jefferson. In 1929 Johnson also waxed a stunning series of guitar duets with white jazz guitarist Eddie Lang that are regarded as masterpieces of the genre. Lonnie Johnson's recordings clearly foreshadow the postwar blues guitar work of B. B. King, Eric Clapton, Otis Rush, Duane Allman, and others. His music illustrates how folk music is able to spread beyond regional and racial boundaries and into popular culture.

Neither was the blues impervious to the impact of popular culture. Some of the hard core, Deep South, down home blues recording artists of the 1920s, such as Six Cylinder Smith, Jim Tompkins, Edward Thompson, or Willie Brown, apparently remained untouched by popular trends. Their handful of recordings are ''pure'' examples of black American folk music; some are considered masterpieces of the genre. But many other blues recording artists whose careers began during the "first wave"—Leroy Carr, Big Bill, Tampa Red—unveiled repertoires that touched upon popular music. Urbane and sophisticated Leroy Carr performed many songs that extended the blues idiom beyond its inherent harmonic language into different song forms. His versions of "Think of Me, Thinking of You," "Love Hides All Faults," "Let's Make Up and Be Friends Again," or "Longing for My Sugar" owe more to Cole Porter and the Gershwins than they do to down home blues. In his later career, Tampa Red showed a distinct fondness for sentimental ballads, as did Lonnie Johnson.

Even though blues no longer has a strong support base within the African American community, white-owned record companies continue to produce this music because it sells. But it is consumed more by a white American and international audience. Alligator, a small, **independent record company** based in Chicago, has built a substantial catalogue by recording electric blues artists. Austria is home to Johnny Parth, whose Wolfe, Blues Document, and other labels have reissued the greatest number of blues records from the 1920s and 1930s. Even Japanese Sony, through its Columbia operation in the United States, had a smash blues reissue when its Robert Johnson set (originally recorded in 1936–37) remained among the top fifty selling releases for much of 1991. Doubtless, most of these sets have been sold to a white audience.

Country Music over the Airwaves

The history of modern American folk music remains inseparably tied to the evolution of the radio and phonograph industries. Although the commercial recording industry began in the late 1800s, their strong, symbiotic relationship began in 1920 when the first commercial radio station, **KDKA** in Pittsburgh, Pennsylvania, initiated its regular broadcasts. Within a matter of months, stations erected by entrepreneurs in other major cities began broadcasting. By 1924 scores of radio stations beamed their virtually unregulated signals throughout the United States. These early radio stations relied almost exclusively upon local talent to entertain their audiences with music, drama, comedy, recitations, and news. Almost as quickly as commercial radio stations sprang up, country music became part of their regularly scheduled daily broadcasts. Weekly "barn dance" shows featuring country music were established by broadcasters eager to serve their rural listeners. **Barn dance radio shows** were by no means a uniquely Southern phenomenon. As early as 1925, the powerful 50,000-watt signal of WLS in Chicago presented "hillbilly" talent to its vast Midwestern audience. The most famous of these shows, **"The Grand Ole Opry,"** has been a Nashville, WSM, and country music institution since its 1924 debut.

Radio was very tentative and exploratory during its first ten years of existence—1920 through 1930. It was so new that nobody was certain what would work. By the mid-1920s, regular country music jamborees were broadcast over WBAP in Fort Worth and WLS in Chicago. By the Depression's onset, radio stations were found across the entire United States, and they proliferated during the 1930s. What began as a big-city phenomenon spread to small cities and towns, which proudly boasted of their own radio stations. This meant that even more talent was needed to fill the demand created by the spread of local radio. Traditional music, especially country music, filled part of this void. The centralized radio networks brought national talent to local stations. Sometimes local grass-roots talent came to the broadcast headquarters in order to go nationwide.

The opportunity to go nationwide occurred to the Roanoke Entertainers, who were recommended to the CBS network by their hometown station, WDBJ. Their appearance was such a novelty that the *Roanoke Times and World News* sent a reporter along on their February 1931 trip to New York City:

> It isn't often the diners of the Memphis Special have a real old time string band to furnish ''music with their meals,'' but that's what happened last week when the Roanoke Entertainers, radio performers from WDBJ, and Hayden Huddleston, the red headed announcer, left here for New York. There were six in the party, five musicians with their banjos, guitars, and fiddles, and the announcer who drawls and slurs his R's. They had a drawing room, for this gang of Roanokers was traveling in style.
>
> They were on their way to the Big Town to play before the Columbia Broadcasting System audition board. . . . At 2 o'clock John Mayo, Columbia announcer, introduced the band with ''Ladies and Gentlemen, presenting a program of unusual entertainment, the Roanoke Entertainers under the personal direction of Hayden Huddleston. . . .'' With that, the Roanoke Entertainers went on the air, playing ''Lights in the Valley.'' The band played six numbers, including the popular tune, ''Smokey Mountain Bill,'' and it was not long before the telegrams began coming in. The Entertainers went over with a bang. But, like everything else, there is an end to all good things. The Entertainers remembered that Roanoke awaited them, so Saturday night they again boarded the train. The boys played for about an hour, then came sleep—welcome after two wild and hectic days in the Big City.
>
> The Roanoke Entertainers, first of the local musicians to play over a national network, are back home today carrying on in their everyday life. For this band is made up of men who work every day. They are not professional musicians. . . . A lot of folks heard about Roanoke, Virginia, Saturday that never heard it mentioned before. Such is the power of radio.

WDBJ is typical in its use of local hillbilly groups, such as the McCray Family, N & W Stringband, Blue Ridge Fox Chasers, and Floyd County Ramblers. By the 1930s, cowboy music and Western swing by groups such as the Texas Troubadours (who predate Ernest Tubb's band by at least two years) became part of its daily programming. The biggest names on Roanoke country radio, Roy Hall and the Blue Ridge Entertainers (1939–43) and Flatt and Scruggs (1947), comforted Roanoke Valley listeners with their own blend of humor, string-band music, and informal commercials.

For many country musicians, radio became more than a performance vehicle. The radio broadcasts themselves paid rather poorly (or not at all), but they allowed the musicians to announce their live **show dates** and personal appearances. Thus, radio became their most effective source for advertising the true financial basis for their musical careers—lucrative live appearances at which they sold autographed pictures and songbooks. An immediate, intimate link between performer and audience helped these fifteen- to thirty-minute shows develop into more than a musical event. Performers responded to the musical requests that came by way of the telephone, mail, and telegraph wires, talked about the weather, and poked fun at one another. Once country artists worked an area "dry" and the requests for show dates slowed down, they either moved on to more fertile ground or temporarily retired from music as a full-time occupation.

The bias of country music broadcasting is clearly towards the South and the "border" region of the Midwest and Middle Atlantic states. The truth is that country music, whose roots are tied to traditional Anglo-American styles, existed in all parts of the United States. Very little has been written about country music outside of the South, though its impact proved to be nationwide. Even the cold Northern climate of upstate New York was not impervious to the charms of **hillbilly music.** This Southern emphasis underscores the inescapable importance of regionalism in folk music; Americans expect hillbilly music to be from the South where it is bred in the bone.

Consequently, we are more hard-pressed to describe the broadcasting of early country music outside of the South. The recording industry also largely ignored white country music north of the Mason-Dixon line, and the statewide collecting projects were largely initiated by scholarly types in search of ballads: British, American, and occupational. The books they published in the first half of this century focus on these aspects of the northern Anglo tradition. Comparably few commercial and field recordings of non-Southern folk music

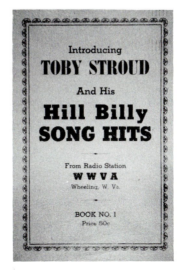

Toby Stroud sold songbooks while he was on the air in the early 1940s.
Kip Lornell.

were made prior to the advent of easily portable equipment in the 1950s. In the halcyon days before the Depression, the commercial companies themselves did not go out of their way to scout non-Southern hillbilly talent. Most of their recordings were done at studios in New York City or Chicago. Victor used its Camden, New Jersey, facilities for recordings and made field trips to a variety of Southern cities in search of vernacular musical talent. With the exception of several trips to the West Coast and one brief session in Butte, Montana, their vision turned ever southward.

But not even all Southern born "rural" talent heard over the airwaves and produced by the Northern-based record companies was factually represented. **Vernon Dalhart,** born Marion Try Slaughter on April 6, 1883, in northeastern Texas, received conservatory vocal training in Dallas before moving to New York City early in the century. Dalhart went on to become one of the era's most prolific recording artists, whose talents knew no arbitrary musical boundaries. Some of his records were marketed as "country," most notably those on Columbia's 15,000 "Old-Time" series. In reality, Dalhart's country records foreshadowed the "city billy" sound heard in the early 1960s. His Tin Pan Alley songs also appealed to the rapidly developing country music clientele, who flocked to purchase his versions of "Wreck of the Old '97" and "The Death of Floyd Collins." This music was far removed from Dalhart's Texas heritage, which he left behind after moving to New York City. Nonetheless, Dalhart literally coined the genre of **pop country,** a term that would not come into currency for several decades.

Throughout the 1940s, country music radio was largely Southern-based. Some radio stations in rural areas outside of the South featured country music early in the morning and surrounding the daily farm reports and prices. Live broadcasts remained the rule of the day for most radio stations until well after the close of World War II. By the early 1950s, however, the radio industry was undergoing an evolutionary upheaval caused partially by television. Established radio stars like Arthur Godfrey and Art Linkletter jumped ship and moved into television's more glamorized spotlight. Networks proliferated and an even greater demand for national talent caused radio stations to move away from their local identities, resulting in an ever-diminishing number of "live" slots for local grass roots and country musicians. For all practical purposes, in-studio musical performances became passé when the nation was engulfed by the rock 'n' roll revolution. The most notable exception is Garrison Keillor's highly successful "American Radio Company" on American Public Radio, which in 1990 superceded "A Prairie Home Companion." These two shows have been a distinct anachronism in today's world of Arbitron ratings and inflexible playlists on commercial radio stations.

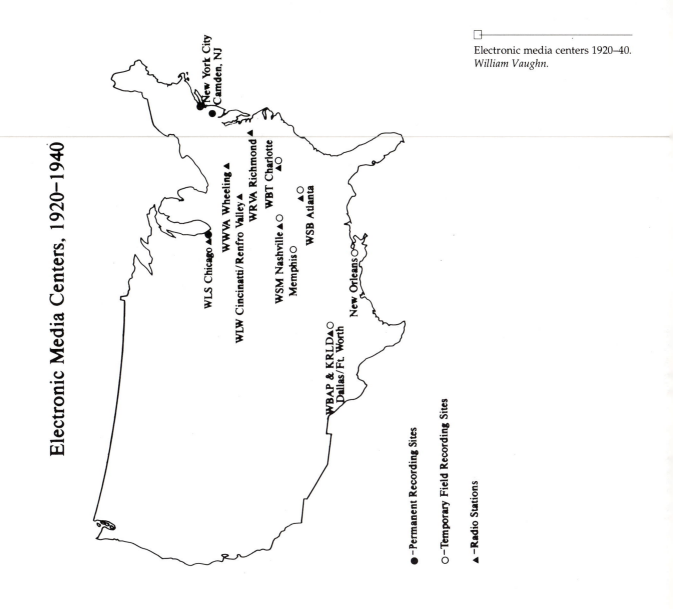

Electronic Media Centers, 1920–1940

New York City
Camden, NJ

WWVA Wheeling ▲
WLW Cincinatti/Renfro Valley ▲
WRVA Richmond ▲
WBT Charlotte ▲○
WLS Chicago ▲●
WSM Nashville ▲○
Memphis○
WSB Atlanta ▲○
New Orleans○○
WBAP & KRLD▲○
Dallas/Ft. Worth

●–Permanent Recording Sites

○–Temporary Field Recording Sites

▲–Radio Stations

Electronic media centers 1920–40.
William Vaughn.

43

Record Companies and Folk Music

Commercial record companies began seriously recording regional country, blues, and gospel artists simultaneous to radio's first days. Although cylinder phonograph records had been marketed early in the 1890s, performers of grass roots American music were largely ignored. A meager number of black gospel groups—most notably, the Dinwiddie Colored Quartet of Dinwiddie, Virginia; Richmond, Virginia's Old South Quartette; and the Fisk (University) Jubilee Singers—recorded prior to World War I. In 1920 the General Phonograph Company's OKeh label recorded cabaret singer Mamie Smith performing "Crazy Blues," which quickly lit the way for blues and other forms of black secular music on disc.

After a general recording slump in 1921 and 1922, blues, gospel, and country music finally caught the attention of record company officials. Victor took a chance with Texas fiddler Eck Robertson, who was accompanied by Henry Gilliland, in the summer of 1922. His pre-electric recording of the old dance tune "Sallie Goodin'" is widely acknowledged as the first country music recording. But the commercial country music industry really got started in 1923 with Fiddlin' John Carson, an older musician from Atlanta, Georgia. By 1925 this market enjoyed a steady stream of releases by banjo pickers, string bands, and fiddle/guitar duets. Victor, OKeh, Paramount, Columbia, Gennett, and Black Patti recorded thousands of blues, country, and gospel performances until the Depression nearly wiped out the entire industry.

These records were distributed across the country and sold in furniture stores by the same people who wanted you to purchase a windup Victrola. Mail order was another important outlet for the fragile 78-rpm recordings. Newspapers and magazines advertised the most recent monthly releases in a series of stylized ads. The companies themselves distinguished between black and white artists by segregating the series. All of the selections by African American artists were issued as part of the "race" catalogue, while the white artists were labeled as "old-time," "hillbilly," or "country." For instance, Columbia Records reserved its 13/14,000 series exclusively for black

Ralph Peer in the 1930s.
Courtesy: Peer-Southern Organization.

performers, while secular and sacred country music appeared on their 15,000 ''Old-Time'' series.

A and R (Artists and Repertoire) **men** supervised all of the recording sessions; their aesthetic and commercial sensibilities helped to shape the direction of American music. Ralph Peer, Art Saitherly, and Frank Walker worked with an enormous number of musicians, relying upon a network of musicians, local furniture dealers, and even newspaper advertisements to locate talent. Musicians whose records sold well came back to the studios on numerous occasions. The openness of early talent scouting led to the recording of poor-selling and obscure but exceptionally interesting folk music talent like the Weems String Band (Arkansas), Blind Willie Reynolds (Louisiana), and the Memphis Sanctified Singers. While the best-regarded artists generally sold no more than fifty thousand copies of a record, these regional lightweights were lucky to sell several hundred copies of one of their discs.

The Depression struck the entire country, altering the record industry. A conservative pallor settled over the business of selling records, and comparatively little out-of-the-way talent was recorded. Instead, the companies relied upon proven artists with a formula for selling records: Big Bill (Broonzy), the Carter Family, Washboard Sam, the Delmore Brothers, and Peetie Wheatstraw

This 1939 Vocalion catalogue underscores the popularity of Big Bill.
Kip Lornell.

RECORDINGS BY AMERICA'S LEADING RACE ARTISTS:
VOCAL BLUES, HOT DANCE, SPIRITUALS AND SACREDS

JOHN HENRY BARBEE
(Vocal Blues with Inst. Acc.)
04417 God Knows I Can't Help It
04417 Six Week Old Blues

BARREL HOUSE ANNIE
(Vocal Blues with Inst. Acc.)
03542 Ain't Gonna Give It Away
03542 Must Get Mine in Front

WILLIE BEE
(Vocal Blues with Inst. Acc.)
03907 Can't Control My Mind
03907 Ramblin' Mind Blues

BIG BILL

(Vocal Blues with Inst. Acc.)
04706 Baby I Done Got Wise
04829 Baby Don't You Remember
03337 Border Blues
03122 Come Home Early
04642 Don't You Lay It On Me
03147 Evil Hearted Me
03337 Good Boy

04532 Good Time Tonight
04095 Got to Get Ready Tonight
03252 Hattie Blues
04532 Hell Ain't But a Mile and a Quarter
03304 I Want My Hands On It
04041 I Want You By My Side
04642 I'll Do Anything for You
04095 I'll Start Cutting on You
03252 It's Too Late Now
04280 It's Your Time Now
04706 Just A Dream
04760 Just Got to Hold You Tight
05043 Just Wondering
04990 Keep on A-Smilin'
03075 Let Me Be Your Winder
04591 Let Me Dig It
02944 Let's Reel and Rock
04429 Living on Easy Street
03075 Louise, Louise Blues
03304 Made a Date with an Angel
04760 Mary Blues
04280 Mill Man Blues, The
03170 My Big Money
03147 My Gal is Gone
03122 My Old Lizzie
03170 My Woman Mistreats Me
04149 New Shake 'Em On Down
04149 Night Time is the Right Time No. 2
03400 Play Your Hand
04938 Please Be My So and So
04884 Ride, Alberta ,Ride
04486 Rider Rider Blues
04378 Sad Pencil Blues
04884 She Never
03400 Somebody's Got To Go
04041 Sweetheart Land
05043 That's All Right, Baby
04591 Trouble and Lying Woman
04205 Trucking Little Woman
04486 Trucking Little Woman No. 2

04378 Unemployment Stomp
04205 Why Did You Do That to Me
04938 Woodie Woodie
04429 WPA Rag
04990 You Can't Win
02944 You Do Me Any Old Way
04829 You Can't Sell 'Em in Here

BLACK BOY SHINE
(Vocal Blues with Guitar Acc.)
04003 Bad Luck Town Blues
04003 Hobo Blues

BLIND BOY FULLER

(Vocal Blues with Inst. Acc.)
02964 Ain't It a Crying Shame
04391 Ain't No Gettin' Along
03098 Babe You Got to Do Better
02956 Baby, I Don't Have to Worry
05083 Baby Quit Your Low Down Ways
03014 Baby You Gotta Change Your Mind
03351 Been Your Dog
03123 Big Bed Blues

(the Devil's Son-in-Law). Just as World War II began pulling record companies out of their prolonged slump, the **Petrillo Ban** (American Federation of Musicians Union) and a shortage of shellac virtually shut down the entire industry for eighteen months in late 1942 and 1943.

By war's end, a new breed of record entrepreneurs slowly infiltrated the industry, challenging the way the major companies did business. While the major companies looked more towards popular music and displayed less interest in blues, country, and gospel, new labels began taking up the slack. The Chess brothers in Chicago, Bernie Bessman (Apollo) in New York City, and Houston's Don Robey (Duke/Peacock) explored the grass roots of American music. Significantly, Sam Phillips's small Memphis operation helped to launch the rock 'n' roll revolution when Elvis Presley walked into his studio in 1954 looking for an opportunity. Within a few years, many of the small labels looked towards rock 'n' roll and its permutations for their livelihood.

Nonetheless, traditional music continues to sell to a select audience. Since the "folk boom" of the early to middle 1960s, the number of small labels devoted to grass roots music has increased. Arhoolie, Rounder, and Flyright (England) help to insure an outlet for contemporary performers of folk and folk based music. These and other companies also devote part of their catalogue to reissuing vintage performances. Although such companies do not have the financial backing or distribution of major labels, they do offer opportunities for artists who would otherwise be overlooked.

Uncle Dave Macon and the Electronic Media

Born in 1870 in central Tennessee, **Uncle Dave Macon** was firmly middle-aged when he first recorded. For many years, Macon farmed and ran the Macon Midway Mule and Wagon Transportation Company, hauling freight between Murfreesboro and Woodbury, Tennessee. He also learned banjo picking under the expert tutelage of minstrel and circus veteran Joel Davidson, who exposed Uncle Dave to his own repertoire and taught him the importance of raconteurship. In 1920 Macon quit the hauling trade and soon after turned to music full time. He played locally but quickly joined the vaudeville circuit, bringing his considerable skills to engagements arranged by the Loew's organization.

From 1923 until his death in 1952, Uncle Dave Macon entertained people with his music and stories. Inspired by the success of Fiddlin' John Carson, Sterchi Brothers Furniture Company (Nashville's Vocalion Record distributors) arranged for Macon and his partner, Sid Harkreader, to record in New York City. Macon's first session in July 1924 suggests the breadth of his experiences, interests, and tastes all tempered by what Macon knew the people wanted. He combined elements of his stage act, including his popular comic piece "Chewing Gum," with traditional material, "The Fox Chase," and his own version of "Little Old Log Cabin in the Lane." Future sessions were equally broad in their interpretation of "country music" for the masses. One of his most famous sessions came in May 1927 with his Fruit Jar Drinkers performing classic renditions of Anglo-American fiddle tunes and lyric songs: ''Sail Away Ladies,'' ''Carve That Possum,'' and ''Tommy and Jerry,'' as well as eight sacred numbers. ''Carve That Possum,'' written by black minstrel performer Sam Lucas and published in the middle 1870s, shows off Macon's own minstrel roots. Its humor relies on racial and rural stereotypes that seem far removed from those living in an urban, high-tech world. This performance features a response by the band, which is shown in parentheses:

> My dog treed, I went to see (Carve him to the heart).
> Dar was a possum up dat tree (Carve him to the heart).
> And dat possum begin to grin (Carve him to the heart).
> I reached up and took a pin (Carve him to the heart).
>
> **Refrain:** Oh, carve that possum, carve that possum children.
> Carve that possum, children, oh carve him to his heart.
>
> Carried him home and dressed him off (Carve . . .).
> Hung him out that night in the frost (Carve . . .).
> But the way to cook the possum sound (Carve . . .).
> First parboil, then bake him brown (Carve . . .).
>
> **Refrain:**
>
> Possum meat am good to eat (Carve . . .).
> Always fat and good and sweet (Carve . . .).
> Grease potatoes in the pan (Carve . . .).
> Sweetest eating in the land (Carve . . .).
>
> **Refrain:**
>
> Some eat early and some eat soon (Carve . . .).
> Some like possum and some like coon (Carve . . .).
> That possum just the thing for me (Carve . . .).
> Old Rattler's got another one up a tree (Carve . . .).
>
> **Refrain:**

Macon recorded nearly 180 songs during his lengthy commercial recording career, which stretched well into the 1930s. His final selections were done by folklorist Charles Faulkner Bryant in 1950, shortly before his death.

Not only did Macon sell records and appear on the stage, he became one of hillbilly music's early radio artists. His debut came late in 1925 over Nashville's WSM, home of the recently established ''Grand Ole Opry,'' where he remained a fixture for fifteen years and regular performer until his death. Macon was not limited to the three-to-five-minute confines of the contemporary Opry; he often had fifteen-to-thirty-minute blocks of improvisatory time, permitting him to stretch out by telling jokes, comic tales, and performing music. Over his nearly thirty-year radio career, Macon reached the ears and hearts of millions of Americans.

Perhaps more than any other Anglo-American ''folk'' musician of the first half of the twentieth century, Uncle Dave Macon stretched across the gap between minstrelsy and rock 'n' roll. He very clearly recognized the vital impact of radio and records as forces in disseminating his music to an audience far more vast than touring could ever hope to reach. Unlike Virginia's Ernest V. Stoneman, who stayed away from radio and touring until the renaissance of his musical career in the late 1950s, Macon embraced both aspects of the new technology in order to further his professional career. By the end of his life, Uncle Dave was a true anachronism. He remained true to his creative muse. As a fiercely individualistic, perhaps eccentric, man, Macon brought his nineteenth-century musical vision to people across modern-day America.

Border Radio

Border radio stations provided another wonderfully unconventional opportunity for America's early country musicians like the Carter Family, Slim Rheinhart and Patsy Montana, Asher Sizemore and Little Jimmie, the Pickard Family, Bob Wills, and onetime Texas senator W. Lee O'Daniel and the Hillbilly Boys. Beginning in the early 1930s, these unregulated stations located just inside the Mexican border blasted their northern neighbors with signals approaching half a million watts. Dr. J. R. Brinkley became the most famous wildcat broadcaster, pitching the notorious goat gland transplant for men whose sex drive had diminished. XERA, his base of operations in Villa Acuña, Mexico, offered a myriad of products to treat the range of human maladies.

Nearly a score of these stations ranged along the Mexican-American border from the Gulf of Mexico to Tijuana. Border stations featured not only grass roots American music but Mexican popular and folk music, including

In the late 1930s, border radio stations offered songbooks by their artists.
Kip Lornell.

stars such as Lydia Mendoza. Music was one important element of border radio's daily schedule, and Dr. Brinkley emerged as the single most colorful pitchman. Dozens of individuals touted themselves as radio seers, spiritual healers of the airwaves, or medical men with astonishing cures. They hosted shows such as ''The Bible Institute of the Air,'' ''Good Neighbor Get-Together,'' ''The Brother Human Hour,'' and ''Helping Hand.'' Their product was sold on a ''P.I.'' (per inquiry) basis with the hosts and the radio stations sharing in the profits. Nearly all of these men and women were most certainly quacks, but they offered hope, solace, and entertainment to millions of listeners.

Border radio reigned unchecked for more than twenty years, well into the rock 'n' roll era. Its influence diminished in the 1950s as the F.C.C. and the Mexican government began a series of legal actions to limit them. As late as 1960, Wolfman Jack launched his broadcasting career as a disc jockey on XERF in Del Rio. Changing tastes in radio and even more stringent regulations have all but shut down these powerful stations. Well into the 1980s, rock groups like Z. Z. Top and Wall of Voodoo continued to celebrate the zaniness and power of border radio: ''I wish I was in Tijuana, eating barbecued iguana. . . . I'm on a Mexican radio'' (''Mexican Radio'' by Wall of Voodoo, 1982).

Final Thoughts

The electronic media have shaped postmodern America. They help to define and promulgate popular trends in fashion, language, dance, and music. American folk music has been intrinsically linked with radio and the recording industry since their inception, both of which have assisted in the breakdown of the cultural traits that delineate regional American culture and music. But traditional music is far from dead. It continues lurking just beneath the commercial underbelly, infusing younger musicians, who seemingly every year discover the old records of Robert Johnson, Gid Tanner and the Skillet Lickers, Elmore James, the Carter Family, Jimmie Rodgers, and the Golden Gate Quartet. All of them are truly American originals.

Key Figures and Terms

A and R men
aural transmission
barn dance radio shows
blackface
commercialization
Vernon Dalhart
down home
''Grand Ole Opry''
hillbilly music
independent record companies
''Jump Jim Crow''
KDKA
Uncle Dave Macon
minstrel shows
Petrillo Ban
pop country
race records
show dates
vaudeville

Audio

Carter Family. *On Border Radio.* JEMF 101 (LP). A selection of songs taken from border radio between 1938 and 1942.

Early Roanoke Country Radio. BRI 010 (CASS/LP). An album/monograph set that covers the period between 1925 and 1955.

Folk Music Radio. Radiola 1133 (CASS). Vintage radio broadcasts by Woody Guthrie, Pete Seeger, and others.

Louvin Brothers. *Radio Favorites '51–'57.* Country Music Foundation 009 (CASS/LP). The title sums up the contents of this release.

Maddox Brothers and Rose. *On the Air*. Arhoolie 222 (CASS). These performances are from broadcasts that originally aired shortly after World War II.

Red Hot and Blue—Classic Radio Transcriptions. Zu Zazz 2012 (LP). Live radio programs from Memphis (WDIA) from the middle 1950s.

Books

Crawford, Bill, and Gene Fowler. 1987. *Border Radio*. Austin: Texas Monthly Press. An entertaining and informative historical account of Mexican border radio.

Dixon, Robert, and John Godrich. 1971. *Recording the Blues*. London: Studio Vista. A study of the blues recording industry up to 1943.

McNamara, Brooks. 1976. *Step Right Up*. New York: Doubleday and Co. The definitive book about the development and history of medicine shows.

Toll, Robert. 1974. *Blacking Up: The Minstrel Show in Nineteenth-Century America*. New York: Oxford University Press. Toll's work is a comprehensive examination of minstrelsy during its heyday.

Video

On Air Country. Blue Ridge Institute, Ferrum College, 1988. A half-hour documentary that complements audio recording BRI 010, *Early Roanoke Country Radio*.

Anglo-American Secular Folk Music

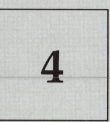

Introducing American Folk Music is gradually exposing you to the wide variety of styles that you've probably never before encountered. In this chapter, however, you will find some quintessential American folk music. Many of the figures discussed here are obscure, while others are quite well known because of their exposure in the commercial media: Gene Autry, Bill Monroe, Ernest V. Stoneman, and Bob Wills, among others. Their folk songs, ranging from a cowboy's lament to the native American ballads celebrating train wrecks, are discussed in the following pages.

This music largely developed from our ancestors who came from the English-speaking British Isles. Typically, the subject of ballads arises in discussions of Anglo-American folk song, and a small number of British ballads remain part of our culture. Even a few songs, such as the ballad ''The Unfortunate Rake'' (better known as the cowboy song, ''The Streets of Laredo'') and the fiddle tune ''Paddy on the Turnpike,'' are still played and sung by folk musicians on both continents. Much of this music eventually went into the brew that evolved into two strains: the ''Nashville'' sound and rock music in the post World War II era.

Tommy Jarrell keeps the tradition alive during the 1982 Festival of American Folklife.
Smithsonian Institution.

Ballads, frequently considered a ''purer'' literary folk tradition, exerted an important influence upon early Anglo-American music. These are the older British ballads, songs with a clear, usually linear story line. Certainly the later **Tin Pan Alley** writers were interested in storytelling, but the classic old-world ballads belong in a separate category because their antiquity and intent differ so greatly from the professional authors. The ballads in James Francis Child's canon, for instance, generally migrated to the United States during its settlement. Child idealized these oral stories purely as products of the unsullied ''folk,'' who preserved these songs as part of an ongoing oral process that was passed down from one generation of semiliterate (at best) folk to another. Many of these songs were transmitted by written means: texts printed in rough ''chapbooks'' or copied by the singers themselves in notebooks.

The early ballad singers generally performed alone and with no instrumental accompaniment. Scholars beginning with James Francis Child have generally been intent upon merely collecting the words to these songs. In recent years, a more holistic approach has prevailed, with not only the text but the tune and the context gaining more status among collectors of folk songs. Bill McNeil's recent compilations, *Southern Ballads,* exemplify this trend, as does Tom Burton's regional study. Bertrand Bronson's important work with the tunes of **Child ballads** also adds greatly to our knowledge of the music associated with these venerable songs.

By definition, ballads tell a story, but they also contain characteristics that make them different from other forms of narrative songs. Ballads are impersonal in tone and compress their action to focus upon a single event. The action is usually vividly portrayed with plenty of drama and romance, and with occasional sorties into melodrama. In these regards, a ballad is similar to a newspaper story, particularly a tabloid bannered with headlines about aliens, Elvis Presley, and wonder diets. Several well-known British ballads imported to this country would make very impressive headline fodder: ''Farmer Sells Wife's Soul to Devil'' (''Farmer's Curst Wife''—Child 278), ''Cuckold Husband Mistakes Wife's Lover for a Cabbagehead'' (''Our Goodman''—Child 274), ''Lover Wins Last Minute Reprieve with Gold Offer'' (''The Maid Freed from the Gallows''—Child 95), or ''Enemy Ship Sunk by Greedy, Love-Crazed Cabin Boy'' (''The Golden Vanity''—Child 286).

Ballads invariably use plotted action. Typically, there is an unsettled situation and its resolution, which makes for suspenseful drama. They tend to gloss over the unsettled early situation and concentrate on the more consequential action of the second section. Ballad scholars have labeled this **''leaping and lingering''**: leaping over the background details in order to linger on the powerful and dramatic scenes. But even the most climactic action unfolds in objective prose, while the most gruesome or emotional scenes are revealed dispassionately and without critical comment. They often unfold as though they are being recounted by a jaded, veteran court reporter who has seen it all dozens of times before.

Ballads

While the British ballads in James Francis Child's canon contain stories about Robin Hood and England's battles with European countries, such tales are not encountered in the United States. The Child ballads that survived into twentieth-century America contain more universal themes with generalized plots: the love of Barbara Allen, tragic events between two sisters, or the roguish charm of Black Jack Davie. The basic appeal of such stories is apparent, especially in eighteenth- and nineteenth-century America where so many people were closer to British culture and lacked the formal education to read and write. It is important to remember that ballads are not perpetuated only among the rural, illiterate poor.

Well into the twentieth century, Edwin Kirkland collected and recorded some fine versions of British ballads from his colleagues and peers at the University of Tennessee in Knoxville. Most of the late twentieth-century ballad singers tend to be from the South, particularly from the Appalachian or Blue Ridge mountains. A few outstanding ballad singers, such as Sarah Cleveland, have been "discovered" in the Midwest and the Northeast. Some of the best of them, such as Horton Barker (Virginia) or Aunt Molly Jackson (Kentucky), sang without musical accompaniment but with great emotional force. However, their performance style tended to be formal, almost Calvinistic in its delivery. Other singers of older ballads, such as Frank Proffitt (North Carolina) and Jean Ritchie (Kentucky), often used their own stringed instrumental accompaniment. A capella singing permits greater freedom from both meter and strict phrasing; it also encourages more ornamentation.

Broadsides

Not all of the ballads with British roots are contained in Child's collection, which was selective and labeled as "popular." Another category of non-American, English ballads is called "broadsides" because they were printed pieces with strong journalistic ties. Broadside ballads are ephemeral by their very nature and few survived into oral circulation, particularly in the United States. Such ballads tend to be topical, placing immediate temporal limitations on them. The human interest element, along with simplicity and general themes, once more helps to perpetuate ballads in oral tradition.

Broadside ballads are usually considered inferior to the classic Child ballads by scholars, who suggest that they lack the refinements and polish of good poetry. Formulas are an important feature of broadside ballads, most often through the use of stock phrases such as the **"come ye all"** salutation that opens "When the Battle It Was Won" (J 23):

> Come all you aged people, I pray you lend an ear,
> You'll hear my feeling story, you can't but shed a tear.
> 'Twas of an aged couple that had one only son;
> He was shot as a deserter when the battle it was won.

Broadside ballads often take the first person perspective, rely upon stereotyped characters, and frequently lack the objectivity of Child ballads.

M u s i c a l   E x a m p l e

Ms. Ritchie comes from an exceptionally musical family in Kentucky. She has made many recordings of ballads, including this version of "The House Carpenter" from the middle 1950s. Some of the literary characteristics of ballads can be seen in this version of "The House Carpenter." This popular British ballad easily jumped the Atlantic Ocean into the repertoire of American singers because of its treatment of romance, heroism, and bold action. The American edition displays many of the traits previously described; it leaps over superfluous details, concentrating instead upon action. The action makes emotional sense and the story moves briskly along. But listeners are left wondering about details: What are the names of the people involved? Where in Italy were they bound? What caused the ship to "spring a leak?" [Folkways 2301]

Title "The House Carpenter" (Child 243)
Performer Jean Ritchie
Instruments one voice
Length 4:19
Notable Features

1. The a capella singing creates a monophonic texture.
2. The form of this ballad is strophic.
3. You can hear very minor variations in melodic and the occasional rhythmic inflections.
4. Her voice is at ease and falls into the lower middle register.
5. Ms. Ritchie uses a pentatonic (five-note) scale for this song.

Well met, well met, my own true love,
Well met, well met, said he,
I've come from far across the sea,
And it's all for the sake of thee.

I could have married the king's daughter fair,
And she would have married me,
But I have forsaken the crowns of gold,
And it's all for the sake of thee.

If you could've married a king's daughter fair,
I'm sure I'm not to blame,
For I have married me a house carpenter
For I'm sure he's a fine young man.

Oh will you leave your house carpenter
And sail away with me?
I'll take you where the grass grows green
Down in sweet Italy.

Oh if I leave my house carpenter
And sail away with ye,
What will ye have to maintain me upon
When we are far away?

Oh I have seven ships upon the sea,
Seven ships upon the land,
Four hundred and fifty bold sailor men
To be at your command.

She turned herself three times around,
She kissed her babies three;
Farewell, farewell, you sweet little babes,
Keep your father sweet company.

They hadn't been sailin' but about two weeks,
I'm sure it was not three,
When this fair lady begin for to weep,
And she wept most bitterly.

Are you weepin' for your house carpenter,
Are you weepin' for your store,
Or are you weepin' for your sweet little babes,
That you never shall see anymore?

Not a-weepin' for my house carpenter,
Not a-weepin' for my store,
Yes, I'm weepin' for my sweet little babes
That I never will see any more.

They hadn't been sailin' but about three weeks,
I'm sure it was not four,
When the ship sprung a leak and down she sank,
And she sank to rise no more.

What hills, what hills so fair and so bright,
What hills so white and fair?
Oh those be the hills of heaven, my dear,
But you won't never go there.

What hills, what hills down in yonder sea,
What hills so black as coal?
Oh those be the hills of hell, my dear,
Where we must surely go.

They are also often subject to recomposition, often with condensation of plot and sometimes with not so subtle shifts in details.

Because they are largely part of an oral tradition, ballads are subject to alterations in time, place, or other details. If the ballad is immediately recognizable and changed only in minor ways, it is said to be a version of some older, usually printed, text. Major changes can be fashioned, but if the fundamental plot is unaltered, it is considered a **variant. G. Malcolm Laws** (1957) undertook the most intensive study of broadside ballads, classifying them thematically and assigning them a numerical symbol: ''War (J),'' ''Sailors and the Sea (K),'' ''Crimes and Criminals (L),'' ''Family Opposition to Lovers (M),'' ''Lovers' Disguises and Tricks (N),'' ''Faithful Lovers (O),'' ''Unfaithful Lovers (P),'' ''Humorous and Miscellaneous Ballads (Q).'' The categories themselves underscore the types of themes most often found in broadside ballads and reflect the interests of the people who sang them.

Though they sound very distant from postmodern America, some broadside ballads have survived well into the twentieth century. Ballads about war, sailors, and crime are not as well preserved as those related to love and its consequences. Many versions and variants of broadside ballads about love were collected up through World War II by English professors and others interested in ballads. Broadsides such as ''The Drowsy Sleeper'' (M 4), ''The Banks of Dundee'' (M 25), ''The Girl I Left Behind'' (P 1), and ''The Butcher Boy'' (P 24) are found from Maine to California. Broadside ballads have circulated through the medium of commercial recordings, too.

In the middle 1960s, the California folk rock group the Byrds recorded ''John Riley'' (N 36), about a soldier who returns from war in disguise so that he can test his love's fidelity. Not surprisingly, early hillbilly recordings reflect the importance of broadsides with Gid Tanner and the Skillet Lickers, Kelly Harrell, and the Dixon Brothers among the many who dipped into this well. Perhaps the most famous broadside ballad related to the problems of love, ''The Bad Girl's Lament'' (Q 26), is related to another broadside, ''The Unfortunate Rake.'' In America it is known as ''St. James' Hospital (or Infirmary),'' ''The Streets of Laredo,'' ''The Young Girl Cut Down in Her Prime,'' or the ''Cowboy's Lament.'' It has been recorded many times since the 1920s and relates, in very oblique language, the consequence of contracting a venereal disease. Perhaps the scourge of the late twentieth century, AIDS, will bring about a revival of this broadside.

Native American Ballads

With this strong ballad tradition in folk music from the British Isles, the emergence of native American ballads seems inevitable. As soon as the Puritans settled in New England, the process began in the United States. However, nearly all of the best-known native American ballads, such as ''John Henry,'' ''The Titanic,'' and ''Casey Jones,'' come from the second half of the nineteenth or the early twentieth century. Ballad making in the United States was not dissimilar to the British broadside tradition, especially in its stereotyping of character and situation. The authorship of native American ballads is almost always anonymous; until the twentieth century, their dissemination was by way of oral or written means. Not surprisingly, their topics encompass the same human impulses that have attracted ballad singers for decades: love, violence, scandals, and tragic events or disasters.

American ballads are often categorized according to a genre or attributed to an occupational or folk group such as miners, sailors, cowboys, or African Americans. Many early ballad scholars such as James Francis Child, Phillips Barre, or Gordon Hall Gerould tended to downplay native American ballads because they lacked both the antiquity and the poetic qualities of their British counterparts. Eventually, collectors compiling the state and regional collections that began in the 1920s and continued through the 1950s recognized the importance and unique qualities of native American ballads. This trend was driven both by waves of nationalism that swept the country and the championing spirit of popularizers like Alan Lomax, Carl Sandburg, and Ben Botkin. By the 1950s, most such collections gave equal weight to Child, broadside, and **native American ballads.**

In 1964 G. Malcolm Laws published a revision of *Native American Balladry,* the major collection in the field. Laws divide native American ballads into nine primary categories:

A. War Ballads
B. Ballads of Cowboys and Pioneers
C. Ballads of Lumberjacks
D. Ballads of Sailors and the Sea
E. Ballads about Criminals and Outlaws
F. Murder Ballads
G. Ballads of Tragedies and Disasters
H. Ballads on Various Topics
I. Ballads of the Negro

The qualities found in native American ballads are similar to British oral poetry, especially the broadsides. They also leap and linger, downplay detail, and concentrate on the overtly dramatic. Like broadsides, native American ballads are often recounted in the first person or from a less objective perspective. The events, though, are distinctly American in their origin.

Similarly, the senseless, gruesome murder in 1896 of an Indiana girl, Pearl Bryant, by two dental students was disseminated to the entire nation because of its newspaper coverage. During the early twentieth century, a ballad about this murder circulated across the country and later appeared on country music recordings of the 1920s. Notice the typical greeting, a variant of ''come ye all,'' that opens this ballad, and its somber, warning tone:

1.   Young ladies if you'll listen, a story I'll relate,
       Which happened near St. Thomas in the old Kentucky state.
       It was January the 31st, that awful deed was done,
       By Jackson and Walling. How cold Pearl's blood did run!

M u s i c a l   E x a m p l e

The story of ''Young Monroe's'' tragic death while freeing a logjam and the subsequent grief of his true love, ''fair Clara,'' is known by lumberjacks as ''The Jam on Gerry's Rock.'' It is one of the best known of the occupational ballads. This version was collected by Sydney Robertson Cowell, who was married to the famous twentieth-century composer Henry Cowell. Ms. Cowell was an avid field collector of folk songs who worked extensively in the 1930s and 1940s. This selection was recorded on Christmas Day of 1938 in Central Valley, California, though Ford himself grew up in Wisconsin. [Folkways 4001]

Title ''Young Monroe''
Performer Warde Ford
Instruments one voice
Length 2:33
Notable Features

1. The melody is very contiguous.
2. You hear a little rhythmic and melodic variation from one verse to the next.
3. This a capella performance is, of course, monophonic in texture.
4. Ford's voice is relaxed and falls in the medium register.

Come all you brave young shanty boys, a tale to you I'll relate.
Concerning a young riverman and his untimely fate,
Concerning a young riverman, so manly, true, and brave,
'Twas a jam on Gerry's Rock where he met his watery grave.

'Twas on a Sunday morning, as you will quickly hear.
Our logs were piled up mountain high, we could not keep them clear,
Then up stepped our young foreman, said ''Who'll volunteer to go
And break the jam on Gerry's Rock with your foreman, Young Monroe?''

Now some of them were willing, while others they were not.
For to work on Sunday they did not think they'd ought.
But six of those bold rivermen did volunteer to go
And break the jam on Gerry's Rock with their foreman, Young Monroe.

Now they had not cleared off many logs when they heard his clear voice say:
''I'll have you boys be on your guard, for the jam will soon give way.''
These words he's scarcely spoken when the jam did break and go,
Taking with it six of these brave boys and their foreman, Young Monroe.

Now, when these other shanty boys the sad news come to hear,
They all pulled for the river, for Gerry's Rock did steer
Where six of those brave rivermen a-floating down did go
While crushed and bleeding on the bank lay their foreman, Young Monroe.

They lifted him from his watery grave, brushed back his raven hair.
There was one fair form among them whose cries did rend the air
One fair form among them, a girl from Saginaw town,
Whose cries rose to the misty skies for her lover who's gone down.

Fair Clara was the lady's name, the riverman's true friend,
Who with her aged mother lived at the river's bend.
She was to wed Young Monroe some sunny day in May.
And the boys made up a generous sum and gave to them next day.

2.   But little did Pearl Bryant think when she left her happy home,
That the grip she carried in her hand would hide her head away.
She thought it was a lover's hand she could trust both night and day.
But alas! it was a lover's hand that took her life away.

3.   But little did Pearl's parents think when she left her happy home,
That their darling child in you would never more return.
Her aged parents, you know well, a fortune they would give,
If Pearl could but return to them a natural life to live.

4.   Now all young girls take warning, for all men are unjust.
It may be your truest lover; you know not whom to trust.
Pearl Bryant died away from home on a dark and lonely spot.
My God, believe me girls, don't let this be your lot.

These ballads touched not only the general population but singers, too. They were especially important to the new generation of aspiring hillbilly musicians, who recognized their immediate appeal to a mass audience and suspected that the fledgling country music audience would enjoy these ballads. These singers apparently did not make strong distinctions among the ballad types, certainly not like the contemporary scholars who carefully pigeonholed each specimen, searching for examples in other printed collections, and listing the possible variants. Many circulated orally, but their printed version would do just as well.

It is indeed ironic that phonograph records from the 1920s helped to keep some native American ballads in our minds and hearts. The fact is that many traditional American ballads were documented and disseminated by way of phonograph records. The Columbia "Old-Time" country series of the middle 1920s through the early 1930s, for example, included the cowboy ballads ''Bandit Cole Younger'' and ''On the Old Chisholm Trail'' among its releases.

Ballads are also found far to the west and as an integral part of the cowboy tradition. Cowboy songs describe their life and, quite often, their work. The early (late nineteenth century and early twentieth century) **cowboy singers** represent a musical genre unto themselves. Montana, Idaho, Wyoming, New Mexico, and the other Western states were largely the domain of first- or second-generation pioneers. They lived, worked, and performed music in a world quite separate from the country music that developed in the Southeast and Midwest.

Although we frequently refer to commercial country music as ''country and western,'' this moniker did not develop until the middle 1930s. Tex Ritter, Roy Rogers, Rex Allen, Jimmy Wakely, and all of the other movie cowboys literally rode the cowboy image onto movie screens across the United States. But it was **Gene Autry,** with songs that he popularized on the silver screen such as ''Back in the Saddle Again'' and ''Riding Down the Canyon,'' who initially mythologized and romanticized cowboys by way of the electronic media.

Autry's early career included stints as a musician and comedian with Fields Brothers Marvelous Medicine Show and a relief telegraph operator. In 1929 he traveled to New York City and recorded for RCA Victor, Champion, and several other companies. Determined to stay in music, Autry returned to Tulsa and broadcast over KVOO as ''Oklahoma's Singing Cowboy.'' His local popularity brought him to the attention of the American Record Company, which enabled him to move to the ''National Barn Dance'' on Chicago's WLS. On the strength of Autry's puckish good looks, the radio broadcasts, and his first hit record, ''That Silver Haired Daddy of Mine,'' Republic Pictures signed him to the movies. Gene Autry eventually made a fortune exploiting

Singing Cowboys

Gene Autry riding high in the late 1930s.
Southern Folklife Collection, Wilson Library, University of NC–Chapel Hill, Chapel Hill, NC 27599–3926.

this image in films and on records and the radio. Today he is the owner of the California Angels baseball team and a real-estate magnate in the Los Angeles metropolitan area. He recently established a cowboy museum there, which is a destination for fans of the Old West who come from across the world.

Autry's success in **Tumbling Tumbleweeds** and other grade B westerns helped to open the gates for others to follow and helped to solidify the connection between country music and a Western image. This image remained strong for over twenty years. From Massachusetts to Oregon, local country performers adopted names like ''Tex'' and wore bolo ties and cowboy boots. His or her backup musicians were likely to be called ''the Lonesome Cowpunchers.'' The ''Western'' conception in country music faded in the 1950s as Nashville's dominance of commercial country music rose. Nonetheless, it was a powerful symbol that has not entirely dissipated.

But cowboy music before Gene Autry was really closer to the reality of rural life in the West, rather than the image of the West. Such songs were first written and sung by cowboys as they drove cattle, mended fences, branded calves, and other related ranch work. By the 1890s, cowboy songs began showing up in newspapers and magazines, often as a poem or a broadside, or in songbooks. They often appeared as ballads whose structure and melody owed much to contemporary folk and popular tunes. In 1908 the first important printed collection, *Songs of the Cowboy* by N. H. Thorp, was published, which was followed almost immediately by John A. Lomax's seminal *Cowboy Songs and Other Frontier Ballads* (1910).

Some cowboy songs began life as poems that were eventually put to a familiar tune. Cowboy poetry, a related genre of oral folklore, has enjoyed a renaissance since the 1980s. Cowboy poetry gatherings have grown in size and now attract participants and audiences from around the country. Some cowboy poets are also singers, further blurring the lines between music and the spoken word.

Many cowboy songs, which are also native American ballads, were composed between 1880 and 1930. The genre became so well known that Tin Pan Alley composers (who are discussed in the next section) also began writing songs with cowboy motifs just at the turn of the century. Some of the best-known cowboy songs, ''Bury Me Not on the Lone Prairie,'' ''The Dying Ranger,'' and ''Home on the Range'' were first heard in the middle nineteenth century. One of the classic cowboy songs, ''Western Pioneer,'' seems to have originated in the 1870s. Notice the opening lines, which use the standard formula so often heard in broadside and native American ballads:

> Come, give me your attention and see the right and the wrong.
> It is a simple story and it won't detain you long;
> I'll try to tell the reason why we are bound to roam,
> And why we are so friendless and never have a home.

M u s i c a l   E x a m p l e

Harry Jackson was a cowboy who worked the Western plains, mostly in the Southwestern states, during the 1930s and 1940s. He learned many songs and poems during his life, many of which were recorded in the 1950s and released by Moe Asch. This selection was well known to cowboy singers at the turn of the century and bears the unmistakable influence of a rather maudlin Tin Pan Alley composition. [Folkways 5723]

Title ''When the Work's All Done This Fall''
Performer Harry Jackson
Instrument one voice
Length 2:24
Notable Features

1. Jackson's solo voice is in the middle register.
2. The form of this piece is strophic.
3. He uses a major scale.
4. Several times during the song, he uses a distinctive leap of a major fifth.
5. ''When the Work's All Done This Fall'' has a monophonic texture.

A group of jolly cowboys discussing plans at ease,
Says one ''I'll tell you something, boys, if you will listen please;
I am an old cow-puncher, and here I'm dressed in rags,
I used to be a good one, boys, and go on them great jags.''

''Well, I have got a home, boys, a good one you all know,
Although I have not seen it since long, long ago;
And I have got a mother who's waiting for me, that's all,
And I shall see my mother when the work's all done this fall.''

That very night this cowboy went out to stand his guard,
The night was very dreary and stormin' very hard;
Them cattle they got frightened and rushed in wild stampede,
And he was a-tryin' to head them and turn them at full speed.

While ridin' in the darkness, and givin' the cattle call,
His saddle horse did stumble, boys, and on him he did fall;
Next morning we did find him, no hat upon his head,
We picked him up so gently, we thought the poor boy dead.

We carried him to the wagon and put him on his bed,
He opened wide his blue eyes, and this is what he said;
''I'll ne'er again go ridin', nor give the cattle call,
And I'll not go see my mother, when the work's all done this fall.''

My home is in the saddle, upon a pony's back,
I am a roving cowboy and find the hostile track;
They say I am a sure shot, and danger I never knew;
But I often heard a story which I'll relate to you.

In eighteen hundred and sixty-three a little emigrant band
Was massacred by Indians, bound West by overland;
They scalped our noble soldiers, and the emigrants had to die,
And the living captives were two small girls and I.

We were rescued from the Indians by a brave and noble man,
Who trailed the thieving Indians and fought them hand to hand;
He was noted for his bravery while on an enemy's track;
He had a noble history, his name is Texas Jack.

Old Jack could tell a story, if he was only here,
Of the trouble and the hardships of the Western pioneer.
He would tell you how your fathers and mothers lost their lives.
And how our aged parents were scalped before our eyes.

I am a roving cowboy, I've worked upon the trail,
I've shot the shaggy buffalo and heard the coyote's wail;
I have slept upon my saddle, all covered by the moon;
I expect to keep it up, dear friends, until I meet my doom.

I am a roving cowboy, my saddle is my home,
And I'll always be a cowboy, no difference where I roam;
And like our noble heroes my help I'll volunteer,
And try to be of service to the Western pioneer.

Cowboy songs were among the first folk songs to be recorded in the 1920s. **Carl T. Sprague,** the "Original Singing Cowboy," was born near Houston in 1895. He grew up working on the family ranch and learned his music firsthand, although he later supplemented his repertoire with songs learned from *Cowboy Songs and Other Frontier Ballads*. At the age of thirty, after graduating from Texas A & M University, Sprague traveled to Camden, New Jersey, where he had arranged an audition with the Victor Company. These Northern record executives were so impressed by Sprague that they immediately released "When the Work's All Done This Fall," which sold well over 100,000 copies in 1925–26. Sprague went on to record other popular cowboy songs for Victor, including "Utah Carroll," "The Last Great Round-up," "The Dying Cowboy," and "The Mormon Cowboy." Before long other real cowboy singers such as the Cartwright Brothers, Goebel Reeves, Jules Verne Allen, J. D. Farley, and Billie Maxwell were recording for some of the major record companies.

There are still cowboy songs in the late twentieth century. For some of today's fans, country music *is* cowboy music, but the older traditions can still be heard. Younger cowboys still learn some of their songs from older musicians and records, though the impact of Nashville songwriters must be given its due. A generation of Western songsters born in the 1930s and 1940s—notably Michael Allen Murphy, Guy Clark, and Mike Williams—have helped to keep Western themes in commercial country music. There are even a small number of performers, such as ex–rodeo champion Chris Le Doux and Canadian Ian Tyson, who really worked as full-time cowboys in addition to their careers as singers. The legacy of the cowboy image in country music can also be seen in the almost ubiquitous use of "Western" attire still worn by many country singers, few of whom have ever wrestled a calf to the ground or even been on a horse in their entire life. This public image, however, remains paramount to the reality of commerical country music in postmodern America.

Tin Pan Alley and Country Music

The songs written by a group of late nineteenth-century American composers touched the repertoires of many Americans, including those rural musicians who pioneered the country-music industry. By the last two decades of the nineteenth century, popular music had become a big business fueled by a new and aggressive cadre of publishers. Some of the songwriters also published their own material; others hired performers to plug their songs to a mass market. In this age just before the dawn of the commercial record industry, sheet-music sales not only affected the dissemination of new popular songs, they were the measure of a song's success. Sheet music was the main product of the music industry, and its goal was sheet-music sales. These songwriters became known as Tin Pan Alley craftsmen, named after a mythical New York City back alley where these songs were cranked out.

The songs of the Tin Pan Alley composers deeply affected the first generation of commercial country artists, born near the close of the nineteenth century and recorded before the Depression. These included Ernest V. Stoneman, the Carter Family, and Vernon Dalhart. The Tin Pan Alley songs of writers like Bob Miller, who composed new pseudocountry disaster ballads like "The Crime of Harry Powers," "1930 Drought," and "Wreck of the N & W Cannon Ball," became part of their everyday repertoire. Such singers emerged from the first generation to grow up with Tin Pan Alley songs. These sentimental, innocent, often heart-touching stories flowed from the pens of professional songwriters and touched Americans from all classes and regional lines.

Paul Dresser, brother of the highly regarded novelist Theodore Dreiser, qualifies as an important early member of this songwriting fraternity. A failure in the music publishing business, Dresser's show business career began with a minstrel show stint during Reconstruction. He settled in New York City, eventually writing such successes as "The Letter That Never Came," "Just Tell Them That You Saw Me," and "My Gal Sal." The words and music for dozens of patriotic, funny, and topical ditties flowed from his pen before his death in 1906 at the age of forty-nine.

Charles K. Harris (1867–1930) remains one of the most prolific and well-respected members of the early Tin Pan Alley writers. In 1885 he went into the songwriting profession in Milwaukee after boldly hanging out the shingle ''Songs Written to Order.'' His first major success, ''After the Ball,'' arrived after the song was included in the hit musical revue, ''A Trip to Chinatown.'' ''After the Ball'' eventually brought thousands of dollars into the coffers of Harris's publishing firm, which went on to open New York and Chicago offices. Harris's prolific pen produced '''Mid the Green Fields of Virginia,'' ''Hello Central, Give Me Heaven,'' ''Break the News to Mother,'' and scores of others.

These songs, along with the work of **Harry von Tilzer,** who wrote ''Good-bye Liza Jane'' and ''I Want a Girl Just Like the One That Married Dear Old Dad,'' later turned up in the repertoires of hillbilly groups—the Carter Family, the Delmore Brothers, Walter ''Kid'' Smith, and countless others. This early generation of recording artists venerated the innocence, pastoral vision, and maudlin simplicity of ''Little Old Log Cabin in the Lane,'' ''Nobody's Darling on Earth,'' ''I'll Remember You, Love, in My Prayers,'' ''The Little Rosewood Casket,'' ''In the Baggage Coach Ahead,'' and ''The Letter Edged in Black.'' Their importance to white audiences is underscored by the frequency with which these songs appeared in the early record catalogues of the hillbilly artists. They also recorded some of the instrumentals, such as ''Over the Waves'' and ''Wednesday Night Waltz,'' which appeared on sheet music early in the twentieth century. It is no accident, I suspect, that the first recorded country-music selection, ''Little Old Log Cabin in the Lane'' by Fiddlin' John Carson in 1923, fits into this category. The song itself was published by William Shakespeare Hays in 1871, only three years after Carson's birth.

This Tin Pan Alley song became a hit for the Leake County Revellers, a string band that recorded for Columbia in the late 1920s.
Kip Lornell.

M u s i c a l   E x a m p l e

Tex Isley and Clarence Ashley had musical careers that spanned more than fifty years. Both also benefited from the folk revival of the late 1950s and early 1960s, which revived their careers in the twilight of their lives. They were often paired together in the late 1960s, playing at many festivals and other musical gatherings. Ashley, who lived near Mountain City, Tennessee, and Isley, from Reidsville, North Carolina, possessed repertoires that included fiddle tunes, native American ballads, and older sentimental songs. [Folkways 2350]

Title "Little Old Log Cabin in the Lane"
Performers Clarence Ashley—guitar and vocal; Tex Isley—
   Autoharp
Instruments guitar, voice, and Autoharp
Length 4:11
Notable Features

1. The performance is played in a relaxed duple meter.
2. Ashley's voice is slightly tense and in the upper/middle register.
3. Its format is verse/refrain.
4. Its texture is homophonic, and both instruments are used almost entirely for rhythmic and harmonic underpinning.
5. The harmonic foundation is built upon the three primary chords.

Oh, I'm getting old and feeble, I can no longer work.
My rusty bladed hoe I've laid to rest.
Oh Mahssy and old Mistus they are sleeping side by side,
While their spirits am a-wandering with the blessed.

Refrain: Oh, the chimney's falling down, the roof is tumbling in.
The leak lets in the sunshine and the rain.
The only friend I've got now is this good old dog of mine
In that little old log cabin in the lane.

Oh, it was such happy times not many years ago.
My friends and loved ones gathered 'round the door,
They would sing and dance at night while they played the old banjo.
But, alas, they cannot play it any more.

Refrain

The hinges they have rusted, the door is falling down,
The roof lets in the sunshine and the rain.
The only friend I've got now is this good old dog of mine
In that little old log cabin in the lane.

Refrain

The paths they have growed up that led us around the hill,
The fences have all gone to decay.
The streams they have dried up where we used to go to mill.
Everything has changed its course another way.

Refrain

I ain't got long to stay here, what little time I've got.
I try to rest contented while I stay,
Until the day death calls me to find a better home,
Than this little old log cabin in the lane.

Refrain

Ernest Stoneman's Repertoire

Ernest V. Stoneman, one of the pioneering commercial country music artists, was born in Carroll County, Virginia, in 1888. A musician such as Ernest V. Stoneman certainly enjoyed these songs, which had been circulated by way of sheet music and cylinders for better than twenty-five years before Stoneman's own recording debut in 1924. Not surprisingly, he chose a topical disaster ballad, ''The Titanic,'' for his own recording debut. A retelling of the famous sinking of the world-class ocean liner that had occurred one dozen years before, it is deliciously ironic that this famous ''folk artist'' learned his version from a published source. In later years, Stoneman recalls that he obtained the words for ''The Titanic'' from a poem published in a newspaper. He told American music expert Dick Spottswood that the lyrics came from a contemporaneous folk song collection published by West Virginia folklorist John Cox, *Folk-Songs of the South.*

The fact remains that this early country music artist from the backwoods of the Blue Ridge Mountains was clearly moved by the sentimental songs that he heard all around him. Stoneman himself truly enjoyed these songs, and his early recorded repertoire is peppered with nostalgic, gently ironic songs. During the first few months of his recording career, Stoneman waxed versions of ''Give My Love to Nell'' (William Gray, 1894), ''The Lightning Express'' (Helf and Moran, 1898), and ''The Dying Girl's Farewell'' (J. D. Patton, 1894). He also recorded another topical ballad, ''Wreck on the C & O,'' which was also derived from the pages of Professor Cox's book.

Stoneman's 1920s repertoire is filled with these older songs from written and oral tradition. His second Asheville, North Carolina, session (April 1926) illustrates these influences upon Stoneman. He included a cowboy ballad, ''The Texas Ranger,'' learned from two neighbors, Bertha and Myrtle Hawks, who may have ultimately picked it up from John Lomax's cowboy song collection. ''The Religious Critic,'' a gently sardonic song about religious hypocrisy, later became better known as ''S-A-V-E-D,'' while the comic Tin Pan Alley ditty ''When Will My Wife Return to Me'' came from the pen of Charles D. Vann in 1889. Two pieces of sentimental American Victoriana, ''Sweet Kitty Wells'' (1860) and ''In the Shadow of the Pine'' (1895), were sandwiched in between a turn-of-the-century lament, ''The Orphan Girl,'' and a railroad song, ''Asleep at the Switch.'' Evidence of the impact of the rapidly growing record industry is illustrated by Stoneman's ''covering'' of popular discs by other artists. He waxed his version of Charlie Poole's successful ''Don't Let Your Deal Go Down'' several months after Columbia released the original. This trend portended the future, for in his next session, Stoneman reworked two of Texas artist Carl T. Sprague's popular Victor recordings, ''Bad Companions'' and ''When the Work's All Done This Fall.''

Despite this varied repertoire, Stoneman's performance style was fairly conservative. His family was steeped in a tradition of playing stringed instruments for themselves and local parties. The importance of string band music in this social fabric is underscored by older brother Burton Stoneman's (born 1881) comments during a 1941 Library of Congress interview:

> We'd go to places, gatherin's, have a good time, all play music; people'd all go home, everybody'd be satisfied, friendly. . . . I recollect you'd go to a party and they'd bring it [whiskey] in a bucket with a dipper in it, set it on a table. People'd come in with their music—banjo and fiddle—that was mostly all they had in that day and time.
>
> I never seen a guitar till I was about twelve years old, I reckon. Just a fiddle and banjo was all we had. . . . They'd dance, they'd fiddle, they'd dance, every-body'd go peaceable . . . never have no disturbances at all in them days when I was a small boy.

The Father of Bluegrass

By far the most influential brothers group, **Bill Monroe** (born September 13, 1911) and his older brothers Charlie and Birch, began playing together as children in western Kentucky. They heard the traditional fiddle tunes, learned shape-note hymns, came under the sway of local old-time musicians, and purchased the latest hillbilly records by Jimmie Rodgers and the Carter Family. One of Bill's earliest direct mentors, Arnold Schultz, an African American fiddle and guitar player, left a deep impression on the fledgling mandolin player. Monroe's father died when Bill was young and he lived with Uncle Pen Vandiver, who profoundly affected Bill as a role model for life and secondarily for his fiddle playing. The well-known ''Uncle Pen'' is named for Vandiver, who himself passed away in 1933.

By the late 1920s, all three brothers had migrated to Detroit in search of more lucrative employment. Their love of music moved north, too. Birch, Charlie, and Bill slid into a semiprofessional musical career in the early 1930s as an adjunct to jobs in the ailing industrial plants. Unlike Stoneman, the Monroes found and thrived on radio work. Between 1932 and 1934, they played a string of radio jobs and show dates in metropolitan Chicago. The trio's music reached large audiences during this tenure; their 1932 WLS broadcasts reached much of the United States at night because of its 50,000-watt signal. By 1934 they had left Chicago and turned to full-time music making on radio and the vaudeville stage. This grime time of unemployment, migration to the land of "milk and honey" (California), and its resulting social upheaval proved relatively easy for the Monroes because of their steady work on radio stations in Shenandoah, Iowa, and Omaha, Nebraska. The sponsorship of a cathartic formula, Texas Crystals, underwrote most of their midwestern radio airtime. By this time, the group had been reduced by one when Birch decided to stay at a newly found refinery job that brought in steady income to help support the rest of the family.

Nineteen thirty-five found them closer to home, wandering among radio stations in North and South Carolina. Bill and Charlie worked as a brother duet, with a sound akin to the Blue Sky Boys (Bill and Earl Bolick). But the Monroes were innovators—they played at faster tempos, while Bill's exciting mandolin style demonstrated that it could handle the chores as a lead instrument. Their tight harmonies, featuring Charlie's high, piercing lead and Bill's tenor voice supported by a highly integrated mandolin/guitar backup, didn't sound quite like anyone else. Their repertoire was not nearly as creative: a durable mixture of religious tunes or already established favorites. Nonetheless, they imbued "Roll in My Sweet Baby's Arms," "He Will Set Your Fields on Fire," "Weeping Willow Tree," "The Saints Go Marching In," and "Darlin' Corey" with a unique fervor and tenderness.

Some of these Carolina Piedmont and Appalachian mountain bands also included a three-finger picked banjo, an element critical to the development of **bluegrass.** This basic regional style was first documented in the middle to late 1920s on country music records by Charlie Poole and the North Carolina Ramblers and Jack Reedy and his Walker Mountain Stringband. During the middle 1930s, "Snuffy" Jenkins was the acknowledged king of the modern Carolina banjo pickers, due in large part to his appearances on the "Crazy Water Crystals Barn Dance" radio shows broadcast over Charlotte's WBT. Jenkins's forward-looking banjo work was often paired with the fiddle of Homer "Pappy" Sherrill during broadcasts and on show dates. These musicians, along with other modernists like J. E. Mainer's Mountaineers (Asheville) and the Washboard Wonders (Charlotte), influenced musicians throughout the Carolinas. They helped to reshape the older string band tradition into a new form that slowly inched its way towards bluegrass. Bill and Charlie Monroe soon integrated themselves into this same circuit; their music quickly became assimilated by local musicians and fans.

Their first encounter with the twentieth century's other important electronic medium occurred on February 17, 1936, when veteran A and R man Eli Oberstein interrupted a recording session by Fiddlin' Arthur Smith and the Delmore Brothers in order to fit in Bill and Charlie. Busy with radio work and unexcited by the prospect of lackluster record sales, the Monroe Brothers first turned Oberstein down. A telephone call finally convinced the duo to try, and every five or six months thereafter, Victor brought them into the studio for a Bluebird session that came out like clockwork. These highly successful records concretized the Monroe Brothers sound, enabling fans and musicians to study their musical vision. Only a breakup of the duet in 1938 stopped their successful recording string. Both men were proud, creative, and stubborn. Possessed by mercurial tempers, they clashed once too often, and Bill went off on his own in search of an expanded musical vision that he could not achieve with Charlie. Bill's peripatetic search lead him across the South: Little Rock, Atlanta, and back to the Carolinas. In 1939 Monroe found himself in Greenville, South Carolina, with Cleo Davis (guitar) and Art Wooten (fiddle), carefully remolding his sound. Bill calculatingly and unceasingly instructed both musicians. For many weeks, they worked to perfect their instrumental roles to coincide with Monroe's vision of a small string music ensemble.

With the addition of Amos Garen as a lead singer for sacred quartet singing, Monroe covered the religious field as well. This part of his repertoire was inspired by popular black, Carolina based gospel quartets such as the Heavenly Gospel Singers and the Golden Gate Jubilee Quartet, as well as their white counterparts like the numerous groups sponsored by the Stamps-Baxter Publishing Company. The bluegrass gospel that developed also owes an obvious debt to revival hymns and the shape-note tradition. It is a unique synthesis that exploits the unconventional (for common-practice Western art music theory) harmonies found in shape-note books and utilizes the syncopation, ornamented slides, and tonal possibilities suggested by black singers to create a tense, high-pitched vocal quartet. In the middle 1980s, bluegrass gospel quartets underwent a moderate renaissance, due in part to the renewed interest in black gospel quartets. Inspired by a capella black quartets, such as the Harps of Melody and the Gospel Writers, and their own reverence for the early Monroe recordings, contemporary groups like Doyle Lawson and Quicksilver and the Nashville Bluegrass Band include quartet selections as part of their everyday repertoire.

Just as the leaves turned golden and red in 1939, Bill felt his new band was ready. Armed with the new ''Blue Grass Boys'' moniker, they traveled west, headed for Nashville and a Grand Ole Opry audition. The Blue Grass Boys caused an instant sensation in Nashville, winning immediate acclaim. Their WSM broadcasts brought in a veritable flood of show date requests, and soon they were performing across the entire South. Based in Nashville, the band went through several personnel changes prior to its first recording session in October 1940. Georgia native Tommy Magness joined as the fiddler, Clyde Moody replaced Davis, and comedian Cousin Wilbur (Willie Westbrooks) joined the Blue Grass Boys as its bass player. Such personnel alterations became standard for the Blue Grass Boys, for its grueling travel schedule and Monroe's often temperamental leadership resulted in frequent changes.

Despite Bill Monroe's prominence and innovation in the field, several other bands were also on the cutting edge in the earliest days of bluegrass.

Significantly, all of these groups had strong roots or ties to western North Carolina. Roy Hall and the Blue Ridge Entertainers and J. E. Mainer's Mountaineers had each worked on WWNC in Asheville, North Carolina, before moving on to new territory. Their sound on 1940 recordings was not too far removed from Monroe's, though it was clearly not bluegrass in the now classic sense.

In 1941 the Blue Grass Boys returned to Atlanta for an important session, very close to the music that Monroe would be playing in ten years. Tuned a half step above standard pitch, Monroe's band sounded flashier and brighter than even one year before. His standard repertoire shaped the session, which included one certifiable classic, "The Orange Blossom Special." It is a masterful performance with elements of comedy in its dialogue, duet singing, and the precise, flashy fiddling of Art Wooten. The lack of a five-string banjo is the only missing element from the standard instrumentation.

In an effort to get as many people under one roof at a time (due to gas rationing and other related constraints), the war years were spent touring as packaged tent shows with other Opry performers. Monroe's band soon split off on its own with a small, well-rounded tent show featuring comedy, religious quartet singing, fiddle tunes, even a baseball game with members of the Blue Grass Boys challenging local clubs. Monroe's musical life continued to prosper following the cessation of World War II. The sheer volume of live performances soared, with dates as far flung as northern Florida; Ontario, Canada; and Tulsa, Oklahoma. Records for Columbia and Decca kept the Blue Grass Boys in the public's eye.

Late in 1946, Earl Scruggs joined the band, bringing his three-finger banjo roll to the Blue Grass Boys. This final link provided the Blue Grass Boys with the quintessential bluegrass instrumentation and performance styles. Their Columbia records from the early Scruggs and Lester Flatt period are the first instantly recognizable bluegrass records: "Mother's Only Sleeping" and "Blue

Bill Monroe's band from the middle 1940s, in the early days of bluegrass. *Kip Lornell.*

Moon of Kentucky'' remain two of the finest examples. In the ensuing five years, Monroe went on to record many examples of traditional bluegrass that are now recognized as classic performances of American music.

Monroe's dynamic new sound proclaimed a bold move into new musical territory. Partly because he sought individual variety within the band itself, the Blue Grass Boys occasionally echoed the ensemble sound of classic New Orleans jazz ensembles like King Oliver's Creole Jazz Band. The Blue Grass Boys' rhythmic feeling also reflected a black influence, especially in the up-tempo 2/4 tunes that at times sound dangerously close to the popular swing bands of the day. Unlike the other hillbilly bands of the day, Monroe allowed (even encouraged) his musicians to solo. Robert Cantwell describes taped performances of Monroe's first true bluegrass band as they appeared on the Grand Ole Opry in 1945 and 1946: ''. . . a wildly accelerated, almost violently high-pitched frenzy of mountain music, one which while treading very close to the edge of the bizarre displays an incredible virtuosity which audiences in those days saw, and were plainly encouraged to see, as a prodigy. With Monroe's voice blasting like an air-raid siren and Scruggs's banjo hurrying forward on ten thousand wheels, that band came at you like the Normandy invasion'' (Cantwell 1984, 76).

Some of the other first generation bluegrass artists were not far behind the Blue Grass Boys, both in artistic and commercial terms. The fertile tri-state area where Tennessee, Virginia, and North Carolina meet produced many of the best early bluegrass bands. Curly King and the Tennessee Hilltoppers, the Stanley Brothers, and the Clinch Mountain Boys worked this area, gaining prominence by way of their broadcasts over Bristol, Tennessee's WCYB. They were also assisted by the emergence of the postwar independent record companies. Mr. King worked with King Records of Cincinnati, Ohio, while Rich-R-Tone (Kingsport, Tennessee) helped bolster the Stanleys' career. The Briarhopper's Band in Charlotte pioneered bluegrass in Piedmont, North Carolina, by way of WBT's fifty thousand watts of power and the Cowboy Record Company. Lester Flatt and Earl Scruggs left Monroe and by 1948 had landed a Columbia recording contract.

By 1950 this music could be heard across the South. It remained a genre of country music without a clear identity of its own. Country music itself was becoming increasingly bland as Nashville emerged as the potent force in driving country music to its present polished, rather homogenized state. The Blue Grass Boys were the only group exploiting the Kentucky nickname, and ''bluegrass'' was not widely applied to the genre. Nonetheless, this first generation of bluegrass musicians left a marked impact upon Anglo-American traditions and, consequently, commercial country music. Hundreds of bands were playing this music and its impact had spread far beyond its hearth area, spilling across the entire South and into the Midwest. Surprisingly, the word ''bluegrass'' does not seem to have gained favor until the early-to-middle 1950s when it began to be applied to this music. No one knows exactly when this occurred, but by 1956 it was used in print.

M u s i c a l   E x a m p l e

Red Allen is one of the many bluegrass musicians who was born and raised in the heart of bluegrass country, Kentucky. He started playing this music following World War II and has enjoyed a long professional and semiprofessional career, recording on numerous occasions. This version of Flatt and Scruggs's classic "Darlin' Corey" was recorded in the middle 1970s with a strong group that included several relatives and the ace fiddler Vasser Clements. [Folkways 31088]

Title "Dig a Hole in the Meadow" (a.k.a. "Darlin' Corey")
Performers Red Allen and Friends
Instruments guitar, mandolin, fiddle, banjo, bass, three voices
Length 2:20
Notable Features

1. The instrumentation is for a "classic" bluegrass band.
2. Note the high-pitched vocals, especially the "high" tenor vocal on the chorus.
3. Its texture is basically homophonic and becomes richer as the various instruments are added near the beginning.
4. This song is performed in a minor key.
5. On several occasions, improvised "breaks" or "leads" are taken by fiddle and mandolin.
6. It is performed in highly regular, duple meter (2/4 time).

Today bluegrass musicians are found across the world. They play at festivals, record for both major and independent labels, and have spawned creative forms. Other musicians who began in bluegrass eventually proved to be innovators in country music. By the early 1960s, Bill Keith and Bobby Thompson had begun playing intricate, chromatic melodies on the banjo, while the single-string, lead guitar work of Tony Rice and Clarence White inspired a new generation of bluegrass musicians. These creative musicians kept many of the basic elements of bluegrass, but they spawned groups that played "New Grass," "Progressive Bluegrass," and even "Dawg" music—a jazz/bluegrass fusion pioneered by David Grissman in the middle 1970s. Despite these changes, all bluegrass performers pay homage to its progenitor, Bill Monroe, acknowledging his role as its "king."

Honky-Tonk

Just as bluegrass began a slow rise to nationwide acceptance outside of its Southern hearth area, the two last grass roots forms of twentieth-century grass has basically remained conservative in its instrumentation, repertoire, and worldview. Hard-core bluegrass musicians eschew amplified instruments, revere Bill Monroe's pioneering work, and are loath to add instruments beyond the basic five—guitar, banjo, mandolin, fiddle, and string bass.

In contrast, honky-tonk rose out of the fecund Lone Star State with an unfettered view towards the commercial marketplace. Honky-tonk updated the values found in earlier commercial country music and reflected the slow merging of regional styles into the national, anonymous ''country music'' sound churned out in today's Nashville studios. Its roots lie in the **Western swing** bands of the mid-to-late 1930s, whose noisy beer hall workplaces invited musicians like Rex Griffen, Floyd Tillman, Moon Mullican, and Ernest Tubb to write songs about drinking, extramarital love, and divorce. Similar themes could be found in both black and white rural music, but honky-tonk songs almost celebrated the dissolution of the family unit and the strains on ''traditional American values.'' Honky-tonk's beat was as well-defined as its working class values: live hard and get your pleasure where you can.

The quintessential honky-tonk hit of the early 1940s, Al Dexter's ''Pistol Packin' Mama,'' stayed on jukeboxes throughout the country for several years. Beer drinking music lovers might then drop their nickels in the slot to hear Merle Travis's ''Divorce Me COD'' or Ted Daffen's ''Born to Lose.'' These musicians paved the road for **Hank Williams** and the Drifting Cowboys, whose music dominated the country music charts between 1949 and

The sheet music for ''Pistol Packin' Mama'' helped to reinforce the song's popularity.
Kip Lornell.

1952. Williams's fidelity to a honky-tonk lifestyle is reflected in his own turbulent marriages, chronic bouts with alcoholism, frequent emotional upheavals, and his tempestuous relationships with the management of the Grand Ole Opry and an important Shreveport radio program, the ''Louisiana Hayride.'' Honky-tonk music continued to roll through the 1950s with Texans Ray Price and George Jones carrying the torch, while more recent exponents include Buck Owens, Gary Stewart, and Joe Ely. Just as honky-tonk music was reaching its commerical peak, rockabilly emerged in Memphis. Rockabilly, however, will be discussed later in this book.

Western Swing

Honky-tonk drew much of its strength from another southwestern phenomenon, Western swing, one of the most interesting and diverse American musical hybrids. Long a cultural crossroads, Texas birthed Western swing. It looked towards the **string bands** and norteño music of Mexico, the Cajuns of Louisiana, and the German American communities of the hill country near Austin and San Antonio. From black musicians came blues and jazz. Combine these influences with cowboy songs and fiddle tunes and you get Western swing.

Bob Wills remains the undisputed king of this genre. He pioneered Western swing, and Wills's first band was a small late-1920s hillbilly outfit, the Wills Fiddle Band. By 1931 they became known as the Light Crust Doughboys, named in honor of their radio sponsor—Light Crust Dough. The band slowly expanded its size and scope, along with its local popularity. Bob Wills and his Texas Playboys, complete with string bass, tenor banjo, and piano, became their new name in 1933. This expansion reflects their affinity for swing music and a desire for increased musical flexibility. Shortly thereafter, the Wills band shifted from Waco, Texas, to Tulsa, Oklahoma, where they remained until 1941.

About 1933 Milton Brown and his Musical Brownies emerged from a minor schism in the Bob Wills band. Using Fort Worth as his base, Brown toured Texas playing for dances. Fiddler Cliff Brunner, steel player Bob Dunn, and tenor banjoist Ocie Stockard emerged as the band's leading instrumentalists with improvised solos that impressed their fellow musicians. Their broadcasts and Decca records reached a large audience before the group disbanded following a traffic accident that killed Milton Brown in April of 1936.

The mid-1930s repertoire of Bob Wills and his Texas Playboys reveals the breadth of Western swing's most influential band. Their 1935 and 1936 ARC (Columbia) records demonstrate their catholic approach to music: ''I Can't Give You Anything But Love,'' ''Oklahoma Rag,'' ''Just Friends,'' ''Mexicali Rose,'' ''There's a Quaker Girl in Old Quaker Town,'' and ''Get Along Home Cindy.'' But above all were their interpretations of black blues, especially the lighthearted double entendre songs taken from records by Tampa Red, Big Bill, Frankie Jaxon, Memphis Minnie, and others: ''Fan It,'' ''No Matter How She Done It,'' ''What's the Matter with the Mill?'' and ''Sitting on Top of the

World." This strong dose of the blues underscores not only the influence of the mass media upon Wills but his love for black music.

By the late 1930s, the more free spirited Western swing bands included a complement of horn and reed players in the groups. Inspired by the success of Tommy Dorsey, Benny Goodman, and Glenn Miller, Western swing bands began using jazz-influenced musicians who soloed over the pulsing 2/4 meter provided by the rhythm section. The orchestras led by African American band-leaders like Duke Ellington, Count Basie, Jimmie Lunceford, and Fletcher Henderson also informed Wills. Their vocalist, Tommy Duncan, could croon with the best of the big band singers.

Only Texas in the 1930s could produce bands such as Adolph Hopner's, led by an accordion playing Czech American. Another San Antonio band, the Tune Wranglers, recorded popular tunes such as "Texas Sand" that further solidified the importance of "Texas nationalism" in this music. Dallas was home to Roy Newman and his Boys, another jazz-influenced group that wood-shedded with black jazz records before recording "Tin Roof Blues," "Sadie Green, the Vamp from New Orleans," and "Tiger Rag." Gene Sullivan, Newman's prized singer, later teamed with Wiley Walker to form one of the more enduring pop vocal teams of the 1940s.

East Texas Western swing groups mingled with other artists who combined Cajun music with country sounds. Cliff Brunner played out of Beaumont, Texas, on the edge of Cajun country. He helped bring country swing into Louisiana, inspiring Leo Soileau to form his Cajun swing band, the Four Aces. The Rayne-Bo and Hackberry Ramblers followed Soileau in mixing blues, swing, and hillbilly with Cajun two-steps.

Bob Wills's impact was nationwide, but the Sons of the Pioneers proved to be nearly as influential. This small ensemble brought cowboy swing to the entire country by way of their syndicated radio programs and an extensive recording career that began in the middle 1930s. The Farr Brothers (Hugh and Karl) and Bob Nolen forged a unique string band that eschewed horns in favor of virtuoso musicianship and nostalgic songs about cowboy life. This irresistible blend also helped to establish a movie career that saw them on the screen with Tom Mix, Hopalong Cassidy, and Gene Autry. The Sons of the Pioneers were moved by the duets of the gypsy guitarist Django Reinhardt and his fiddle playing partner, Stephane Grappelli. These wonderful improvised swing recordings are still regarded as jazz classics. It's ironic that French musicians playing swing music should exert such a strong influence over a group of Western singers—a global musical village decades before the concept became fashionable.

Western swing continued as a strong regional tradition well into the early 1950s, when rock 'n' roll hit the Texas airways. This music undergoes periodic revivals, and Wills's name remains magical in Texas despite his death in 1975. The eventual dissemination of Western swing beyond its Texas/Oklahoma birthplace suggests the importance of cultural geography in understanding American vernacular music. Both Western swing and bluegrass rather quickly

Mary McClain and her violin in
Arkansas circa 1936.
Library of Congress.

emerged from their hearth areas, moving out across the entire country. Bob
Wills found enough transplanted Texans in California to relocate his band
there in 1946. Significantly, he did not move to Marquette, Michigan, or
Miami, Florida, in search of an audience to support his music. When people
move, their love of regional music, food, and expressions migrates with them.

Final Thoughts

Anglo-American folk music forms the
basis for today's commercial country
music. British and native American
balladry paved the way for the
storytelling aspect of Nashville's
songwriters. The evolution of folk
music into commercial music is well
illustrated by the popularity of
Western swing and honky-tonk in the
1940s and 1950s. This process
underscores the ongoing interaction
between popular and folk music that
marks our postmodern world.

Key Figures and Terms

Gene Autry
bluegrass
Child ballads
"come ye all"
cowboy singers
honky-tonk

G. Malcolm Laws
leaping and lingering
Bill Monroe
native American ballads
Carl T. Sprague
string bands
Tin Pan Alley
variant
Harry von Tilzer
Western swing
Hank Williams
Bob Wills

Audio

Back in the Saddle Again. New World
314/315 (CASS). This two-cassette
package includes early recordings
by Gene Autry, Patsy Montana,
Jimmie Rodgers, and others.

Ballads and Songs. Old-Timey 102
(LP). A nice cross section of native
American ballads and songs that

first appeared on early commercial
recordings.

Burris, John. *Cowboy Songs and
Country Hymns.* Documentary Arts
(CASS). The title summarizes this
nice sampler by this West Texas
cowboy singer.

Carson, Fiddlin' John. *The Old Hen
Cackled.* Rounder 1003 (LP). An
excellent survey of the work by
this pioneering commercial
hillbilly musician.

Cleveland, Sara. *Sara Cleveland of
Brant Lake, New York.*
Folk-Legacy FSA-33 (LP). This
album documents the repertoire of
this ballad singer from upstate New
York.

Cowboy Songs on Folkways. Smithsonian/Folkways 40043 (CASS/CD). An anthology that encompasses some of the best performances from its vast catalogue, including older-style ballads.

Fine Times at Our House. Folkways 3809 (CASS). A well-rounded sampling of ballads, songs, and instruments recorded in Indiana.

Macon, Uncle Dave. *Early Recordings.* County 521 (CASS/LP). This set includes some of Macon's finest solo and group performances from the 1920s and 1930s.

Monroe, Bill. *The Original Bluegrass Band.* Rounder SS-06 (CASS). These are the classic early recordings with Lester Flatt and Earl Scruggs.

Native Virginia Ballads. BRI 004 (LP). This album of native American/native Virginian ballads comes from a comprehensive booklet.

OKeh Western Swing. Columbia Special Products 37324 (CASS/CD). An overview of this genre inludes vintage recordings by Spade Cooley, the Sons of the Pioneers, and Hank Penny.

Old Love Songs and Ballads from the Big Laurel, North Carolina. Folkways 2309 (CASS). These solo, a capella vocals cover a wide range of material.

Old-Time Ballads from the Southern Mountains. County 522 (CASS/LP). A survey of ballads that first appeared on commerical records during the 1920s and 1930s.

Riddle, Almeda. *Ballads and Hymns from the Ozarks.* Rounder 0017 (LP). This album surveys Riddle's vast repertoire of native American and British ballads.

Rodgers, Jimmie. *First Sessions—1927–28.* Rounder 1056 (all formats). The first in a comprehensive series that will reissue all of the recordings by America's "blue yodeler."

Tanner, Gid, and the Skillet Lickers. *Hear These New Southern Fiddle and Guitar Records.* Rounder 1005 (LP). An overview of recordings, originally made in the late 1920s, by this compelling and fun string band.

Wills, Bob. *Anthology: 1935–1976.* Rhino 70744 (CASS/CD). A first-rate sampling of Wills's important and influential Western swing.

Books

Abrahams, Roger, and George Foss. 1962. *Anglo-American Folksong Style*. Englewood Cliffs, N.J.: Prentice-Hall. The authors explore a wide variety of mostly Southern styles and include texts, some musical transcriptions, and classifications.

Bronner, Simon. 1987. *Old-Time Music Makers of New York State*. Syracuse, N.Y.: Syracuse University Press. A folklorist's view of the varied musical culture of twentieth-century hillbilly music in upstate New York.

Bronson, Bertrand. 1969. *The Ballad as Song*. Berkeley: University of California Press. The regional collection of Frank C. Brown (North Carolina), Cecil Sharpe's Southern explorations, and others are the subjects of Bronson's insightful essays.

Cantwell, Robert, 1984. Bluegrass Breakdown: *The Making of the Old Southern Sound*. Urbana: University of Illinois Press. This book explores bluegrass not only historically but as a phenomenon of American culture.

Cohen, Norm. 1981. *Long Steel Rail*. Urbana: University of Illinois Press. The book's subtitle, ''The Railroad in American Folksong,'' sums up the focus of this exhaustive study, which contains many native American ballads.

Green, Archie. 1972. *Only a Minor*. Urbana: University of Illinois Press. The approaches of musicology, literary studies, anthropology, and folklore inform this unique study of mining songs.

Laws, G. Malcolm. 1957. *American Balladry from British Broadsides*. Austin: University of Texas Press. A classic work in American ballad studies.

Malone, Bill. 1985. *Country Music, U.S.A.* Rev. ed. Austin: University of Texas Press. The breadth of this genre is covered in this broad and masterly survey.

McNeil, W. K. 1987–88. *Southern Folk Ballads*—2 vols. Little Rock, Ark.: August House. These two volumes constitute a fine overview of this field, including Cajun and Tex-Mex material.

Porterfield, Nolan. 1979. *Jimmie Rodgers: The Life and Times of America's Blue Yodeler*. Urbana: University of Illinois Press. A richly rewarding study of this influential country singer.

Ritchie, Jean. 1968. Singing Family of the Cumberlands. New York: Oak Publications. A personal look at the rich musical legacy and daily life of this Kentucky family.

Rosenberg, Neil. 1985. *Bluegrass: A History*. Urbana: University of Illinois Press. The most complete and well-balanced history of the genre.

Video

Doc Watson. CMNS 212–1103. 30 minutes. Watson is joined by his older neighbors and mentors Clint Howard and Fred Price in the performance of folk songs from western North Carolina.

Legends of Country Music. CMNS 272–6. 60 minutes. A sampler of performances, mostly from the 1960s, including the Louvin Brothers, Bill Monroe, Moon Mullican, and the Carter Family.

Sprout Wings and Fly. Flower Films. 30 minutes. One in a series of strong ethnographic/music films by Les Blank, this one focusing on North Carolina fiddler Tommy Jarrell.

Stanley Brothers and the Clinch Mountain Boys with Cousin Emmy. Rainbow Quest 212–1105. 52 minutes. This is part of a series taken from television shows hosted by Pete Seeger in the 1960s. This one features the bluegrass pioneers playing ''It Takes a Worried Man,'' ''Clinch Mountain Backstep,'' and others. [Note: Other artists in the ''Rainbow Quest Series'' include the Greenbrier Boys, Woody Guthrie, and the New Lost City Ramblers.]

Anglo–American Country Music, Pre–1945

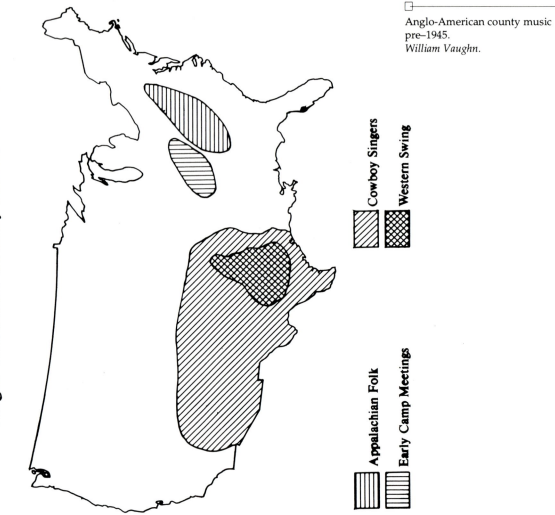

Anglo-American county music
pre–1945.
William Vaughn.

Cowboy Singers

Western Swing

Appalachian Folk

Early Camp Meetings

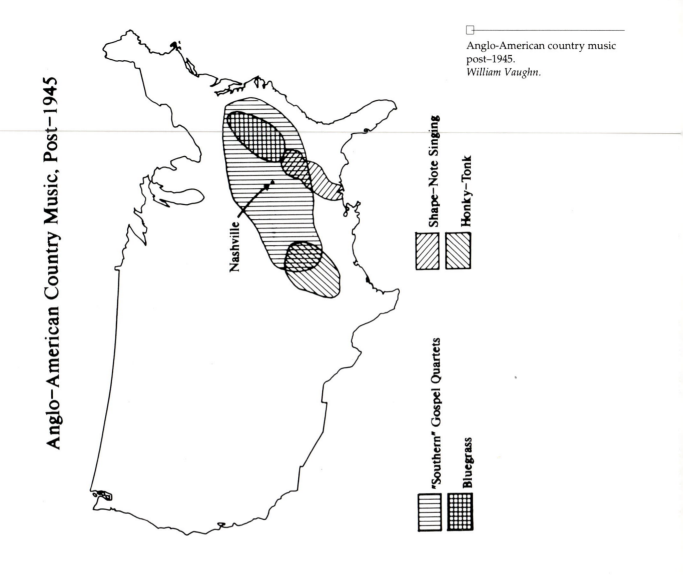

Anglo-American Country Music, Post–1945

"Southern" Gospel Quartets

Bluegrass

Shape-Note Singing

Honky-Tonk

Nashville

Anglo-American country music
post–1945.
William Vaughn.

5 | Anglo-American Sacred Folk Music

Religious beliefs of all kinds remain at the core of American values and life. And religious music is a vitally important, often underappreciated aspect of traditional music. The early English-speaking settlers brought their own church songs with them, most notably psalms. It's very likely that psalms were the first European music sung here; for the first few decades of the establishment of the "New World," psalm singing was the only form of music generally allowed in colonial churches. Within one hundred years, singing schools had developed throughout the colonies, helping to teach religious singing to the musically illiterate. This method of teaching gradually cultivated the shape-note tradition that flourished in the South following the Great Awakening.

As the United States expanded following Reconstruction, folk and folk-like styles of religious folk music continued to evolve and flourish. Revival hymns, spiritual songs, and gospel hymns emerged in the later part of the nineteenth century, helping to shape postmodern religious music. Despite all of the nineteenth- and twentieth-century innovations, Anglo-American religious folk-song practices tend to be fairly conservative. But, as we shall see, many distinctly American folk styles of religious singing gradually developed out of these essentially European practices.

Psalmody

Psalm singing grew out of the practice of chanting psalms from the Bible, and it was eventually replaced by composed hymns. The chanting tradition came over with the first English settlers and was promoted through books such as Thomas Ravenscroft's *Whole Booke of Psalms,* published in London in 1621. In fact, Ravenscroft's tome eventually inspired the first book published in the American colonies, the **Bay Psalm Book** (1640). Its texts are largely unique, though the musical notation was not added for another sixty years when it was reprinted with some of Ravenscroft's own four-part settings. Early white Americans were also likely to have used Henry Ainsworth's *Book of Psalms: Englished Both in Prose and Metre,* which had also been brought over by very early settlers. Calvinist theology suggested that this music be sung without instrumental accompaniment and in keeping with the congregation's abilities. Some New Englanders learned the melodies and words from books. But for most seventeenth-century white residents, psalm singing was an oral tradition.

Gradually, the old-world ties to religious singing grew weaker and more tenuous as the initial settlers' formal musical skills decreased. However, this led to the use of a greater number of oral elements, such as slides and other related embellishments, and antiphonal singing. A lack of literacy helped to contribute to the call-and-response style, which helped to encourage more ornate singing from the congregation. These factors all contributed to a unique, identifiable Anglo-American style of religious folk singing by the early eighteenth century.

This new way of singing did not suit everyone. Cotton Mather and several other important New England clergymen complained that this newly developed style was improper. They called for a reform, which lead to the establishment of **singing schools.** Such schools offered instructions under a ''trained'' musician who could teach vocal techniques and how to read standard Western notation. People taught at singing schools were supposed to return to their congregation and reinforce the ''regular singing'' of their forebears.

But the Anglo-American style had such strong adherents that graduates of singing schools met with only limited success. Many enjoyed the new freedom to partially improvise and express oneself. But the idea of printed songbooks with a preface, instructions on singing, and a collection of well-known psalms did catch on. The first of these, John Tufts's *A Very Plain and Easy Introduction to the Singing of Psalm Tunes* (1721), went through eleven editions in twenty-three years. Most of the subsequent 350 or so songbooks published over the next eighty years were aimed at the singing school market. One of the most significant of these, *A Collection of Psalms and Hymns,* printed in Charlestown, Georgia, was the first book by John and Charles Wesley, two brothers whose names are now inseparably linked with the Methodist church.

Singing schools and songbooks helped to encourage a few individuals to became part-time singing-school teachers. These men were among the first professional musicians in North America. They taught that a nice blend of voices and vocal production were important traits for congregational singing. These factors constitute the basis of the Protestant church choirs that later emerged in New England.

By the close of the eighteenth century, a small school of men writing psalms for American consumption had emerged in New England. *Urania,* a 198-page opus published by James Lyon in 1761, helped to set the standard for later collections. Lyon included not only contemporary English psalms but truly American creations as well. His landmark compilation was followed in short order by Josiah Flagg's *A Collection of the Best Psalm Tunes* and Aaron Williams's *Universal Psalmodist.* Shortly after the Revolution, the number of new American songbooks had increased tenfold over a fifty-year period.

Shape Notes

The first widely recognized form of white religious folk music was found in the shape-note tunebooks first published in the wake of the Second Great Awakening after 1800. The shapes themselves represent a simplified system to help people who were not conversant with standard Western notation. This system is known widely as fasola, referring to the last three syllables used in sight singing—fa, sol, and la. It is also known as **sacred-harp singing** because of the very popular book *The Sacred Harp.* These Southern and Eastern tunesmiths carried on a New England tradition that is considered at least partially folk because it is so often maintained through oral tradition. The late eighteenth-century New England shape-note books contain many musical examples that appear in later tunebooks from other parts of the United States. They also established the practice of including a pedagogical section to assist singing-school teachers with their craft. The first widely used book with all of these components, *The Easy Instructor* by William Little and William Smith, was initially published in 1798.

The vernacular roots of these tunebooks are evident in their utilization of a system that uses from four to seven shapes to help the inexperienced quickly sing without a working knowledge of key signatures or an ability to recognize pitches. The appearance of anthems and fuguing tunes by American composers drawn from oral tradition further establishes its folk roots. These facets are readily apparent in the first Southern tunebook, which was compiled by Ananias Davisson, *Kentucky Harmony,* in 1816. Davisson was a singing school master who used the book to help teach his classes in the Shenandoah Valley of Virginia. This system eliminated the need to memorize key signatures, thus streamlining the three- or four-day schools taught by Davisson and his colleagues.

The tunes are presented in four-part harmony with the main melody given to the tenor voices. The voices are unusually independent, marking a move away from the harmonizing of a melody so commonly found during this time. The tunes themselves (the melody lines) often came from broadside ballads, fiddle pieces, or popular songs of the day, which the tunebook compilers reworked rather than created. They are written in a mixture of major and minor keys, with some modal tunes also occurring. Some of the most stringent rules of Western music composition are routinely broken in these tunes: parallel fifths, octaves, and unisons abound, while inner voices cross to higher and lower levels. In these tunes alone, the arrangers proved themselves to be American originals. Although such tunes did have some parallels in eighteenth and nineteenth century hymnody, these writers undeniably created a

A page from the *Social Harp* book.
Kip Lornell.

M u s i c a l   E x a m p l e

This group of older singers was recorded by George Pullen Jackson in northeastern Tennessee in the early 1950s. Most of the singers were older because at this time relatively few younger people were involved with shape-note singing in this section of Tennessee. ''Wondrous Love'' is found in a variety of shape-note books from across the southern United States and is a very popular, beloved song that is universally sung at a slow, deliberate tempo. At the beginning of the song, you can hear the names of the shapes being sung before they launch into the words themselves. [Folkways 2356]

Title ''Wondrous Love''
Performers Old Harp Singers of Eastern Tennessee
Instruments eight voices
Length 2:05
Notable Features

1.   The singers weave the four lines into a polyphonic texture.
2.   Its melody is conjunctive and you hear a minor key.
3.   The tempo is slow and quite deliberately somber.
4.   The song uses a simple *ab* form.

What wondrous love is this, oh my soul, oh my soul.
What wondrous love is this, oh my soul.
What wondrous love is this, that cause the Lord of bliss,
To lend a dreadful curse for my soul, for my soul.
To lend a dreadful curse for my soul.

distinctive sound that would seem a bit unruly to those trained in the standard European classical music.

Because they proved so popular and practical, many people eventually followed Davisson's lead. In 1831, the Reverend James Carrell of Lebanon, Virginia, published *The Virginia Harmony*. William Moore of Wilson County, Tennessee, brought out *The Columbian Harmony* in 1825, while another Tennesseean, William Caldwell of Maryville, presented *The Union Harmony* in 1837. Perhaps the second most popular shape-note book, after *The Sacred Harp* by B. F. White, came out in 1835 and went through five editions. *The Southern Harmony* by William Walker of Spartanburg, South Carolina, touched the consciousness of religious singers throughout the South. Unlike *The Sacred Harp*, Walker's book was set almost entirely in three parts.

"Singin' Billy" Walker was part of the social and economic class of people who used such books. *The Southern Harmony* presented itself as "A Choice Collection of Tunes, Hymns, Psalms, Odes, and Anthems; Selected from the Most Eminent Authors in the United States," though its authors did include a European composer named George Frideric Handel. Some very familiar songs, most notably "Amazing Grace," appear in these shape-note collections. Other compositions often found in these pages include "Sherburne" and "The Good Old Way."

In the 1840s, a slow shift from four to seven shape-note books began to occur. They argued that since there were seven distinctive tones in the major and minor scales, each one should have its own name: mi, fa, sol, la, ti, do, re. This was viewed as "progressive" by younger singers, and publishers eventually moved to fill the need for new books. Jesse Aikin's *The Christian Minstrel* (1846) was perhaps the first popular book to use seven shapes, but it was quickly followed by others. Many of these publishers were once more concentrated in the Shenandoah Valley of Virginia. Joseph Funk was the most notable, and his seven-shape *Harmonia Sacra* (1851) was so successful that it went through six editions in nine years.

These books all contained a wide variety of material. Their texts came from English hymnody, anthems composed by New Englanders, Southern spirituals, and camp-meeting songs, among others. The music is from equally eclectic sources, with only the tunes from spirituals and camp-meeting songs being closely related to the ballads and fiddle tunes that were so often used to accompany folk songs and dancing. Shape-note singing contains elements of our aural and elite culture, and thus it is at least partly tied to folk music.

Shape-note singing is, above all, a social form of religious music. The singing-school teachers brought people together in order to instruct them in the rudiments of the four-note (later back to the seven-note) system. People also gathered in small and large groups for the express purpose of singing this music. By the late 1800s, formal singing conventions were being held across the South. These lasted for varying lengths of time, from an afternoon to several days, depending on the gathering's size and the distance people had to travel. Contemporary singing conventions are held not only at churches but in other public buildings. The singers sit in sections arranged by the distribution of the four voices. A different singer often leads each song, which is first sung with the syllables to familiarize everyone and then with the words. The leaders often choose their favorites, leading the same tune or tunes at each convention; sometimes they are identified with these tunes. The singers participate for the spiritual movement of the singing itself and secondarily for the fellowship afforded to the singers as they greet old friends. These conventions often also involve food, usually potlucks, and frequently a religious service. The sessions themselves open and close with a prayer.

Contemporary folk shape-note singing continues with its strongest following in Alabama and Georgia. With song leaders and singing school teachers such as Hugh McGraw of northern Georgia and Mrs. Helen Nance Church of

Wm. Clay Neal and assistant teacher Etta Stewart, Logan County, Kentucky, 1890.
Kentucky Library, Western Kentucky University.

Yadkin County, North Carolina, spreading the word, the tradition has remained alive. Although it has never disappeared from our cultural landscape, this style of singing has undergone something of a renaissance over the past twenty years. I first encountered shape-note singing while a student at the University of North Carolina at Chapel Hill in the middle 1970s; our singings involved a mixture of local folks and students. There are now many other "revival" groups across the country, including New England where this type of singing went largely unheard during its days of greatest popularity. Nonetheless, traditional shape-note singing almost entirely remains within the borders of the South, and *The Sacred Harp* remains in enough demand that a new edition came out in 1991.

Camp Meetings

During the first decade of the nineteenth century, a revival of hymns and spiritual songs was sweeping across the United States. The Methodism of John Wesley was behind the movement; circuit-riding ministers rode their horses across the frontier in order to meet with the widely scattered settlements. **Camp meetings** developed in the early nineteenth century as it became clear that efficiency came through numbers and people gathered together in worship. Caught up in a grass roots movement, the first camp meeting convened in July of 1800 in Logan County, Kentucky. Baptist and Presbyterian preachers soon became part of the camp meeting revival, promoting salvation through conversation and unfettered contact with God through the acceptance of Jesus Christ. Methodists predominated the early camp meetings because of their body of popular and familiar revival hymns, many of which appeared in the often reprinted *The Pocket Hymn Book* of 1797. By the early 1800s, several camp meeting songbook collections had appeared, such as John Totten's *A Collection of the Most Admired Hymns and Spiritual Songs, With Choruses Affixed As Usually Sung at Camp Meetings* (1809) and Lornezo and Peggy Dow's 1816 *A Collection of Camp Meeting Hymns.*

The camp meetings themselves were lively and spirited religious events. Imagine several thousand frontier women, children, and men camped together for worship—blacks, though segregated, often participated, too. These uplifting conclaves often lasted several days, with people "witnessing" their faith, reaffirmed by preachers shouting about hellfire with the nearby campfires roaring brightly. Perhaps most striking were the "jerking" masses of humanity caught up in their holy whirling with visions of heaven dancing through their brains. Their happy frenzy was oft-described by contemporary witnesses struck by the unlikely sight of the nightly contortions, replete with wild gesticulations, leaping, and shouting. Not surprisingly, the term "holy roller" came from this fervent period. Such happy, willing, and photogenic congregations would no doubt be admired and coveted by today's televangelists.

At the edge of this new frontier, the older methods of Christian education were strained by a lack of trained ministers and a low level of literacy. The major Protestant denominations turned to revivals as a means of reaching a great number of people who would otherwise go unserved by ministers of God. Methodists became particularly successful at revivals. One of the main reasons was their new songs, which reached directly for the spirit and soul of each individual.

Camp meeting singing appears to have taken the mid-to-late eighteenth-century New England revival hymns one step closer to the masses. Many of the camp meeting hymns were constructed from the verses of already familiar religious songs using a simple strophic structure—verse and chorus—that permitted almost unlimited improvisation within a theme. ''Satan's Kingdom,'' first published in *Revival Hymns* (H. W. Day, Boston, 1842) is a good example

---

M u s i c a l   E x a m p l e

The Phipps Family of eastern Kentucky blends a secular and sacred repertoire; they are heavily influenced by the pioneering country music group, the Carter Family, who came from nearby Maces Spring, Virginia. This selection is structured like many other camp-meeting songs, and its verse/chorus structure is very easy to learn. The incremental textual substitutions of ''father,'' ''brother,'' etc., help to increase the song's length and enable it to encompass more segments of the family. [Folkways 2375]

Title ''Away Over in the Promised Land''
Performers The Phipps Family
Instruments Autoharp, two guitars, three voices
Length 2:15
Notable Features

1. Its texture is homophonic.
2. The vocals are quite relaxed and in the middle range.
3. A 2/4, duple meter is heard throughout the song.
4. The dynamic range is limited and moderate.
5. The chorus is sung in unison.

I've got a father in the promised land (repeat)
I hope someday we'll all get there
Away over in the promised land

Refrain: Away over in the promised land (repeat)
I hope someday we'll all get there
Away over in the promised land

I've got a mother in the promised land (repeat)
I hope someday we'll all get there
Away over in the promised land.

Refrain:

I've got a brother in the promised land (repeat)
I hope someday we'll all get there
Away over in the promised land

Refrain:

Sister is a-waiting in the promised land (repeat)
I hope we'll all get there
Away over in the promised land

Refrain:

Gonna see my saviour in the promised land (repeat)
I hope someday we'll all get there
Away over in the promised land

Refrain:

of this style. No one knows, of course, exactly what such hymns actually sounded like, but contemporary performance practice suggests that most camp meeting songs might have been sung in a major key in a spirited, simple duple meter.

Such themes will be well known to many contemporary Americans as they still echo through evangelical circles in the late twentieth century: crossing the River of Jordan, pilgrims wandering through this troubled world, laying down one's burden to rest awhile. Repetition is one of the keys to the success of camp meeting songs, for it serves to reinforce the fervor and the message. This type of thematic recombination has an impact on an emotional level similar to that of the blues.

Camp meetings continued to grow in popularity during the first four decades of the nineteenth century. They spread from their Mid-South hearth by way of contagious diffusion that disregarded social and economic status in favor of religious conviction. The powerful message of direct communication with God swayed many people to join the ranks of the saved, a process no doubt assisted by the beauty and directness of the a capella hymns. By the 1850s, camp meetings were commonplace throughout the South and were not unknown in the Midwest and back East. Just as any manifestation of popular culture must slowly lose its power, the camp meeting revivals had lost much of their punch by the beginning of the Civil War. The songs, however, continued to be sung throughout the country, but most especially in the South.

Shakers

Shakerism is one minor and unique offshoot of the camp-meeting movement. Started by Mother Ann, who came to the United States at the beginning of the Revolution, the **Shakers** were always a small, self-contained religious movement whose music has been related to their rituals or ''laboring exercises.'' Although there were some eight to ten thousand songs in surviving Shaker manuscripts, very few have survived in oral tradition to the late twentieth century. An astounding number of them were written between 1837–47. Playful and simple by nature, Shakers believed that life should combine hard, clean work with a spiritual vision that was sometimes manifested by ''gift'' songs. The best-known Shaker song is ''Simple Gifts,'' which Aaron Copland used as part of *Appalachian Spring* and Judy Collins recorded in the middle 1960s. Other important Shaker folk songs that are still sung today include the ''quick dance'' tune ''Come Life, Shaker Life'' and ''Willow Tree'':

> I will bow and be simple, I will bow and be free,
> I will bow and be humble, Yea bow like the willow tree.
> I will be, this is a token, I will wear the easy yoke,
> I will lie low and be broken, I will fall upon the rock.

Unfortunately, there will be no more Shaker songs, for it is truly a moribund religion with only a handful of members living in Sabbath Day Lake, Maine.

Later Hymnody and Gospel Songs

These revival hymns and camp meeting songs set the stage for the final third of the nineteenth century. A new wave of evangelism, which emphasized revival ''song-services'' with sweet, lyrical compositions, flourished after the close of the War Between the States. Ira D. **Sankey** and Dwight **Moody** were two of the key figures in this movement, and they collaborated on a number of **gospel song** collections between 1874 and 1894. This duo helped to popularize gospel hymns, such as ''Sweet Hour of Prayer,'' that proved fashionable among both black and white Christians. They delivered an evangelical message that was as simple and direct as their advertising slogan, ''Mr. Moody will preach the gospel and Mr. Sankey will sing the gospel.''

Singers, evangelists, and publishers began forming new alliances. ''Normal Singing Schools,'' intensive music education courses that taught all of the rudiments of music using religious texts and songs, began replacing the shorter singing schools. The Ruebush-Kieffer Publishers of New Market, Virginia, conducted the first such school in 1874. Ten years later, A. J. Showalter, manager of Ruebush-Kieffer's Southern office, began his own company at Dalton, Georgia. He also began teaching normal singing schools. These songbook publishers also began printing monthly or quarterly newspapers that expedited communication between singers and teachers. *The Musical Millions,* published by Ruebush-Kieffer, began in 1870 and continued for forty-five years.

These new hymnals appealed to a wide audience because of their catchy melodies and their often strophic form, which made them easy to remember. Some of the tunes came from well-known secular songs. *Gospel Hymns and Sacred Songs by P. P. Bliss and Ira D. Sankey, As Used by Them in Gospel Meetings* (1875) achieved such immediate and widespread use that it went through four versions within sixteen years. Such books were used all across the country, but they gained particular favor in the South.

The singings themselves were becoming more organized, first on a regional basis within a state. The statewide "conventions" did not occur for many years. Alabama, for example, held its first statewide singing in 1918. Larger conventions met once or twice a year, while local sings often transpired on a monthly basis. The repertoire became so well known that many people knew the songs by heart; new songs were sometimes introduced aurally. But the demand for new books was constant and a handful of new publishers sprang up to meet this demand.

Vaughan Publishers of Lawrenceburg, Tennessee, and **Stamps-Baxter** of Dallas, Texas, emerged at the forefront of these new houses. Beginning at the turn of the century, these two companies promoted gospel songbooks, which were used in normal singing schools. They published many of the early gospel songs that are today considered classics of the genre. Songs that have passed into oral tradition, such as "The Sweetest Gift, a Mother's Smile" and "I'll Fly Away," are actually composed pieces that first appeared in Vaughan or Stamps-Baxter songbooks early in this century. Many other songbook publishers sprang up from Texas through Georgia, but none had the strength and impact of the big two.

Before long these publishers began sponsoring their own small groups, usually quartets, to sing out of and promote their songbooks. They were actually placed on a salary, which the publishers could afford because their books were selling so well. Vaughan, for instance, sold in excess of one hundred thousand songbooks in 1915, a fact that could be attributed in part to touring quartets that had gone on the road about five years previously. Stamps-Baxter soon followed this lead and both companies maintained quartets for several decades. These groups kept up a regular routine of performing, and by the middle 1920s had added radio appearances and record dates to their schedules.

Folk hymns and gospel music were also favored by evangelists because they had become so well known. Homer Rodeheaver and Billy Sunday were two of the most influential early twentieth-century evangelists that wanted to reach the "common folk" through this type of music. Rodeheaver worked throughout the United States from his Midwestern base. He even began a publishing company in 1910 and a record company in the early 1920s. Once more, songs such as "The Old Rugged Cross" and "His Eye Is on the Sparrow" that we assume are "folk" really began as composed turn-of-the-century hymns.

Charles H. Gabriel's ''Brighten the Corner Where You Are'' is typical of these songs. It is *ab* (verse/chorus) in form, and its ''Brighten the corner where you are; Someone far from harbor may guide across the bar; Brighten the corner where you are'' refrain helped to strengthen its popularity. The song is usually performed in duple meter (4/4) with an easy-to-recall, nearly stepwise melody. Its rhythm is predominated by quarter notes, though the occasional dotted half note or eighth note can be found.

The performance of early twentieth-century white religious folk music lacks the emotional intensity of the pre–Civil War revivals. Except for Pentecostal churches, such emotionalism was discouraged, and the music emphasized nicely blended voices and well-controlled performances. These trends have a parallel in the Tin Pan Alley school of popular songwriting that flourished in the last two decades of the nineteenth century. Both segments produced sentimental songs that were widely disseminated by way of commercial publications and that eventually passed into tradition. They are most evident on the commercial phonograph records by some of the ''family'' groups of the 1920s and 1930s.

Sacred singing, in fact, is often the province of family ensembles. This holds true for Ernest V. Stoneman's religious recordings, the first of which came almost exactly two years after his 1924 debut. He and several friends and neighbors journeyed to New York City for a three day Victor session, where the Dixie Mountaineers joined voices to produce ''The Resurrection,'' ''Sinless Summer,'' and ''The Great Reaping Day,'' among others. The strongest religious sides were three songs first published in the late nineteenth century: ''Are You Washed in the Blood of the Lamb?,'' ''I Am Sweeping through the Gates,'' and ''Going down the Valley.'' The last was composed by Jessie Brown and J. H. Fillmore about 1890. Stoneman's version utilizes a less complex melody and more simple harmony, though its words are very close to printed texts:

> We are going down the valley one by one,
> With our faces toward the setting of the sun.

The famous evanglist, Homer Rodeheaver, recorded for his own record company in the early 1920s. *Kip Lornell.*

Down the valley where the mournful cypress grows,
Where the stream of death in silence onward flows.

Refrain:

We are going down the valley, going down the valley,
Going toward the setting of the sun.
We are going down the valley, going down the valley,
Going down the valley one by one.

We are going down the valley one by one,
When the labors of the weary day are done.
One by one, the cares of earth forever past,
We shall stand upon the river bank at last.

Refrain:

We are going down the valley one by one.
Human comrade you or I will there have none,
But a tender hand will guide us lest we fall.
Christ is going down the valley with us all.

Refrain:

These songs featured a parlor-hall style of instrumentation underpinned by Irma Frost's organ, Ernest's rhythm guitar, and the modest ornamentation of fiddlers Kahle Brewer or Uncle Eck Dunford.

An example such as this is considered folk, or at least folk based, because of a process it has gone through from the composer's pen to its performance by Stoneman and his group. First, the origins of the song may be obscured to the singers by time: an old song they've heard sung in their church for many years. Second, their rendition makes no conscious attempt to replicate the original published version. Stoneman's version eliminates the accidentals and most chromatic notes, and considerably simplifies the rather elaborate melodies. Third, this rendition adapts the piece to folk performance practices found among singers in Carrol County, Virginia, by assigning the lead male and female voices in octaves. Finally, the singers use a somewhat nasal tone, which would have been shunned by contemporary popular singers and abhorred by classically trained vocalists.

Other early country music recording artists also mixed sacred and secular repertoires. The Monroe Brothers' (Bill and Charlie) first recording session for Bluebird in 1936 featured a number of late nineteenth-century hymns, including "What Would You Give in Exchange?" and "God Holds the Future in His Hands." The Blue Sky Boys and other brother groups often utilized sacred numbers on their radio shows and records. Many of these mainly Southern groups grew up in homes where Sunday church attendance was mandatory, which greatly affected their musical interests. Northern duos, such as Gardner and McFarland, mined similar territory during the late 1920s and into the 1930s. When bluegrass emerged in the middle 1940s, many of these groups also included religious numbers. Some even worked up four part–harmony gospel songs that they performed as part of their show.

M u s i c a l   E x a m p l e

Many of the examples of later-composed hymnody are almost as sentimental as their Tin Pan Alley counterparts. Many of them praise similar virtues of mother, home, family, and God. Despite being recorded in the early 1980s, this performance by Joe Miller and Lawrence Humphries underscores the pathos heard in this genre for many decades. This song which was composed by J. W. Vaughan in 1933, is still popular in many areas of the South. [Folkways 31107]

Title ''The Old Country Church''
Performers The Georgia Pals
Instruments two guitars and two voices
Length 2:43
Notable Features

1. Listen for the close and smooth two-part harmony.
2. The performance is in duple meter (2/4).
3. Both voices are relaxed and the tenor is in the high range, which is characteristic for this genre.
4. There is a slight syncopation in the chorus.
5. The guitars and voices create a homophonic texture.
6. One guitar plays lead figures reminiscent of a mandolin.

There's a place near to me where I'm longing to be
With my friends at the old country church.
There with mother we went, our Sunday's we spent
With our friends at the old country church.

Refrain:

Precious memories (sweet memories)
Oh what joy (joy, great joy) it brings to me (brings to me),
How I long (how I long) once more to be
With my friends at the old country church.

As a small country boy, how my heart beat with joy
When I knelt at the old country church.
For the Saviour above, I had wonderful love,
Save my soul in the old country church.

Refrain:

How I wish that today, all the people would pray
As we prayed in the old country church,
And would only confess Jesus surely would bless
As he did in the old country church.

Refrain:

Oh my thoughts make me weep, for so many asleep
In that grave in the old country church.
And someday I might rest with my friends I love best
In a grave near the old country church.

Refrain:

Gospel Boogie

The rise to prominence of gospel performances on the radio and records as well as live performances helped to change the face of white religious folk music. Here we shift from music that can be considered largely folk to that which is popular but clearly folk based. The tradition of singing out of shape-note books declined rapidly, and the communal spirit of the old-fashioned camp meetings and friendly singing conventions was lost. Touring singers were no longer directly linked to, and supported by, publishers because the groups could support themselves. White religious music, specifically the new gospel music, was quickly becoming a full-time professional business that could sustain a community of singers, songwriters, promoters, publishers, and broadcasters.

Gospel quartets were at the forefront of this movement. By the late 1930s, several Stamps-Baxter–associated quartets were holding regular **all-night sings** over Dallas radio station KRLD. Stamps-Baxter groups were popular enough to hold a successful all-night sing that all but filled the Cotton Bowl stadium in Dallas. But changes were coming. This became clear in 1941 when one of Vaughan's most popular groups, which was led by Claude Sharpe, resigned in order to join the Grand Ole Opry as the Old Hickory Singers.

Following World War II, the popularity of white gospel quartets rose to even greater heights. Grand Ole Opry star **Wally Fowler** left his band to concentrate on his gospel quartet career. By 1948 he was a full time quartet singer and a busy promoter who occasionally set up as many as five programs on a single night! Every Friday night he staged an all-night sing at the home of the Grand Ole Opry, the Rhyman Auditorium. About the same time, the **Blackwood Brothers Quartet** used their Shenandoah, Iowa, base to launch a career in gospel music. They started out on their own small record label and with broadcasts over local radio stations. However, by the early 1950s, the Black-wood Brothers realized that the South offered them more professional opportunities so they moved to Memphis and began recording for the RCA-Victor Company.

Anglo-American gospel music was moving into the mainstream of American music. This type of gospel music quickly echoed some of the themes exploited in popular songs. ''Gospel Boogie,'' copyrighted in November 1947 and first recorded by the Homeland Harmony Quartet in early 1948, became an instant sensation. It was quickly covered by nearly a dozen black and white artists, some of whom recorded it under the alternate title ''A Wonderful Time Up There.'' The popularity of ''Gospel Boogie'' created a controversy within the gospel community. Some of the older singers felt that the popularity of groups such as the Speer Family, Chuck Wagon Gang, the Statesmen Quartet, and the Johnson Family was built upon an ephemeral foundation. Fowler and his cohorts suggested that nothing but good could result from spreading the message of the gospel to more people. The battle took place on all types of grounds: backstage at programs, in churches, at all-night sings, and in newspaper letters to the editor. Ultimately, the argument became moot as the younger gospel singers reached a larger audience and the quartets became stronger.

Some of the best and most popular songs performed by these singers were authored by **Albert E. Brumley,** whose ''I'll Fly Away'' has been recorded more than five hundred times. Brumley was born on October 29, 1905, in rural eastern Oklahoma. Attending his first singing school in 1922, he was struck by the power and beauty of what he heard and continued to study at the Hartford Music Company in Arkansas. This small, regional publisher issued one or two songbooks annually, which were based on the seven-shape system. By the late

This 1927 songbook came from the high-water mark of the shape-note singing convention movement. *Charles Wolfe.*

1920s, he began composing songs for Hartford, including ''I'll Fly Away'' in 1932.

Over the next twelve years, Brumley unleashed some of his best compositions upon the gospel world: ''Jesus Hold My Hand'' (1932), ''I'll Meet You in the Morning'' (1936), ''Turn Your Radio On'' (1938), and ''If We Ever Meet Again'' (1945). Most of these early compositions were promoted at conventions, over radio broadcasts, and in other live contexts. The first songbook dedicated specifically to his work, *Albert E. Brumley's Book of Radio Favorites* (1937), helped to spread his fame. But it was not until he switched to Stamps-Baxter in 1937 that his written songs reached a nationwide audience.

Within ten years, Brumley had bought out the old Hartford Music Company in order to form Brumley-Hartford, which is still operated by his family in southern Missouri. He continued to write songs and run his publishing company until his death in 1977. Performers as diverse as the Chuck Wagon Gang, Elvis Presley, and Hank Williams have recorded his songs, which are firmly in the early twentieth-century gospel mold. ''I'll Fly Away,'' for example, uses the same melody as the well-known ''Prisoner's Song,'' and it opens with the catchy line ''If I had the wings of an angel.''

If this music was being exploited by the mass media and reaching millions of people, can it be considered ''folk''? In many of these performances, we can find folk elements similar to those used by Ernest Stoneman's version of late nineteenth-century hymnody, which leads to a qualified yes. These elements include a nasal vocal technique; a repertoire that encompassed not only new compositions but older gospel hymns and spirituals; simple harmonic structures that were readily accessible to any piano or guitar player; and easily remembered melodies. The message of these songs was equally straightforward: help your neighbors, live a ''clean'' life, worship God regularly, and then find eternal bliss in heaven.

Final Thoughts

The English brought their psalmody tradition across the Atlantic Ocean, and since then sacred music has been part of white American music. But many decades passed before American religious folk songs developed. However, the last two hundred years have witnessed the gradual evolution of uniquely American styles from the rejuvenating camp meeting songs to the gospel boogie of the late 1940s.

Since the middle of the twentieth century, there has been an expanding relationship between folk and popular forms of religious music. Despite the commercialization of Anglo-American sacred folk songs, the shape-note tradition and gospel hymnody remain a part of life in the South and parts of the Midwest.

Key Figures and Terms

all-night sings

Bay Psalm Book
Blackwood Brothers Quartet
Albert Brumley
camp meetings
Wally Fowler
gospel song
psalmody
sacred-harp singing
Sankey and Moody
Shakers
singing schools
''Singin' Billy'' Walker
Stamps-Baxter

Audio

Brighten the Corner Where You Are. New World NW-224 (LP). Both black and white hymnody and gospel songs are heard on this collection.

Chuck Wagon Gang. Columbia Historic Edition FC-40152 (CASS/LP). An assemblage of some of their best-known recordings from the 1940s and early 1950s.

Country Gospel Song. RBF 19 (CASS). This record contains a selection of (mostly white) performers originally recorded prior to World War II.

Early Shaker Spirituals. Rounder 0078 (CASS/LP). Mildred Barker and other members of the United Society of Shakers perform spirituals from the nineteenth and twentieth centuries.

Favorite Sacred Songs. King CD 556 (CD). A nice sampler of country gospel songs recorded by the Delmore Brothers, Grandpa Jones, Wayne Rainey, and others in the late 1940s and early 1950s.

The Gospel Ship: Baptist Hymns and White Spirituals from the Southern Mountains. New World NW-294 (LP). Alan Lomax assembled this sample of selections, which focuses on performances recorded after World War II.

Lester Flatt and Earl Scruggs with the Foggy Mountain Quartet. County 111 (CASS/LP). Flatt, Scruggs and their quartet explore a selection of bluegrass gospel numbers.

Old Harp Singers. Folkways 2356 (CASS). This recording presents some strong examples of sacred-harp singing in Tennessee in the 1950s.

Social Harp: American Shape-Note Singing. Rounder 0094 (LP). The tunes from this recording from Georgia in the 1970s are found in the *Social Harp* tunebook.

Something Got a Hold of Me. RCA 2100–2–R (CASS/CD). An anthology of white gospel recordings from the 1930s by the Carter Family, Monroe Brothers, Dixon Brothers, and others.

Books

Bruce, Dickson, Jr. 1974. *And They All Sang Hallelujah: Plain-Folk Camp Meeting Religion 1800–1845.* Knoxville: University of Tennessee Press. A straightforward accounting of the Anglo-American camp meeting movement.

Hively, Kay, and Albert Brumley, Jr. 1990. *I'll Fly Away: The Life Story of Albert E. Brumley.* Branson, Mo.: Mountaineer Books. An entertaining, insider's view of one of the most important twentieth-century gospel composers.

Jackson, George Pullen. 1933. *White Spirituals in the Southern Uplands.* Chapel Hill: University of North Carolina Press. The standard book about Appalachian religious folk song, specifically shape-note singing, from the late nineteenth into the early twentieth century.

Montell, Lynwood. 1991. *Singing the Glory Down.* Lexington: University of Kentucky Press. A detailed study of amateur gospel music in twentieth-century South Central Kentucky.

Sankey, Ira, et al. 1972. *Gospel Hymns Nos. 1 to 6 Complete.* New York, 1895. Reprint. New York: Da Capo Press. An important reprint of gospel hymns from the late nineteenth century.

Sizer, Sandra. 1978. *Gospel Hymns and Social Religion: The Rhetoric of Nineteenth-Century Revivalism.* Philadelphia: Temple University Press. This book covers the development of gospel hymns and describes its social context during the post-Reconstruction era.

Video

Chase the Devil: Religious Music of the Appalachians. SHAN-V1208. 60 minutes. This BBC documentary was shot in the early 1980s and features holiness singing along with other local styles.

African American Sacred Folk Music

The cliche that churches form the backbone of black American life contains a great deal of truth. This need for social cohesiveness and leadership was particularly pressing in the eighteenth and nineteenth centuries during the decades of legalized slavery. Even following Reconstruction, they have served as social-services networks, rallying points for civil rights, and public spokespersons, among other functions. Although the federal government has finally sanctioned full civil and legal rights for African Americans, traditionally black churches remain at the core of life for many people in the United States.

It is abundantly true that religious music remains **the** clear stronghold for traditional music in the African American community. Because the music of most mainstream black churches tends to be conservative, this is not surprising. Technological innovations, such as the adaptation of electric bass guitars or electronic organs, can be heard in many churches. The core framework of black sacred music, however, remains more closely tied to its roots. This is most evident in important elements such as repertoire, training techniques, and vocal styles.

A strong symbiotic relationship between secular and sacred black music has also existed since the beginning of the United States. Some singers and instrumentalists have always been devoted exclusively to their religious calling, but many others have mediated between both ''worlds.'' Post-Reconstruction ''songsters'' (rural black musicians with varied musical interests) played for Saturday night square dances and then got up the next morning to provide music for their churches. In our postmodern world, however, the monetary stakes have been raised to extraordinary heights. These enticements have lured traditionally trained sacred singers such as Aretha Franklin and Sam Cooke from their churches to pursue careers on the popular stage. As we shall see in chapter 10, there are many elements of folk music in late twentieth-century African American popular music.

The Great Awakening and Camp Meetings

The Great Awakening of the 1730s brought several important changes to American religious life, one of which was the enlivening of the tunes and words sung during services. Hymns based on religiously inspired poems rather than the psalms taken from biblical scripture gained favor. The popularity of Dr. Isaac Watts's books, *Hymns and Spiritual Songs* (1707) and *The Psalms of David, Imitated in the Language of the New Testament and Apply'd to the Christian State and Worship* (1719), was so strong that Protestants soon came to prefer ''**Dr. Watts hymns**.'' By the 1740s, both whites and blacks who attended church were singing hymns as part of each worship service.

The Second Great Awakening was the next religious movement to greatly impact upon America. A frontier revival phenomenon, its greatest force was felt between 1790 and 1830. **Camp meetings** where great numbers of people lived and worshiped for at least several days in temporary tents became the norm. Methodists slowly came to dominate camp meetings, and Methodist hymns were sung in meetings that by the early nineteenth century had spread across all of the Middle Atlantic states into the Deep South. Unlike most aspects of contemporary American life, camp meetings were not entirely segregated. Groups upwards of three thousand camp meeters gathered to sing and hear preaching, with blacks and whites keeping separate quarters on the grounds. Whether standing or seated, blacks attended camp meetings, sometimes participating as preachers. Such modest integration resulted in mutual influences and the emergence of ''spiritual songs'' that found favor among both black and white singers.

Camp-meeting singing was congregational. Contemporary accounts suggest that blacks often sang louder than whites and that blacks often stayed up singing long after their counterparts had retired for the night. These late night gatherings gave black singers a forum for experimentation not previously available to them. Away from the watching eyes of whites, black singing began to shift away from the camp meeting hymns. Blacks began improvising by adding lines from biblical verses and prayers to the well-known Watts hymns, which became solidified by the frequent addition of choruses and refrains. The tunes, too, veered from the acceptable European melodies towards the banjo and fiddle dance tunes favored in folk music. These new songs

Veteran song leader Dewey Williams begins a song at a southern Alabama shape-note sing circa 1980. *Smithsonian Institution.*

contained enough familiar elements to gain swift and widespread acceptance as a new genre, "spiritual songs."

In New England, where blacks constituted a smaller number and percentage of the population, slaves sometimes became part of the worship service held by whites. Seated in segregated pews (a presentiment of the "separate but equal" doctrine), blacks were exposed to the religious practices of northern Europeans, an experience steeped in ritual that possibly reminded them of the importance of their own ceremonies. However, the music itself must have seemed exceptionally tame by comparison with their own background. The white religious music—music most often from Dutch Reformed, Congregational, Methodist, or other related sects—lacked the fervor and rhythmic punch of West African music. Drums, often playing improvisational patterns and indispensable to their rituals, were simply not found in these churches. An African connection, call and response, was part of at least one church, the Dutch Reformed. Any black attending a Dutch Reformed service would have recognized the "lining out" performance practice so often found in black African music. Lining out a psalm provided an easy way for white and black churchgoers to learn the song's text, along with the basic melody, with the song leader providing one line and the congregation responding. This practice, common among blacks singing work songs, proved to be one of the few early direct links between Anglo and African music.

In the South, some whites even became involved with the religious instruction of blacks. On large plantations, slaves were kept in relative cultural and social isolation, a practice reflected in the slave's religious training. Blacks were almost never allowed to attend the weekly religious services, though they could sometimes participate by standing in a separate section in the back of the church. Clergymen were sometimes brought in to lead slaves in their own religious worship. Southern colonies in general were not as strict about the Sabbath as their Northern counterparts. The more conservative Protestant denominations, such as the Dutch Reformed, did not gain widespread currency in the South. Indeed there was far less religious instruction for Southern blacks and much greater social and economic segregation.

Spirituals

Although their origins are not entirely clear, spirituals are among the earliest sacred folk songs attributable to black culture. "Spiritual" has been an encompassing term for black American religious folk songs that are sometimes called anthems, jubilees, or gospel songs. White origins for African American spirituals have been argued, but the considerable interchange between white and black musical traditions prior to the Civil War makes such discussions moot.

The term itself was not used in print prior to the 1860s, but descriptions in travel accounts and diaries of songs that sound like spirituals exist as early as 1819. These descriptions by whites speak of traits such as syncopated hand-clapping and foot stamping that provided the rhythmic fervor absent from

Anglo-American music. Contemporary accounts also list call and response, group participation, and improvised texts as the other notable characteristics of these spirituals. The form of spirituals tended to be similar, with an alternating line and refrain that encouraged the textual improvisation that impressed so many eighteenth-century observers. "In That Great Getting-Up Morning" is a traditional song that contains many of the textual elements found in nineteenth-century spirituals. Note how its structure encourages the singer to improvise new lines to further the story:

> I'm a-going to tell you about the coming of the savior.
> Refrain: In that great getting-up morning, fare you well, fare you well!
> The Lord spoke to Gabriel.
> Refrain
> Go look behind the altar.
> Refrain
> Take down the silver trumpet.
> Refrain
> Blow your trumpet, Gabriel.
> Refrain
> Lord, how loud shall I blow it?
> Refrain
> Blow it right and easy.
> Refrain
> Do not alarm my people.
> Refrain
> Tell 'em to come to judgement.
> Refrain
> Gabriel, blow your trumpet.
> Refrain
> Lord, how loud shall I blow it?
> Refrain
> Loud as seven peals of thunder.
> Refrain
> Wake up the living nations.
> Refrain

Spiritual texts are often characterized as sad or even sorrowful. They usually lament the trials and difficulties of a life that was made doubly difficult by slavery. "Nobody Knows the Trouble I've Seen" and "Roll, Jordan, Roll" are two well-known spirituals. The refrain "Motherless children have a hard time when their mother's dead" exemplifies the motifs of loss and separation. Death and escape are two other recurring themes in spirituals, and it is often suggested that such themes serve a dual purpose. One purpose is to lament earthly hardships and the peace of dying and eternal life, while the other is a code from the black underground. Blacks could express the hope of "stealing away" from slavery and into the freedom of the North. In later years, particularly during the civil rights movement that began in the 1950s, spirituals were sung to protest economic and social conditions in the South, with refrains about ''crossing the River of Jordan'' and creating a new vision of America.

The earliest spiritual collection, *Slave Songs of the United States* (1867) by William Francis Allen, Charles Pickard Ware, and Lucy McKim Garrison, includes some well-known spirituals that continue to be sung in the 1990s: ''Old Ship of Zion,'' ''Michael, Row the Boat Ashore,'' and ''Get on Board, Children.'' Their transcriptions only hint at the complex rhythms and vocal qualities of the songs, while suggesting that early black spirituals used slightly flattened notes, generally the third, fifth, and seventh. The authors readily admit that they could not reduce to standard Western notation all of the various shadings, anticipations, and slurs that they heard, but their admission clearly underscores that some of the vocal techniques heard in gospel music and work songs were present in the spirituals of the 1860s.

Spirituals were most often performed by a small group that accompanied and supported its leader. In addition to call and response, some of these hymns were lined out, a process during which the leader sings a line or two that is repeated by the group. By the late nineteenth century, however, spirituals were commonly found in hymnals and in other printed sources. Their arrangements grew more elaborate, were written in four-part harmony, and moved further from folk practices. The ''Jubilee'' groups sent out by Fisk, Hampton, Tuskegee, and other pioneering colleges for blacks and Native Americans included singers trained in Western musical practices. They were also concertizing, rather than performing for a group of peers in a sacred setting. These factors helped set Jubilee singing groups apart from their sacred counterparts, both in context and performance style.

Still occasionally performed in the late twentieth century, spirituals have been an important part of black folk culture for approximately 150 years. They are still found in the repertoire of many small black church groups and choirs. Even African American singers trained in the European tradition, such as Leontyne Price, often perform and record spirituals. Rising from the musical culture of camp meetings and other evangelical forums, spirituals helped to guide the way for the gospel songs that developed at the dawn of the twentieth century.

Ring Shouts

A **ring shout,** one of the earliest forms of African American religious practice, combines physical movement with song. These songs are almost always spirituals. A ring shout is reminiscent of some West African religious ceremonies and remains one of the closest and clearest connections between black American and African folk culture. Arguably the oldest form of African American folk music to be heard today, ring shouts are one way that participants have of communicating directly with God through spontaneous movement and singing. The concept of divine communication links those who take part in a ring shout with adherents to Pentecostal beliefs.

M u s i c a l   E x a m p l e

Livingston, Alabama, was home to Dock Reed, an exceptionally powerful singer with a vast storehouse of African American folk songs who was born late in the nineteenth century. Reed had first recorded for the Library of Congress several times between 1937 and 1941. In the middle 1950s, folk song collector Harold Courlander "rediscovered" Reed while he was surveying black folk music in central Alabama. Courlander recorded Reed in great depth, further documenting his stories as well as Reed's magnificent voice and his nineteenth-century spirituals. [Folkways 4418]

Title "Jesus Gonna Make Up My Dying Bed"
Performer Dock Reed
Instruments one voice
Length 1:15
Notable Features

1. His a capella voice means this piece has a monophonic texture.
2. The melody is conjunctive and quite smooth.
3. Reed displays a marvelous control over the vibrato in his voice.
4. A "rise" in his voice of a fifth can be heard at the beginning of the first phrase of the first verse (the extended "Oh...") and at several other points.
5. The song is in a modified blues form, basically *aaab*.

Oh, don't you worry 'bout me dyin'!
Oh, don't worry 'bout me dyin'!
Oh, worry 'bout me dying'!
Jesus goin' to make up my dyin' bed.

Oh, I been in this valley! (repeat twice)
Jesus goin' to make up my dyin' bed.

Ah, when you see me dyin'
I don't want you to cry.
All I want you to do for me
Just low my dyin' head.

Ah, I'm sleepin' on Jesus!
Ah, sleepin' on Jesus!
Oh, I'm sleepin' on Jesus!
Jesus goin' to make up my dyin' bed!

Once found across much of the South, ring shouts remain part of religious services in the **Georgia Sea Islands.** These islands have only been easily accessible to the mainland since about 1930 when the first bridges and causeways were built. With a black population of about 90 percent, the people of the Sea Islands are almost all descended from cotton plantation slaves. This combination of factors has made the Georgia Sea Islands a stronghold for folk culture, including Gullah speech, folktales, and ring shouts.

Contemporary ring shouts are held in special "praise houses" where the faithful regularly gather. Most participants have moved past middle age; very few are under the age of forty. The "watch meetings" that draw the greatest number of attenders are held at Christmas and Easter. These are primarily song services without a sermon or separate choir to sing. The singing is done by a "band" of vocalists—a lead singer and responders whose songs are almost always antiphonal. The songs themselves are perhaps best characterized as spirituals. Vocal bands, by the way, are still found today in some Southern and Northern Pentecostal churches. After a long period of singing spirituals such as "Savior Do Not Pass Me By," the ring shout begins.

M u s i c a l   E x a m p l e

This ring shout was recorded at a workshop in Mississippi, but it captures the atmosphere and passion of a Georgia Sea Islands' prayer service. Singers from the Moving Star Hall on St. John's Island have kept this very emotional singing alive for many decades. During the 1960s, when this performance was recorded, the group toured around the United States, appearing at the Newport Folk Festival and many other smaller events. This tradition and the singers face a new challenge as their islands are "developed" for the tourist and retirement trade, which is exemplified by the Hilton Head Resort. [Smithsonian/Folkways 40031]

Title "Talkin' 'bout a Good Time"
Performer Benjamin Bligen (leader)
Instruments four voices
Length 1:11
Notable Features

1. You hear a capella singing accompanied by syncopated handclapping.
2. There is an acceleration in tempo during the performance.
3. It is an antiphonal arrangement with unison singing in the chorus.
4. A crescendo in dynamic level towards the middle of the performance is present.

Although not all of the worshipers actually get up and move around, some shuffle around. Their feet are not supposed to cross or be lifted from the ground—just as the worshipers are in direct contact with God, their contact with the earth is equally constant. During the shout, people are singing, speaking ecstatically (''in tongues''), and clapping polyrhythmically. Most of the participants are able to carry on three different rhythms simultaneously with their feet, hands, and voice. Ring shouts can last for hours, and the important ones often last all night.

Although ring shouts can still be found on a few of the islands just off the coast where Georgia and South Carolina meet, this description of a Christmas shout from an elementary school in 1865 illustrates that this religious practice has changed little in over one hundred years: ''The children move around in a circle, backwards, or sideways, with their feet and arms keeping energetic time, and their whole bodies undergoing most extraordinary contortions, while they sing at the top of their voice the refrain. . .'' (Epstein 1977).

Gospel Songs

Nineteenth-century folk music came from a variety of sources. The themes for the sermons of Baptist preachers draw their inspiration from the Bible and everyday experience, the music of Pentecostal singers was inspired by the holy spirit, while choirs in A.M.E. churches took their messages from everyday experiences and the holy scriptures. By the dawn of the twentieth century, a new wellspring, the **gospel song,** began penetrating and affecting each of these genres. Spirituals arose from the devastating effects of slavery, their message of hope and of flight to a new land capturing the attention of black Americans. Around the turn of the century, just as racism reemerged and blues, ragtime, and jazz began emerging, a younger generation of African Americans started composing simple ''gospel'' songs of praise. Within a decade, these songs had attracted the attention of churchgoers and, significantly, sheet-music and songbook publishers.

Such compositions drew from black secular and sacred experiences to create something new. While hymns are directed towards God, the message of gospel songs are aimed at humankind. The term ''gospel'' is subject to a number of definitions. For some it refers to any type of sacred selection, implying that the phrases ''gospel music'' and ''religious music'' are interchangeable. Others divide ''religious music'' into more specific categories: hymns, spirituals, and jubilees. Hymns are older songs drawn from the published Protestant hymnals of the nineteenth century, also known as ''Dr. Watts hymns.'' They are sometimes ''lined out'' or even performed as solos. Spirituals refer to the largely antebellum songs of unknown authorship that passed through oral tradition. Themes of freedom, movement, and unburdening predominate. Their form is usually *ab* or verse chorus. Jubilee has two distinctive meanings. First are songs about freedom or release from slavery and the happiness at being set free. Or it can mean up-tempo songs performed by black gospel quartets beginning in the 1930s that feature vocal effects, high rhythmic interest, strong lead vocal, and a ''pump'' bass. The **Golden Gate Quartet** pioneered this style of jubilee gospel singing in the middle 1930s.

The specific meaning of ''gospel song'' relates to the fact that it can be traced to a specific composer—**Thomas A. Dorsey,** Cleavant Derricks, Rev. C. A. Tindley, **Rev. William H. Brewster,** or Lucie Campbell. These early gospel songs were also the first type of black sacred music to be transmitted first within small groups and then to a large audience by way of the print media. Gospel songs and performance techniques are sometimes found among both black and white performers.

Early gospel songs incorporated bright imagery and simile to achieve their power and directness. In 1893 W. Henry Sherwood published *The Harp of Zion,* one of the earliest hymnals to use gospel songs. By the 1920s, these newly minted gospel songs impinged upon all aspects of black religious music. This appears to be particularly true for the **guitar evangelists,** whose recorded repertoires are peppered with written compositions. **Blind Willie Johnson,** for example, recorded ''Sweeter as the Years Go By,'' written and published by C. H. Morris in 1912. Blind Joe Taggert, Washington Phillips, and others waxed C. A. Tindley's 1916 song, ''Leave It There'' under the title ''Take Your Burden to the Lord.'' A 1909 composition by Benjamin Franklin Butts, ''It's All Right Now,'' appeared to be a staple of Arizona Dranes's repertoire, as her accomplished recording in 1927 implies. Some of these songs had already entered into oral tradition by the 1920s, while others seem to have been learned from printed sources such as *Gospel Pearls.* The full flowering of gospel publishing did not occur until the 1930s and 1940s when these new compositions hit the black religious community with the force of atomic power.

In 1982, the Smithsonian Institution arranged a conference dedicated to Roberta Martin.
Kip Lornell.

Roberta Martin
and the
Roberta Martin Singers:
The Legacy
and The Music

In the 1930s the gospel scene exploded. The works of the earlier gospel composers continued to gain popularity, primarily through church performances and the print media. Turn-of-the-century composing pioneers such as Rev. C. A. Tindley inspired the younger performers. By the early 1930s, the commercial companies had expanded their recordings of sermons, vocal quartets, and guitar evangelists to include more of the increasingly popular gospel songs. ''Georgia'' Tom Dorsey, often referred to as the ''Father of Gospel Music,'' emerged as the most influential of the early gospel performers whose work was heralded and greatly advanced by the mass media. Dorsey, along with Sisters Sallie Martin, Roberta Martin (no relation), and Willie Mae Ford Smith, soon revamped Chicago into the nodal point for the commercialization of gospel music in the African American community.

Dorsey began his career as a blues performer. His first widespread exposure came with Ma Rainey, for whom he served as pianist and musical director until 1928 when he joined Tampa Red (Hudson Whittaker). This duo proved enormously successful with a series of records with lightly salacious tunes, such as ''Its Tight Like That,'' ''Somebody's Been Using That Thing,''

M u s i c a l   E x a m p l e

This West Coast–based group had a successful pop music career in the late 1960s and early 1970s. Here they betray their roots in the Baptist church with this version of a spiritual-like song that, despite its title, is not related to Albert Brumley's well-known gospel song. This style of gospel singing was first heard in the early 1950s. It features a ''drive section'' towards the middle of the songs in which the chorus is repeated (''Do you feel like shouting?'') while the lead singer improvises. During this section they stay on the tonic chord both to spotlight the lead singer and as a means to heighten the tension and emotion of the song. [Folkways 31008]

Title ''Before You Get to Heaven (I'll Fly Away)''*
Performers The Chambers Brothers
Instruments drums, guitar, and four voices
Length 3:25
Notable Features

1. A duple (2/4) meter is quickly established by the instruments
2. Call and response between the lead singer and chorus
3. Crescendo dynamics during the drive section
4. Gently syncopated rhythm
5. Moderate tempo that increases slightly
6. ''Shouting'' lead vocal includes falsetto singing style

* The lyrics are located on page 124.

''Billie the Grinder,'' ''Stewin' Your Mess,'' and ''The Stuff You Sell.'' Along with Big Bill (Broonzy), they were among the frontline purveyors of ''hokum blues,'' featuring snappy guitar or guitar-piano duets, double entendre or humorous lyrics, and clear vocals. This music was strictly uptown, played for fun, but ultimately unsatisfying for Thomas Dorsey. In 1932 Tampa Red and Georgia Tom broke up their partnership. Red remained with blues and hokum music, but Dorsey turned his full attention to gospel composition and performance.

His gospel recordings, ''How About You?'' and ''If You See My Savior,'' recorded in March 1932, debuted nearly a decade after he began writing gospel songs. His debut sold quite poorly, not surprisingly, because the country was hitting the depths of the Depression and seventy-five cents was too much for even the most uplifting recording. Although Dorsey went on to record a few more religious titles, he quickly proved his worth as a composer. Nearly four hundred songs flowed from his pen, including such American classics as ''Precious Lord, Take My Hand,'' ''If You See My Savior,'' ''Little Wooden Church on the Hill,'' ''Peace in the Valley,'' ''When the Gates Swing Wide,'' ''Hide Me in Thy Bosom,'' and ''Search Me, Lord.'' Many of these enduring compositions initially appeared in the National Baptist Sunday School hymnal, *Gospel Pearls,* first printed in 1921. Dorsey also served as one of the principal organizers of the National Gospel Music Association. He and his fellow Chicagoans founded this organization in 1935, and it rapidly expanded to chapters across the United States. By the late 1930s, gospel music was being performed in black churches throughout the entire country.

Gospel music clearly benefited from the media's attention. Although gospel recordings were not plentiful until after World War II, they did trickle out slowly. Radio proved more helpful as performers with Sunday programs increased, spreading the word to those who could not or did not attend church services that featured this new music. The print media became the most critical factor in disseminating gospel music throughout the community. Small publishing houses began printing songbooks containing the words and simple four-part musical notations for these new compositions. These songbooks sold well as gospel fans looked forward to each new edition. Used as a point of departure, songbooks provided groups with an established reference for embellishing the printed arrangements for their own purposes. In its actual performance, black gospel music is highly dramatic and personal. No printed score could hope to (or want to) limit the singers' vocal techniques, their reworking of harmonies, or the use of syncopation to heighten their performances.

By the late 1930s, Roberta Martin had emerged as one of the most important innovators in gospel music. Her recordings from the 1940s and 1950s suggest that even in the middle of the twentieth century, black gospel music combines West African and western European elements. Her melodies betray an allegiance to black American folk and African traditions in her use of few tones (often pentatonic scales or the mixolydian mode), conjunctive melodies, and a persistent emphasis on one principal tone. Most of the songs adhere to the simple *ab* song form. Her harmonic language is closer to standard western European usage, with a clear emphasis on the primary chords. She also demonstrates a clear preference for **compound duple meters,** especially 12/8.

Another major innovation spawned by this music, the gospel concert/caravan, began in the late 1930s and signals its movement from the grass roots to the popular realm. Gospel programs brought together performers for special shows outside of the church service itself. Of course, this was not distinctly new because out-of-town groups were sometimes invited to sing at special Saturday evening or Sunday afternoon programs. The innovation occurred when singers got together and toured full-time. The community had not previously been able to support such groups, but gospel's newly minted popularity permitted this. Thomas A. Dorsey and his associates hit the road as part of a package that performed on tours, during the week as well as on weekends. Although they were several years ahead of their time, the Soul Stirrers of Houston, Texas, became the first gospel quartet to begin touring, trading their full-time "day" jobs for full-time touring in 1938.

Black gospel music represents a blend of musical as well as cultural innovation. First, it is music whose harmonic and melodic structure was deliberately similar to popular tunes. Composers like Dorsey felt that one way to reach a mass audience with a spiritual message was to package their songs in a familiar musical setting. Second, its message was equally straightforward with themes that appealed to the heartstrings—mother, duty, and home. Third, its simplicity was clearly aimed at an audience that could easily participate and become enveloped in gospel music. Fourth, gospel became the first African American religious music for which direct authorship of songs could be ascribed. Finally, gospel music emerged as the first style packaged with the mass media in mind and clearly aimed towards an increasingly sophisticated audience that looked to their radio, records, and printed sources for sacred music.

Pentecostal Singing and Guitar Evangelists

Holiness sects came into existence during the nineteenth century as people sought to gain a second blessing or sanctification through direct possession or intervention on the part of the Holy Spirit. Holiness services, both black and white, are highly emotional, featuring spirited preaching, equally compelling music, and even more improvisation. Spontaneous "holy dancing," "shouting" (ecstatic speech), and glossalia (speaking in tongues) are three notable aspects of holiness services that occur as congregation members are possessed by the spirit. These ritual acts are part of most **Pentecostal** services, though they are almost never captured on record. One would have to listen to or attend an entire service to taste its true flavor, but several important black Pentecostal performers did record as early as 1926.

By the time of these initial recordings, most of the black holiness sects were no more than thirty years old. The majority of these "Churches of God" were founded in the Deep South between 1895 and 1905. Most significant is the Church of God in Christ, founded in Lexington, Mississippi, by Memphis based minister Charles C. H. Mason in 1895. It remains the largest African American Pentecostal church in a sect that comprises about 4 percent of all black churchgoers, most of whom belong to urban congregations (temples) with small memberships.

Pentecostalists believe in the baptism of the Holy Spirit, the so-called second baptism that people receive because of special calling. This spiritual rebirth or calling is reflected in their fiery music. Holiness singers believe that they are called to praise God with a variety of instruments, as cited in the Book of Psalms. Rev. F. W. McGee, who established a temple on Chicago's South Side in the middle 1920s, and the blind pianist Arizona Dranes were among the outstanding early holiness recording artists. McGee was a preacher whose sermons were recorded by Victor with the accompaniment of various stringed instruments and horns. Other sanctified preachers, such as Rev. D. C. Rice, preferred to lead small ensembles in performances of popular holiness songs. Small jug bands accompanied at least a few of the groups associated with Memphis's holiness groups—Rev. Bryant's Sanctified Singers and the Holy Ghost Singers. Perhaps the most dramatic and musically moving of these performers was Arizona Dranes. Her OKeh recordings of ''Bye and Bye We're Going to See the King'' and ''I'm a Witness'' are masterpieces of this genre. Black sanctified music is characterized by dramatic vocals, the use of instruments (stringed and horns) not usually associated with sacred traditions, cooperative vocal ensembles that eschew close harmony for collective improvisation, and a fierce spontaneity.

Because of the popularity of the guitar—due to its portability, the ability of its strings to bend for flatted tonalities, and its relative low cost—a small group of guitar evangelists also became part of rural black music. The truth is that nearly all rural black musicians played sacred music; however, some specialized in it and a handful of them were recorded beginning in the 1920s. Rev. Edward Clayborn, whose recordings for Vocalion are characterized by a pronounced duple meter and a strong, regular rhythm punctuated by his slide guitar, preferred homiletic, pedantic songs: ''Everybody Ought to Treat Their Mother Right'' and ''Men Don't Forget Your Wives for Your Sweethearts.'' Blind Joe Taggert, thought to be from West Virginia, roamed the Southeastern states preaching and singing. He was occasionally accompanied by a fiddle and second guitar on his recordings. Other evangelists from this period—Blind Roger Hayes, Blind Willie Davis, Blind Mamie Forehand, Blind Gussie Nesbit—seemed attracted to the profession by a love for God and music and because of their physical liabilities, too. The options for visually handicapped blacks born near the turn of the century were as limited as their educational opportunities.

Blind Willie Johnson, born about 1902 near Marlin, Texas, was one of the finest rural black musicians to record and arguably the most accomplished guitar evangelist. He spent much of his life as a street singer and came to the attention of Columbia officials in 1927. A virtuoso guitarist and an arresting

Reverend Leon Pinson from central Mississippi performing at the Festival of American Folklife. *Smithsonian Institution.*

vocalist with an exceptionally wide range, Johnson sang to the accompaniment of his slide guitar. His wife, Angeline, participated on several of his sessions, serving as a wonderful foil to his singing—which ranged from a sweet falsetto to an emotive growl. Their repertoire included many of the most familiar gospel songs: ''Let Your Light Shine on Me,'' ''John the Revelator,'' ''You'll Need Somebody on Your Bond,'' and ''I Know His Blood Will Make Me Whole.'' However, his recorded masterpiece, ''Dark Was the Night—Cold Was the Ground,'' is a solo piece in which his slide recalls the holy moaning of a Baptist church service. ''You'll Need Somebody on Your Bond'' is a vocal duet with his wife and is underpinned by his delicate slide guitar:

> Well, you gonna need somebody on your bond,
> You gonna need somebody on your bond,
> Now it's way, at midnight,
> When Death comes slippin' in your room
> You gonna need ah, somebody on your bond.

Preachers became the first and arguably the most vitally powerful voice to reach the faithful. One of the clearest, most widely recognized voices belonged to **Rev. J. M. Gates** of Atlanta, the spiritual forefather for Martin

Preachers on Record

M u s i c a l   E x a m p l e

Pentecostal sects can be found throughout the United States. They are growing rapidly, although not as quickly as other fundamentalist churches. In predominantly black neighborhoods, they often hold services in small storefront churches. Many parts of the rural South are dotted with Pentecostal churches, though they tend to be strongest in the Deep South. This recording was done on location at the First Independent Holy Church of God—Unity—Prayer in Marion, Alabama, in 1954. The church was founded and fronted by Elder Effie Hall, who leads her small congregation on this piece. [Folkways 2658]

Title "Don't Let His Name Go Down."
Performers Elder Effie Hall and Congregation
Instruments guitar, percussion, tambourine, and four voices
Length 1:23
Notable Features

1. It has a simple, syncopated rhythm.
2. The mix of voices and instruments produces a rich homophonic texture.
3. The song follows a basic two-chord (tonic and dominant) harmonic progression.
4. Unison singing is used by the background voices.
5. A fervent, improvised feel propels the chorus.

Oh, don't let his name go down! (repeat)
Refrain: I'm goin' to do what I can, hold up his hand,
Don't let his name go down!

Well, don't let his name go down! (repeat)
Refrain [substitute "all" for "what"]

His name is holy and sanctified! (repeat)
Refrain

(Repeat the first verse)
Glory!

Luther King. Gates's initial Columbia release, "Death's Black Train Is Coming" (May 1926), proved so wildly successful that the company immediately released its session mate, "I'm Gonna Die with the Staff in My Hand." The Gates phenomenon continued, and by year's end he had visited the studios of Pathé, Plaza, OKeh, Victor, Vocalion, and Gennett. Most of these recordings were accomplished in New York City studios, though the Reverend Gates did stay at home for his first session and for one in November.

Rev. J. M. Gates's success illustrates the power and influence of the electronic media in promoting traditional music. In the spring of 1926, he was a very popular Baptist preacher with a large and devoted congregation in Atlanta, Georgia. Less than one year later, Gates had recorded nearly eighty selections and had visited New York City on two occasions for marathon sessions as he free-lanced. He recorded many of the same titles/themes— "Baptize Me," "Death's Black Train Is Coming," "Dying Gambler," "I Know I Got Religion"—because they were powerful sermons and popular themes. Many of these selections were marketed by title only; the artist was not always listed. Thus Gates's most striking themes were repeated at least in part because of the pressure of record companies to sell products. These factors all worked to propel a respected local religious leader into the forefront of the nationwide "race" record industry in a staggeringly short period. The Reverend Gates's popularity proved long-lived, too, for he continued to record, albeit sporadically, until 1941.

Rev. J. C. Burnett, a Kansas City preacher, soon followed Gates into the Columbia studios. His sermon on "The Downfall of Nebuchadnezzar" sold exceptionally well; apparently record buyers were moved by his interpretation of Daniel 4:14 and his hoarse, emotive preaching. Although Burnett proved to be popular, he stayed with Columbia Records for about three years and did not enjoy the long-lasting success that greeted Gates. Black preachers, none of them "professional," continued to be documented by record companies throughout the 1920s and into the 1930s. By the close of the prewar record era in 1943, seventy preachers had recorded some 750 sermons on a wide variety of subjects ranging from biblical passages; to moral issues such as drinking, drugs, and fidelity; to topical statements about floods, tornadoes, and the flight of Lindbergh. The Reverend Gates warned his listeners of gambling's dangers in a 1926 sermon, "The Dying Gambler" (on OKeh Records 8387), that strayed from his usual biblical stories:

> I have seen the gambler standin' with his cards in his hand. And the fifty-two cards in the deck represent the fifty-two weeks in the year. And the 365 spots on the cards, represent the 365 days in the year. And the highest card, my friends is the Ace; represents on God high over all. And the deuce represents Jesus' law "one of you could seek me and then you would find me." And the trey represents the three Godheads of the Trinity. . . .

One of Gates's most pedantic sermons on a topic of everyday problems urged his listeners to "pay your furniture man"—who collected weekly or monthly for furniture purchased on time-payment plans.

How well did these recorded sermons reflect the experience of attending a church service? Clearly they could not replicate the emotional atmosphere of a live service. Live sermons benefited from the interaction between the preacher and the congregation, whose "amens," "yes, Lords," and other responses punctuated the oration. Studio sermons most often included a ''congregation'' of between two and six voices, but these blanched in comparison to the experience of attending church. Moreover, the sermons were truncated to fit into three-minute packages, all but eliminating certain aspects of a church service and sermon: speaking in tongues, ''anointed speech,'' and the strong, extended ritual interaction (verbal and behavioral) could not be captured on disc. There is no replacement for the experience of attending a church service, but sermon records helped to remind the faithful of their worldly obligations and exposed them to different styles of preaching.

Gospel Quartets

More palatable folk music continued to predominate the mass media as the United States entered World War II. Led by the Golden Gate Quartet, both secular and sacred vocal quartets were beginning their rise to prominence. The Gates (as they were usually referred to) pioneered the ''jubilee'' style of quartet singing from Norfolk, Virginia. This modern ''neo-jubilee'' singing has little to do with Reconstruction jubilee groups; it represents an aesthetic innovation that profoundly affected black American sacred music. Jubilee singing incorporated new lyrical and musical ideas. The lyrics often told a semi-linear story based on Bible parables, such as the Gates' well-known versions of ''Job'' and ''Noah.'' Unlike blues or the earlier spirituals, which tend to be nonlinear and cohere through emotional connections, jubilee songs are closer to sermons or nodal ballads in their ability to relate a story. Jubilee groups also featured a lead singer, whose dramatic but smooth *cante-fable* style clearly foreshadowed popular Motown singers like Smokey Robinson or Levi Stubbs. The pumping, percussive bass helped to create the propulsive polyrhythms and carefully accented syncopations that characterize **jubilee quartet** singing. By way of their popular Bluebird and Columbia recordings and their NBC radio network broadcasts, the Golden Gate Quartet disseminated this music from their New York base throughout the entire country. This happened over a three-year period, profoundly affecting the course of black religious music for the next decade.

The radio, however, continued to broadcast comedy programs and news of the war as well as all types of music into people's homes. Of the major strains of black folk music, only religious traditions were part of radio's standard fare. Fifteen-minute or half-hour broadcasts by black vocal gospel groups became the norm in many cities across the United States. Nashville's Fairfield Four broadcast daily over 50,000-watt WLAC, while just to the east in Knoxville, the Swan Silvertones began their day with a fifteen-minute program on the less powerful WNOX.

By the war's end, there was a pent-up demand for live performances by black gospel quartets, which was fermented by several years of restricted travel and widespread radio broadcasts. Prior to World War II, only a handful of gospel quartets braved the difficulties of life on the road to become full-time touring groups. People now wanted to see and hear the groups that they had enjoyed on radio. Independent record companies helped to fan the flames by issuing records by groups that enjoyed local or regional followings: New York City's Trumpeteers on Score Records, the Harmonizing Four of Richmond (Virginia) on Gotham, and the Spirit of Memphis on King and Peacock. The mass media helped reinforce the interest in gospel quartets by getting this music before the public and moving it into the popular realm. Between 1945 and 1950, this grass roots black music became intensely public as hundreds of quartets toured the country performing in large auditoriums, small churches, and school halls.

A new style, "hard gospel" quartet singing, began competing with and complementing the jubilee groups by the close of the decade. "Hard" refers to the emotionally powerful lead singing epitomized by Ira Tucker of the Dixie Hummingbirds and Julius Cheeks of the Sensational Nightingales. These singers utilized every trick in the repertoire of African American folk singers: falsetto, rasps, growls, moaning, highly ornamented phrasing, etc. Their strongest, most pronounced improvisation came during the "drive" sections of live performances. The drive section, a repetitive groove during which the same chords or ostinato figure is repeated, encourages the lead singer to heighten the emotional or spiritual feelings through improvisation. Hard gospel singing acknowledges the importance and influence of solo performers such as Alex Bradford, Mahalia Jackson, and Rosetta Tharpe.

Many of the black gospel quartets during this period became versatile, featuring singing in both the jubilee and hard gospel style. A capella singing characterized the styles of many of these groups, but by the early 1950s most groups had added at least one instrument (usually a guitar) to their line up. Instruments added a solid rhythmic foundation and provided the harmonic underpinning for the singing. Their repertoires were also undergoing changes, as more of the popular gospel songs like Roberta Martin's "Swing Down, Chariot" or the Reverend Brewster's "Move on Up a Little Higher" became integrated

CBS TRUMPETEERS

One of the premier quartets as they appeared in the early 1950s.
Kip Lornell.

into programs. The role of the bass singer was de-emphasized, probably in light of the addition of instruments that often took the bass line. Two new time signatures, 12/8 and 6/8 or compound duple meters, augmented the standard duple meters. These so-called gospel meters became quite popular and were extensively used for certain songs. Another one of the Reverend Brewster's gospel compositions from the 1940s, ''Surely, God Is Able,'' is regularly performed in 12/8 time.

By the early 1950s, black gospel quartets concentrated on their programs as much as they did on the religiosity of their musical message. Professional groups regularly performed in matching, often brightly colored suits and had elaborate stage performances worked out. Certain groups earned reputations as ''soul killers'' because they put on such dramatic and moving programs. Money became an overriding concern because many of the singers had to support families. On one level, black gospel quartet music had moved well beyond its grass roots status, functioning as a manifestation of popular culture. On the other hand, there were many local community groups singing this music. They would never be stars or even semiprofessional singers, but they sang at local churches and were occasionally in demand for programs out-of-town.

Inevitably, the quartet boom ended. Professional groups such as the Soul Stirrers, Pilgrim Travelers, CBS Trumpeteers, and Spirit of Memphis could no longer support themselves as touring and recording artists. Some quartets disbanded, others retreated to semiprofessional status. Many of the grass roots quartets remained true to the music of their youth, and some are celebrating anniversaries of fifty or more years: Royal Harmony Four (Memphis) and the Sterling Jubilees (Birmingham). This process took several years to wind down, but by the late 1950s it was all but complete.

Popular black gospel music moved into new areas. The soloists, especially Mahalia Jackson but also Cassietta George and Delores Ward, once more rose to prominence. Larger vocal ensembles, notably large choruses and choirs, gradually began to be heard on records and over the radio.

Final Thoughts

Religious music maintains its strong roots in black folk culture. Even the most modern gospel has clear links with the past, most often through the vocal styles that still emphasize the "moans," "growls," and other tricks that have been heard in black churches for decades. The older spirituals are still sometimes performed, but even modern gospel uses older songs. Pentecostal churches retain their conservative values; their updating is more surface: electric instruments, microphones, etc. Of all black folk music, the religious traditions continue to be the most vital and alive.

Key Figures and Terms

Rev. William H. Brewster
camp meeting
compound duple meter
Thomas A. Dorsey
Rev. J. M. Gates
Georgia Sea Islands
Golden Gate Quartet
gospel song
Great Awakening
guitar evangelist
Blind Willie Johnson
jubilee quartet
Pentecostalism
ring shout
Slave Songs of the United States
Dr. Watts hymns

Audio

A Capella Gospel Singing. Folk lyric 9045 (LP). An excellent survey of male gospel quartet singing from the 1920s to the 1950s.

African American Gospel Music. World Music Institute 002 (CASS). Contemporary selections by small community-based and semiprofessional vocal ensembles: the Badgett Sisters, Faithful Harmonizers, Fairfield Four, and others.

Been in the Storm Too Long. Smithsonian/Folkways 40031 (CD/CASS). An anthology of Georgia Sea Island material that includes examples of spirituals, shouts, and prayers recorded in the early 1960s.

Bless My Bones—Memphis Gospel Radio, the Fifties. Rounder 2063 (CASS). A survey of commercial recordings and radio transcriptions that focuses on the Spirit of Memphis Quartet, Sunset Travelers, and other important groups that broadcast over WDIA.

In the Spirit. 2 vols. Origin Jazz Library 12 and 13 (LP). These records provide a cross section of guitar evangelists and songsters, such as Charley Patton and Bukka White, who recorded in the 1920s and 1930s.

Jackson, Mahalia. *Newport 1958.* Columbia Special Products 8071 (LP). An exemplary live performance by this noted soloist.

Johnson, Blind Willie. *Sweeter as the Years Go By.* Yazoo 1058 (CD/CASS). Some of Johnson's best and most moving songs are included on this set.

Mays, Osceola. *Spirituals and Poems.* Documentary Arts (CASS). A collection of (mostly) nineteenth-century a capella spirituals performed solo by this female Texas artist.

The Storm Is Passing Over: Reverends and Their Post War Gospel. Global Village 203 (CASS). A strong sampling of commercial recordings from the 1940s and 1950s, which is important because it also includes sermons.

Books

Broughton, Vic. 1985. *Black Gospel: An Illustrated History of the Gospel Sound.* Dorset: Blandford Press. Broughton, a born-again British writer, surveys the development of black gospel music from the turn of the century through the 1980s.

Carawan, Candie and Guy. 1989. *Ain't We Got a Right to the Tree of Life?* Athens: University of Georgia Press. An ethnographic study of black life on the Georgia Sea Islands that emphasizes musical culture.

Epstein, Dena. 1977. *Sinful Tunes and Spirituals.* Urbana: University of Illinois Press. Epstein examines the sources for eighteenth- and nineteenth-century black folk music.

Heilbut, Tony. 1975. *The Gospel Sound: Good News and Bad Times.* New York: Anchor Books. An overview of commercial gospel music from the Depression through the late 1960s, with sketches about such important figures as Mahalia Jackson, the Soul Stirrers, and Marion Williams.

Lornell, Kip. 1988. *"Happy in the Service of the Lord":* *Afro-American Gospel Quartets in Memphis.* Urbana: University of Illinois Press. This book takes an interdisciplinary look at the quartet tradition in Memphis over a sixty-year period beginning in the 1920s.

Oliver, Paul. 1984. *Songsters and Saints.* Cambridge: Cambridge University Press. Although not strictly about religious music, chapters five through seven provide an important survey of religious music on early records.

Video

The Gospel According to Al Green. Mug-Shot Production/Magnum Entertainment, Inc. 94 minutes. A lengthy examination of this former soul singer's career, including scenes in his Pentecostal church in Memphis.

Say Amen, Somebody. George Neuworth Films. 90 minutes. This stirring documentary covers some of the most important figures in the history of black gospel music.

Singing Stream. Tom Davenport Films. 60 minutes. A documentary that provides a fine contextual and musical look at the Landers family of gospel singers based in Granville County, North Carolina.

---

*"Before You Get to Heaven (I'll Fly Away)"

It's a rough and rocky road, before you get to heaven. (repeat three times)
And I feel like shouting all the time.

You have to cry sometimes, before you get to heaven. (repeat three times)
And I feel like shouting all the time.

You have to pray sometimes, before you get to heaven. (repeat three times)
And I feel like shouting all the time.

You got to love everybody, before you get to heaven. (repeat three times)
And I feel like shouting all the time.

You have to moan sometimes, before you get to heaven. (repeat three times)

And I feel like shouting all the time.
"Drive" section: Do you feel like shouting?
       I feel like shouting!
       etc.

African American Secular Folk Music

It would be difficult to underestimate the profound impact of nineteenth- and twentieth-century black American folk music upon our culture. In this chapter you will learn about the types of secular black folk music that developed in the United States since Reconstruction. Because of slavery's legacy, which left so many African Americans in rural Southern areas, most of this music originated in the South. These innovations represent a move away from the early Africanized styles of folk music and directly into a uniquely and demonstrably African American hybrid, a process that began slowly but inexorably prior to Reconstruction. The changes only accelerated with freedom, which was justifiably celebrated in songs like ''The Year of Jubilee.'' The dawn of the twentieth century saw the creation of ragtime, blues, jazz, and other forms of vernacular music.

This music also reflects its Southern heritage. Some of the instruments, most notably the fifes and drums or quills, are often homemade, partly reflecting the harsh economic conditions under which many blacks lived in the United States. The themes heard in many work songs—separation from loved ones, oppression by one's ''Captain,'' hard work, longing for freedom—further underscore the difficult conditions under which many people lived. The important role played by songsters suggests the importance of all types of music within rural black communities, which were often far removed from the mainstream of American popular culture. Nonetheless, some of this music, especially blues, has now become a universally accepted part of our own vernacular musical vocabulary. The blues has even migrated well beyond our borders to influence popular music in other parts of the world.

Indeed, the music discussed in this section of *Introducing American Folk Music* forms the foundation for much of our contemporary popular music. Virtually all of the forms of twentieth-century popular music, most notably rock 'n' roll, directly evolved from these Southern black roots. Although it might seem like a long distance from Scott Joplin's ragtime to the Gershwin brothers, Elvis Presley, and the hip-hop nation of the 1980s, the direct links to earlier black folk music are there. The precise nature of these relationships is more fully discussed in a later chapter, ''The Folk Roots of Popular Music.''

String Bands

Many rural musicians around the entire United States, and from all racial and national origins, play in informal, small string ensembles. Though it is not well documented, black folk musicians also performed together in **string bands** across the South. In fact, black string bands were once quite widespread, particularly in the Southeastern United States. Some slaves were inevitably exposed to European music in the form of Haydn's sonatas and the music of other popular eighteenth-century composers, but most no doubt played country dance tunes on fiddles. Individual musicians or small string ensembles no doubt also filled the air during less formal occasions: cornhuskings, taverns on a Saturday evening, and parties. Occasionally, blacks were encouraged to develop their musical skills on pianos, violins, as well as a variety of brass instruments. White slave owners often fostered musical interests because blacks sometimes provided musical entertainment. African musical practices, particularly drumming, were almost always discouraged.

Slaves also performed dance tunes on fiddles and banjolike instruments. Across the South, they played for Anglo-American balls and assemblies, but for their own enjoyment and recreation, too. Many brief accounts of black music exist in the diaries, newspapers, and contemporary written accounts of the period between 1700 and 1800. Unfortunately, this music was not notated on staff paper, and since sound recording equipment was not developed until the 1880s, these fleeting recollections must suffice. As early as 1754, one runaway Maryland slave's most distinctive, identifiable trait was as a ''banjer'' player. So pervasive were the accounts of black banjo playing that by the early 1800s, it was described in an ''off-hand'' manner as though it were part of everyday life.

Fiddlers became part of the early African American musical experience, and they performed both for white dances as well as for the diversion of other blacks. The instrument itself was quite popular among the colonists, who used it in formal parlor performances and to accompany dances of all types. Not only did slaves play fiddles, they also crafted them. One early reference to a runaway slave describes him as ''a black Virginia born Negro fellow named Sambo, about 6 ft. high, about 32 years old. He makes fiddles, and can play upon the fiddle, and work at the carpenter's trade'' (Southern, 1983, 64).

Despite the popularity of the banjo and fiddle, the two are rarely mentioned in the same references. Apparently, blacks played one or the other. Nor were these instruments played in tandem, as they are so often paired today. But during the 1830s, such duets had become a staple in early minstrel shows and there are many drawings and paintings of such musicians. By the turn of the century, the guitar and sometimes a mandolin were added to this basic unit, creating a fuller and richer sound. But the fiddle and banjo remained at the core of these string bands.

Joe and Odell Thompson have played string band throughout Orange County, North Carolina, since the 1940s.
Kip Lornell

The instruments used to accompany all-black rural dances almost always included a fiddle or banjo, often augmented by a rhythmic instrument. Rhythms, often polyrhythms, and the use of various percussion instruments are arguably the most fundamentally important black contributions to American music. It could be as simply performed as ''patting **juba**—patting hands together, on thighs, or the chest, the antecedent of the hambone games found among black children today. Sticks or the jawbone of a large animal provided two more percussive instruments.

Based on rather sketchy twentieth-century aural evidence, the following observations about black string bands appear to be true. Banjo playing betrays two basic traits. First, the melody played is simplified to the point that it basically sketches out the melodic line with little improvisation. Second, rhythmic complexities are held in high regard, even to the point of virtuosity. There seem to be some direct links between black banjo playing and early blues guitar playing, particularly in Mississippi. In Piedmont, North Carolina, several of the black banjo players that I documented in the 1970s transposed their banjo technique to guitar, even to the point of tuning their guitar like a banjo. There are also some striking similarities between black banjo-picking techniques and the open-tuned frailing style of a Delta bluesman such as Bukka White.

Similar observations can be made about black fiddle playing. The emphasis is generally upon rhythmic, rather than melodic, improvisation. Their playing seems to be more forceful and intent upon driving the 2/4 or 4/4 beat home for dancing, instead of creating a beautiful melodic line. When the instruments play together, it is usually in a simple *ab* tune form.

Lyrics for other forms of black secular music are even simpler. Prior to the emergence of blues about 1900, a large number of short lyric songs constituted a major body of African American music. Some, such as ''Old Black Joe,'' came from the minstrel stage, but the majority were brief ditties that came from dance tunes. Such tunes were performed for solo dancing as well as for square dances, which were integral to the black tradition well into the twentieth century. Many were part of a shared black/white repertoire that reflects late nineteenth-century rural American life more than it betrays racial origins. Tunes or songs like ''Roundtown Gals,'' ''Molly Put the Kettle On,'' ''Soldier's Joy,'' and **''John Henry''** were favored by rural musicians across much of America; it would be difficult or dangerous to assign racial origins to most of them.

Work Songs

A **work song** is simply any song performed by workers that assists them in carrying out their task. With the exception of sea shanties and possibly some nineteenth-century cowboy songs, they have been principally the domain of black American laborers. Anglo-American shanties flourished throughout the nineteenth century, particularly between 1820 and 1860, but they faded as sailing ships were supplanted by steam vessels. Sea shanties accompanied all types of nautical work, including raising and lowering sails or hauling in an anchor. The songs themselves derive from a variety of sources: the minstrel stage, English ballads, popular contemporary ditties, even military marching songs. As long as the words and tune were well known, almost any song could be used as a sea shanty.

African American work songs constitute a much richer, longer-lasting tradition. Black workers have utilized songs to accompany everything from shoe shining to poling a riverboat. In the nineteenth century, novels, diaries, and other printed sources describe all types of work songs, but it wasn't until the twentieth century that they began to be properly documented. These songs rarely use any harmonization and usually follow a simple, recurrent structure featuring unison singing or some type of call and response. Because so many twentieth-century work songs were collected in prisons, their themes are often related to incarceration. Sometimes even a religious folk song, like ''Sign of Judgement,'' can be transformed into a work song. Most work songs, however, are based on secular themes, often escape or freedom of movement.

Regardless of their origins, work songs fulfill two basic functions. One is to pass the time while workers carry out monotonous, repetitive jobs such as hoeing a row of cotton, chopping or pulling weeds, caulking a boat's hull, or loading a truck. Work songs also provide the singers with a sense of solidarity by participating in a communal act. The singing gives workers a greater measure of control, co-opting that role from their boss or overseer. An even closer tie is forged by those whose task requires special pacing or timing. Jobs demanding special coordination and split-second group effort—such as spike driving, **track laying,** or hauling in fishnets—forces the workers into even greater cooperation. Crushed, mangled fingers result when the timing of a song leader heading a spike driving crew wavers or falters. Understanding the task and an ability to time the work, rather than possessing a marvelously powerful voice, becomes the prime requirement for a respected song leader.

A group of convicts at work in a Texas prison circa 1935. *Library of Congress.*

M u s i c a l   E x a m p l e

Prison work songs are a part of our musical past, though they could be heard in some sections of the South as recently as the 1970s. Such songs were first aurally documented on wire recordings by the Library of Congress in the 1930s and later by other collectors. This selection was recorded in the early 1950s by a group, which included Pete Seeger, that traveled to Texas looking for work songs. They recorded a number of solo ''arhoolies'' as well as group work songs similar to this well-known hoe chopping song about breaking new ground for planting. Its themes of hard work and separation are common in work songs. [Folkways 4475]

Title ''Chopping in the New Ground''
Performers Texas Prisoners
Instruments one lead voice and six voices in response
Length 1:37
Notable Features

1. You hear seven a capella voices singing in antiphonal style.
2. There is a loose, unison response to the song leader.
3. The lead voice sings in a relatively tense vocal style.
4. A conjunctive, pentatonic melody is heard in the response.
5. The piece has a very steady, moderate rhythm.

Oh, Captain Charlie
(Good God A'mighty)
Oh, Captain Charlie
(Oh, my Lord)
[These responses alternate throughout the rest of the song]
I'm chopping in the new ground
I'm chopping in the new ground
I'm chopping my way back
I'm chopping my way back
My way back home, sir
My way back home, sir
Oh, Captain Charlie
Oh, you remember what I told you
If you didn't row, sir
Oh, you would not make it
Make it back to Rosie
To Rosie and the baby
Oh, Captain Charlie
We're chopping in the new ground
We're chopping all day long
Chopping all day long, sir
Oh, Captain Charlie
Oh, do you remember
Remember how she looked, sir

> We're choppin in the live oak
> Way down in Brazos
> Way down in the Brazos
> Oh, Captain Charlie
> Oh, Captain Charlie

Nonetheless, the ability to improvise lyrics and an agreeable voice remain the most valued qualities for a song leader of group work songs.

Work songs relieve boredom as well as regulate the timing of such skilled team-tasks as driving railroad spikes or chopping wood. However, its function is much deeper and more critical. Simply by setting the tempo of work, such songs also give black singers a modicum of control over their reduced circumstances. They also provide a sense of solidarity for the singers, the feeling of being part of a group united in a single action. Finally, these early work songs relieved tension by allowing blacks to complain about their living conditions and treatment by white slave owners.

Though only circumstantial evidence backs this up, work songs tend to be short and repetitive. This permits almost anyone to join in their singing. A work song might consist of a half dozen words repeated by the leader and the chorus of fellow workers. The musical phrases are short, usually no more than four or five measures. But the key to avoiding true repetition is slight melodic and textual variations. The key to the success of a song leader was the ability to improvise, making the singing more interesting. This ability to improvise, as we shall see, is important to the respect accorded to African American musicians.

Today work songs have all but disappeared due to mechanization and, in some states, relatively recent changes in prison systems. The well-documented conservative atmosphere maintained in the Texas penal system remained until the 1970s when court orders forced it to change. Significantly, the work song tradition continued within this inhuman system well into the final third of the twentieth century. In 1972 Bruce Jackson recorded the same songs that previous generations of prisoners sang. One of these, ''Alberta,'' became a group work song sung in unison as the prisoners weeded and is clearly influenced by the blues.

> See Alberta comin' down that road (repeat twice)
> Walkin' just like she got a heavy load.
>
> Wo, 'Berta, don't you hear me gal? (repeat)
> Twenty-one hammers fallin' in a line (repeat twice)
> None a them hammers, boys, that ring a like mine.
> Ring like silver and it shine like gold (repeat twice)
> Price a my hammer, boys, ain't never been told.

Big Leg 'Berta, if you come and be mine (repeat twice)
Have to do nothin' in the summertime (Jackson 1972, 280).

Fife and Drum Bands

Fife and drum band music is perhaps the best example of a regional style of black American folk music undocumented on race series. Once a tradition that existed in several sections of the South, by the race record era, **fife and drum bands** were largely confined to the deep mid-South. This music evolved from military tradition and became transformed by black musicians, veterans of the Civil War. In central and northern Mississippi, fife and drum bands sometimes played for funerals, but they primarily came to provide entertainment for dances and other less somber community functions. Fife and drum bands in some respects were the Mississippi equivalent of the black fiddle and banjo tradition that flourished and still exists in Virginia and North Carolina.

The music itself was played on two primary instruments, drums and cane fifes, constituting a small ensemble. Two snare drums and a bass drum constitute the drum section, while the cane fife usually has four or five holes. The cane provides the main melodic interest, though with a very limited range of less than a fifth. Drums provide this music with its strong rhythmic interest, a marked duple meter (2/4) with an underlying polyrhythmic feeling as one of the drums plays an improvisatory line. Alan Lomax of the Library of Congress's Folksong Archive undertook the only prewar recording of this music: the Hemphill Band of northern Mississippi. This Como County band consisted of family and neighbors who played locally for many years. Hemphill also played the ten-hole quill, another wind instrument that is almost never heard in modern America.

Northern Mississippi remains about the only place that fife and drum band music is still performed. The major summer holidays—Memorial Day, Fourth of July, and Labor Day—provide the context for this music, a throwback to the era when fife and drum bands performed for military affairs. Picnics featuring barbecued goat and plenty of liquor begin in the afternoon and run well into the night, while the fife and drum bands play and people march behind or dance to the music. These are male-dominated functions, both musically and socially, which usually contain a large number of drunken men by night's end.

Ragtime and Coon Songs

Ragtime is yet another black musical style to emerge in the late nineteenth century. Initially a Midwestern innovation, by the turn of the century it was being performed across the country. This music developed among itinerant piano players who made their living performing in rough sporting houses, **juke joints,** and bars where drinking, gambling, and prostitution were commonplace. They started playing highly syncopated tunes (later called rags) based on established and popular polkas, marches, and schottisches.

Ragtimelike tunes were being published and heard on the minstrel stage by the late 1880s.

Ragtime itself synthesized classical piano technique and distinctly African American folk dance tunes, such as the slave dance-derived "cakewalk." J. Russel Robinson, **Scott Joplin,** Tom Turpin, and James Scott were among the pioneering pianists whose rags were eventually published in sheet music and issued on piano rolls. Many people gained their initial exposure to ragtime at Chicago's World's Columbian Exposition in 1893. Several of the era's most prominent ragtime performers, including Scott Joplin, played at this event, which attracted nearly twenty million patrons. The popularity of ragtime dramatically increased following this exposure and the subsequent publication of ragtime on sheet music. The "classic" rags of the first decade of the twentieth century, many of which were published by John Stark, compared favorably with the best contemporary European music. The popular era for ragtime lasted until World War I, when jazz began to establish itself and composers like Zez Confrey began composing popular songs with roots in both idioms.

This dramatic instrumental music was characterized by its use of 6/8 meter in the treble, which often contrasted with 2/4 meter in the bass. Ragtime's classic form tended towards a march (ababa) or a quadrille (abacd). Most rags are written in major keys, though some of their strains are in minor keys or in the relative major. In other words, these different sections often modulate into different keys. The clearest vernacular influence is found in the scales that often feature a flattened third and seventh scale degrees, similar to its contemporary style—blues. Ragtime's commercialization marked the second time that white America had "discovered" black regional music and brought it to the attention of the entire country. What began as an unwritten folk music informally passed from one piano player to another was quickly

Confrey was one of many popular composers who used ragtime as a basis for their writing.
Kip Lornell.

Musical Example

Ann Charters, an English professor and dean at the University of Connecticut, became interested in black American music in the 1950s. Among her many publications is a biography of black vaudeville entertainer Bert Williams. She is married to Sam Charters, the noted blues historian and writer, and is also a proficient ragtime pianist. Charters's interpretation of James Scott's late (1919) composition remains true to the printed version. [Folkways 3563]

Title ''Victory Rag''
Performer Ann Charters
Instrument piano
Length 3:22
Notable Features

1. It is played in a duple (2/4) meter.
2. The tempo is restrained; it is marked ''not fast'' on the sheet music!
3. You can hear moderate syncopation.
4. There is a generally even flow of eighth and sixteenth notes.
5. The key is major, with the contrasting section in its relative minor.

---

embraced by the music publishing business, which reduced ragtime to notation and piano rolls in order to enhance its dissemination.

In addition to the published piano rags, the pens of the Tin Pan Alley songwriters developed the **''coon song''** genre, affording whites another opportunity to lampoon black Americans. Once more white America reveled in its celebration of the musical image of smiling, gap-toothed, chicken pie–eating, and oversexed Negroes. Ernest Hogan's 1896 composition, ''All Coons Look Alike to Me,'' kicked off the coon song era. Another song from this era, Ben Harney's ''Mr. Johnson,'' comes from the same mold:

> A big black coon was lookin' fer chickens
> When a great big bulldog got to raisin' de dickens,
> De coon got higher, de chicken got nigher,
> Just den Johnson opened up fire.
> And now he's playing seben eleben,
> Way up yonder de nigger heaben,
> Oh! Mr. Johnson, made him good.

Such songs inspired a generation of songwriters, including Irving Berlin and George M. Cohan, whose own work greatly influenced twentieth-century American popular song.

The emotion cohering most blues songs contrasts with ballads, another genre in traditional black music. Just as in the Anglo-American tradition, ballads associated with black American culture relate a story. By the early twentieth century, ballads had become integrated into the repertoire of African American rural **songsters.** A singer such as **Leadbelly** was a repository for ballads, particularly those associated with Texas, ''Ella Speed,'' or related to his own life, such as ''Governor O.K. Allen'' and ''The Shreveport Jail.'' Leadbelly's versions of these songs remind us that the **African American ballad** tradition is distinguished from its Anglo-American neighbor by its lack of narrative coherence and linearity, by its subjectivity, and by its tendency to glorify events. Ballads in the black tradition are also often centonical—they borrow thematic elements from a variety of sources in order to build something new. Such songs have generally been called ''blues ballads,'' but more recently the term ''nodal ballad'' has been suggested because they tend to take a theme and use it as a point of departure for casual storytelling.

''John Henry'' is doubtless the most well-known member of this tradition. Popular among both black and white musicians, ''John Henry'' was a steel driving man whose story is believed to have occurred in West Virginia in the 1870s. This song's many versions are archetypal of black ballads for they recount the story of a strong man competing against a steam-powered drill. In most versions, John Henry dies after defeating his mechanical foe and is celebrated as a mighty man. ''John Henry'' has been collected among blacks across the South from the early 1900s to the present and is sometimes played as a fiddle tune. In the late 1920s, Joe Evans and Arthur McClain recorded this rather complete version:

John Henry he was a li'l baby boy
Sittin' on his mama's knee,
Had a nine-pound hammer, holdin' in her arms
Goin' be the death of me. (repeat three times)

John Henry went to that Big Bend tunnel
Hammer in his hand,
John Henry was so small and that rock was so tall
Laid down his hammer and he cried. (repeat three times)

John Henry asked his shaker,
''Shaker did you ever pray?
'Cause if I miss that piece of steel
T'morrow be your buryin' day.'' (repeat three times)

''Who's gonna shoe your pretty little feet,
Who's gonna glove your li'l hand?
Baby who's gonna kiss your rosy cheeks
When I'm in a differ'nt land?'' (repeat three times)

Ballads

John Henry took sick and went to bed,
Sent for the doctor and in he come.
Turned down the side of John Henry's bed,
''Sick and can't get well, oh pardner,
Sick and can't get well.''

While ''John Henry'' is ubiquitous, other nodal ballads have remained regionalized or even more local. The story of ''Railroad Bill'' relates how an Alabama turpentine worker, Morris Slater, became entangled with the law and eventually fronted a series of bold attacks on trains before being shot to death in 1897. This ballad has primarily circulated in the Southeastern states, most widely in Tennessee and Virginia. ''The Mystery of Dunbar's Child'' exemplifies a ballad with exceptionally limited geographic circulation. This song describes the 1912 kidnapping of two children from a picnic in Opelousas, Louisiana. The only known version of ''The Mystery of Dunbar's Child'' comes from Richard ''Rabbit'' Brown, a New Orleans singer/guitarist who recorded it for Victor in 1928. This ballad is also notable for its strong sense of narrative, as it covers a sequence of events in chronological order.

The majority of ballads associated with black culture, however, fall in between the popularity of ''John Henry'' and the obscurity of Rabbit Brown's song. ''Frankie and Albert'' tells of a lovers' quarrel that lead to death for Albert, shot by Frankie after spying him with another woman. This song is also known as ''Frankie and Johnny,'' possibly because the sheet music for the song appeared with this title in 1912. The printed publication of ballads helped them circulate, but black singers always took decided liberties in reshaping them to suit their own needs. The publication in 1909 of ''Casey Jones'' helped to popularize this ballad among both black and white performers. In 1927 Memphis singer Walter ''Furry'' Lewis recorded this song for Victor, though it was also derived from another ballad, ''I'm a Natural Born Eastman.'' An ''eastman'' refers to a hustler, and Lewis's version illustrates how African American singers are willing to improvise on even a supposedly fixed ballad text.

It is not surprising that another man of mythic proportions, Stack O'Lee, has rivaled John Henry for the attention of black songsters. Stack O'Lee (a.k.a. Staggerlee, Stagolee, etc.) was a purely bad man, a bully who in some versions of his tale kills Billy Lyons following a gambling game. Another murderous ''bad man,'' Dupree, who in the somewhat confused narrative promises Betty a diamond ring and ends up hanging for the murder of a policeman and a detective, also circulated among black singers in the late 1920s. ''Dupree Blues'' is in fact derived from a ballad published by Andrew Jenkins, a white composer and recording artist from Atlanta who sang the song as ''Frank Dupree.'' His version is based on a true incident, which resulted in the hanging of Frank Dupree on September 4, 1922. Bad men, murderers, and men of strength seem to have captured the interest of black songsters, because their exploits are more celebrated than those in other ballads. ''Stavin' Chain'' is an intriguing song that appears to straddle the line between ballad and blues. Stavin'

Chain is the nickname for a man who, in black culture, is bigger than life. In the collected and recorded versions of the songs about him, Stavin' Chain was in Parchman Farm (a notorious Mississippi prison) for killing a man, a train engineer of might, a man with sixteen women but who wanted sixteen more, and a dead man who lives in hell with his Stetson hat on. All of these different Stavin' Chains symbolized a man of extraordinary means, electric energy, and sexual power. He appears to have been a hero with chameleon-like virtues who triumphed over many situations and conquered many women. There are numerous balladlike songs about Stavin' Chain, though none can be recounted as true ballads.

Ballads of British origin are not unknown to black performers, but not surprisingly, they are rarely encountered in black musical culture and tend to be among the most popular of the broadside or Child ballads. The bawdy ballad of adultery ''Our Goodman,'' known as ''Drunkard's Special'' or ''Cabbage Head'' among New World performers, was collected during the early part of the twentieth century and later recorded by Dallas-based singer Coley Jones and the Carolina performer Blind Boy Fuller. As recently as 1973, it was recorded by the New Orleans pianist Professor Longhair. The Irish broadside ballad ''The Unfortunate Rake,'' the sad lament of a lad dying of venereal disease, became ''St. James Infirmary'' or the ''Dying Gambler'' as sung by blacks. Two inmates of Ramsey State Convict Farm in Texas recorded by John A. Lomax in 1933, ''Iron-Head'' Baker and Moses ''Clear Rock'' Platt, also performed several British ballads, ''Maid Freed from the Gallows'' (Child 256) and ''The Farmer's Curst Wife'' (Child 276).

Songsters and Rural Music

This term implies that the performer not only possesses a fine voice but knows many songs in a variety of genres. Many of the black rural singers of this century are, in fact, songsters. Record companies and field researchers often billed them as ''blues singers''; however, such versatile musicians as Walter ''Furry'' Lewis (Memphis), Pink Anderson (South Carolina), Jim Jackson (Memphis), Henry ''Rufe'' Johnson (South Carolina), and Mance Lipscomb (Texas) performed blues, work songs, ballads, religious songs, and so forth.

Songsters participated in church music, too. After a Saturday night in the juke joint, at least some of the patrons would adjourn to the mourners bench for the Sunday morning service. The most ''churchified'' citizens of Leigh, Texas (where the well-known songster Leadbelly lived early in the twentieth century), no doubt stayed out of these joints, but many people moved back and forth between the secular and sacred sides of life. Baptist churches drew the largest number of blacks in east Texas at the turn of the century. Gospel music, in the specific sense of songs composed and copyrighted by black writers, had yet to reach Leigh. Spirituals, Dr. Watts hymns, and camp-meeting songs comprised their sacred music: songs that told of freedom, promised great rewards in heaven, and warned of the dangers of spiritual compromise.

M u s i c a l   E x a m p l e

Huddie Ledbetter, a.k.a. ''Leadbelly,'' remains one of the best-known black folk musicians of the twentieth century. He also helped to popularize the twelve–string guitar, which was one of his trademarks. Leadbelly was a quintessential ''songster,'' with a wide repertoire of sacred and secular songs. Following his ''discovery'' by the Library of Congress in 1933, Leadbelly popularized ''Goodnight Irene,'' ''Black Betty,'' ''Midnight Special,'' and a host of other songs. He recorded extensively for the Library of Congress, the American Record Company, RCA Victor and Folkways before his death in 1949. [Smithsonian/Folkways 40001]

Title ''Rock Island Line''
Performer Leadbelly
Instruments voice and guitar
Length 2:31
Notable Features

1. This is a *cante-fable,* a performance that is partially sung and partially spoken.
2. Once the singing begins, the tempo of this song increases.
3. At times, Leadbelly's voice and guitar act in tandem creating internal antiphony.
4. After a rubato introduction, the song settles down into a gently rocking duple (4/4) meter.

Spoken: This is the Rock Island Line. These boys is cutting with pole axes and the man that cuts right-handed he stands opposite side of the other man; the other one cut left-handed, he stand on the other side. Boys, one thing about that Rock Island Line, which is a might good road to ride. In that road, the man going to talk to the depot agent; when he's going to come out to cut with the Rock Island Line freight train, coming back from New 'leans this away. That man blows his whistle different than men's blow whistles here. 'Cause he's talking to the depot agent, tell him something when that switchboard call over that line, that means for that freight train to go into that hold. The man's going to talk to him.
Sung: I got goats. I got sheep. I got hogs. I got cows. I got horses. I got all livestock. I got all livestock.
Spoken: Depot agent let him get by. He got down, going to tell him.
Sung: I fooled you. I fooled you. I got iron. I got all pig-iron. I got all pig-iron. The old Rock Island Line.

Refrain: Oh, the Rock Island Line is a mighty good road.
Oh, the Rock Island Line is a road to ride.
Oh, the Rock Island Line is a mighty good road.
If you want to ride, you gotta ride it like you find it,
Get your ticket at the station for the Rock Island Line.

Jesus died to save our sins, Oh great God, we're gonna meet him again.

Refrain

I may be right, I may be wrong, you know you gonna miss me when I'm gone.

Refrain

ABCWXYZ that's how it goes, but it don't take me.

Refrain (repeat)

New words and new music arrangement by Huddie Ledbetter. Edited with new additional material by Alan Lomax TRO © copyright 1959 (Renewed) Folkways Music Publishers, Inc. New York, NY. Used by permission.

The morning services lasted for several hours, and the music was familiar to all. There was no need for songbooks because everyone knew the selections so well: ''Amazing Grace,'' ''When That Train Comes Along,'' ''Witness for My Lord,'' ''Join the Band,'' and ''Old Time Religion.'' Music held a central place in these services, and a musician of Leadbelly's caliber was welcome to sing and testify. Some songs were ''lined out,'' in which the initial line is sung by a leader and then repeated by the entire congregation. This practice has its roots in eighteenth-century America, particularly in the Dutch Reformed churches of the colonial period, and is heard today in some African American Baptist churches.

Leadbelly's physical movement from Leigh illustrates the most important early means of transmission for regional styles of folk music. Geographers call such movement relocation diffusion, referring to the spread of a new idea or innovation through the migration of an individual or a folk group. Between 1906 and 1911, Leadbelly lived in different places in eastern Texas and Louisiana, calling Shreveport and New Orleans home for short periods. His music traveled with him, and Leadbelly, in turn, picked up new influences and musical ideas.

Wandering black folk musicians were not an uncommon sight early in this century. Folk music provided entertainment, and small rural towns always welcomed a good musician with new ideas and a fresh sound. Some were itinerant musicians who, like Leadbelly, hoboed from town to town. Many other black folk singers found steady employment with traveling minstrel or medicine shows or with a circus. Road shows provided steady employment for peripatetic musicians eager to see the world around them. This tradition harkens back to the antebellum minstrel tradition that first flourished in the 1840s, but by the time of Leadbelly's adolescence at the opening of the twentieth century, minstrelsy was suffering its inevitable decline.

The mobility of certain black musicians, the fact that most of these musicians were musically illiterate (in the sense of reading musical notation), and the orientation of African Americans towards the verbal arts all helped to promote the aural/oral tradition in black folk music. With few exceptions, such as the odd printed broadside or sheet music featuring a folk song, this music has not been transmitted through formal musical channels. There are no formal conservatories for black (or white) musicians to attend and no university courses, such as ''Advanced Blues Singing Techniques,'' ''The Rudiments of African American Accordion Playing,'' or ''Gospel Quartet Ear Training.'' Early in this century, black singers learned their music by way of family members—like Leadbelly, whose accordion technique came from his uncle—or older members of an immediate musical community.

Music was especially important for many blacks living in the rural South at the dawn of the twentieth century. It provided a source of entertainment and escape from a daily diet of hard work and poor food. Racism, both legal and social, was regaining strength with the passage of ''Jim Crow'' laws restricting the right to vote, reinforcing segregation, and reapplying the stranglehold of economic subjugation. Many of the gains won during Reconstruction were slowly eroding into a legal and social mire that brought despair to the black community.

Weekends in the churches and at the rough juke joints provided diversion, offered solace, and brought relief from daily toil. These venues presented the public side of folk music. Within the black community, public musical performances fulfilled several functions—one was purely entertainment. A performer such as Leadbelly played for many public events within his own community. As a youth, he worked at dances, known as breakdowns or sooky jumps, in his section of east Texas, rowdy dances that featured free-flowing liquor, gambling, and mixing of the sexes. These gatherings often served as the social centerpiece for many rural people. From small Texas towns like Leigh to the Mississippi Delta through the Carolinas, Saturday night functions drew the community together to visit, discuss problems, gossip, and relax from six days of demanding work. Because of their activities, Saturday night dances drew adults only. They began at dusk and usually lasted until well into the night, occasionally until sunup.

The actual music heard at such turn-of-the-century dances varied according to the region of the country. In North Carolina, for example, the music was often provided by small string bands consisting of fiddle, banjo, and guitar. Missouri blacks were more likely entertained by a ragtime piano player when they congregated to forget their troubles. In Texas, Leadbelly or one of his contemporaries performed a mixture of lively duple-meter polkas and ''two-steps,'' elegant waltzes, and slower-tempo ''drags,'' which gave the dancers a chance to become better acquainted. People called out requests that the musicians could nearly always fulfill, for this was a tightly knit group composed of people who knew one another quite well.

Well into the twentieth century, most blacks living in the rural South fit into the patterns associated with a classic folk community: insular/isolated, family-oriented, agrarian, conservative, cohesive, homogeneous, and slow to change. This era prior to paved interstate highways, the electronic media, and mass public education helped to reinforce traditional culture. The folk roots of twentieth-century blues and gospel music lie in the antecedents that emerged from such communities.

Blues

Blues first evolved as a distinctive style near the beginning of the twentieth century. The product of multigenesis in the Deep South (east Texas, Mississippi, Louisiana, and Alabama), blues was a synthesis of the traditions that preceded it: dance tunes, minstrel songs, secular ditties, and spirituals. Because of its origins, it is impossible to assign a specific date and geographical location for the first blues performance. There are several reasons why blues developed at this time. First, the period of Jim Crow racism added misery and hard times to the black community. Ku Klux Klan activity gained momentum during the 1890s, too, with the number of lynchings increasing and the per capita income for blacks stagnating or falling. These factors meant that black American citizens lived in an increasingly segregated society, enduring attacks on their civil and legal rights. Reconstruction promised freedom and opportunities for blacks, but thirty years after the ''Year of Jubilee,'' the specter of increased racism shadowed the United States.

Second was the more ready availability of mail-order guitars and their greater popularity among folk musicians. Guitars were perfect for black folk musicians because they were portable, the primary chords (I, IV, and V) were easy to play, and the strings bent easily to accommodate the flatted tonality commonly found in black folk music. Early blues guitarists sometimes tuned their instrument to an open D or E chord and used a knife or the neck of a bottle to increase their ability to produce tonalities outside of their European models. ''Bottleneck'' blues guitar (still an important performance practice) also gave guitarists a voice that was more human in its qualities, allowing them to create an interesting foil between their instrument and their voice. The interactions between guitarist and voice and between singer and audience have become important ingredients of the blues tradition.

Because the early twentieth-century black community closely adheres to our model of an idealized folk society, change and innovation is expected to be gradual. In this instance, it took the blues tradition at least ten years to diffuse across the South and gain acceptability. Nonetheless, blues provided one of the most important, creative outlets in response to increased repression and a renewal of hard times after the heady days of Reconstruction. Blacks (and a few whites) protested in other ways: newspaper editorials, feeble legislative reforms, and the formation of support organizations. But these did not hit the same type of responsive chord as blues, which became an important rallying point for the frustrations of blacks and one of their most important and lasting musical contributions to American culture.

Early blues probably sounded similar to the ''hollers'' sung as people worked hard in the fields and to the secular ditties popular during the 1880s and 1890s. Certainly the subjects would have been similar: mistreatment, money problems, and difficulty between the sexes. **Field hollers** are one of the most immediate precursors of blues, and their free-form structure betrays the relationship to the later innovation. This particular example comes from Virginia in the late teens:

> Ef I had 'bout fo'ty-five dollahs
> All in gol' yas, all in gol'
> I'd be as rich as ol' man Catah.
> I'm gwine back to South Ca'lina;
> Fah away, yas, fah away.
> I'm gwine see my Esmeraldy.
> I can't stay, no, I can't stay. (Scarborough 1925, 219).

Blues are built upon a series of rhymed couplets that speak the ''truth'' about life, one of the principal reasons why this new music appealed to its listeners. As the musician played the ''low-down'' music and sang about mutual concerns, blues promoted a dialogue between musician and audience. Because the early blues were played at house parties and dances rather than formal concert halls, audiences shouted encouragement and sometimes interacted with musicians by joining in the singing. Dancing, another means of releasing energy and frustration as well as creative movement, quickly became another important ingredient in this dialogue.

The first blues songs were of variable length, usually between eight bars and fourteen bars. The standardization that mandated a twelve-bar format did not develop for several decades; therefore musicians could play cycles of whatever bar length suited them. The length of early blues was probably determined by the words being sung. A song like ''Poor Boy'' was perfectly suited to this new style of music and was likely to be recast in the emerging blues style. Sociologist Howard Odum described this song, which he collected in Georgia in 1911. This nascent version was sung to the accompaniment of a guitarist playing with a knife and included lyrics echoed by today's bluespersons:

> I'm a po' boy 'long ways from home,
> Oh, I'm a po' boy 'long ways from home.
> I wish a 'scursion train would run,
> Carry me back where I cum frum.
> Come here, babe, an' sit on yo' papa's knee.

Possibly because this version of ''Poor Boy'' was taken from early field work, this early blues or blueslike song sounds fragmented when compared to later recorded versions. It is likely that the singer himself organized the song this

Downhome Blues Hearths and Migration Patterns

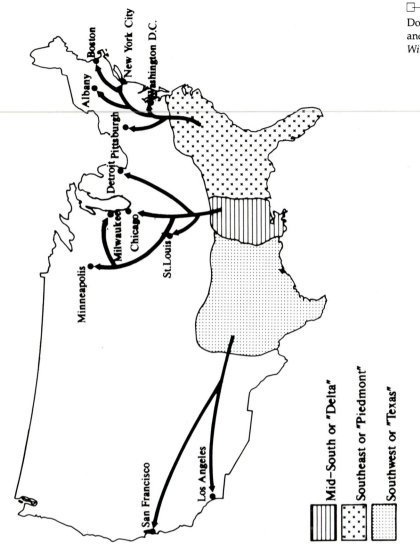

Boston
Albany
New York City
Washington D.C.
Detroit
Pittsburgh
Milwaukee
Chicago
St. Louis
Minneapolis
San Francisco
Los Angeles

Mid–South or "Delta"
Southeast or "Piedmont"
Southwest or "Texas"

Down home blues hearth areas
and migration patterns.
William Vaughn.

way, punctuating the heartfelt lyrics with ringing slide guitar. Almost certainly the song was performed in an eight-bar format, much like a secular ditty rather than the more polished, stylized blues that had been codified by the 1920s.

Blues singers demonstrated many musical characteristics that are regional in nature. The early down home blues styles can be assigned to three general regions: Southwest, Mid-South and Southeast. When singers from these areas

---

M u s i c a l   E x a m p l e

Big Joe Williams lived as an itinerant blues singer and musician until his death in 1982. Born near the turn of the century, Williams spent his formative years in the Mississippi Delta as a contemporary of the legendary blues singers Charlie Patton and Son House before moving to Chicago in the middle 1930s. His gruff, intense vocals are reminiscent of the field hollers that rang throughout the South during the early twentieth century. Though he kept a trailer in Crawford, Mississippi, in later years Williams rambled throughout the United States and also played concerts in Europe. [Folkways 31004]

Title ''Night Cap Blues''
Performer Big Joe Williams
Instruments guitar and voice
Length 2:53
Notable Features

1. The tonality is major and it's played in duple (4/4) meter.
2. Williams sticks to the basic blues form.
3. His voice and guitar are used as a foil to one another, almost like an internal call and response.
4. The tempo of the song increases during the performance.
5. The highly syncopated guitar accompaniment underlies its homophonic texture, resulting in a full texture.

Put on your night cap, woman, I'm gonna buy you an evening gown.
(repeat)
I'm taking you out tomorrow night, baby, and I swear we sure gonna break 'em on down.

I'm gonna pack my bucket, baby, gonna move back to the piney woods.
I'm gonna get my bucket baby. . . move back to the woods.
I'm gonna leave here, darling, 'cause you don't mean me no good.

I ain't never been to Georgia, boys, but the half ain't never been told.
(repeat)
Tell me them women down there got something sweet, sweet as jelly roll.

(Repeat the first verse.)

When you raise sweet potatoes, boy, raise you a Nancy Hall.
If you want a sweet potato, boy, raise a Nancy Hall.
If you want a good woman, I swear you better marry one long and tall.

Put on your night cap, baby, I'm gonna buy an evening gown.
I'm going out Saturday night and I am sure gonna break 'em on down.

migrated outside of the ''hearth'' areas, they carried their music with them. Figure 7.4 illustrates the location and migration patterns for Southern blues singers. Big Joe William's musical example illustrates the Mid-South or ''Delta'' style well.

Modern Blues

Black popular music began to evolve into new forms. Jazz-influenced singers such as Billy Eckstine, Ella Fitzgerald, Johnny Hartman, and Sarah Vaughan rose to prominence during the middle to late 1940s. Rhythm and blues (R and B) became popular beginning in the late 1940s: Bull Moose Jackson, Tiny Bradshaw, Johnny Otis, and others were recording for the same independent labels as the gospel singers. Their music was not only popular, it was based on the blues, which were undergoing another transformation.

Down home blues continued to be popular in the South and among southerners transplanted to the North. However, the blues that appeared on commercial discs slowly changed during the 1940s as popular music tastes altered. Small ensembles all but supplanted the single artists that so often appeared on records during the 1920s and into the 1930s. The late 1930s recordings by Sonny Boy Williamson (John Lee Williamson), Washboard Sam (Robert Brown), Tampa Red and his Chicago Five, Lonnie Johnson, and others foreshadowed the new trends in commercial blues. The ensembles frequently consisted of a bass, drums (or washboard), guitar, piano, harmonica, or horns. These additional instruments smoothed out many of the harmonic and stylistic idiosyncrasies of the **folk blues** performers, routinizing the music into a more predictable pattern. As commercial record companies learned very well, predictability, albeit spiced with a dash of creativity, is what sells records. The wonderfully individual sounds of Mr. Freddie Spruell, Otto Virgial, and George Clarke all but disappeared following the record industry's reactivation in 1945. An even more pronounced ensemble sound emerged on records and, to a far lesser degree, over the radio following the end of the war against the Axis powers. In New York City, the music centered around the East Coast

Lonnie Johnson cut a dapper figure in the mid-1940s.
Folkways Archive, Smithsonian Institution.

musicians who had migrated northward: Brownie and Sticks McGhee, Sonny Terry, Larry Dale, and others. Their sound, on record at least, was distinctly ''country,'' updated somewhat but not truly transformed. In Los Angeles, many of the musicians came from Texas in search of work. The R and B sound of Charles Brown and Amos Milburn tended to predominate West Coast commercial blues.

But the true musical and popular revolution in blues was going on in Chicago. The majority of Chicago's migrants, from the turn of the century onward, arrived from the Mid-South: Arkansas, Mississippi, and western Tennessee. This influx of residents from an area where the blues were deep and well developed combined ·with the electrification of guitars to create a vital, vibrant sound. At the forefront of this movement were **Muddy Waters** (McKinley Morganfield), Howlin' Wolf (Chester Burnett), Elmore James, and Walter Horton. Each of them arrived in Chicago with highly developed musical skills, full of the fire and emotional rawness that characterized the blues that developed along the Mississippi Delta. These men truly created an important new form by transforming the music of masters such as **Charley Patton,** Eddie ''Son'' House, Willie Brown, Will Shade, and Robert Johnson into the roots of rock 'n' roll.

The transformation began in the middle 1940s, about the same time that another revolution in black music, bebop, was capturing the other ear of black music aficionados. The transitional records of Muddy Waters, Big Joe Williams, and Snooky Pryor (with Moody Jones) came out in the late 1940s and sounds like Mississippi blues in a modern setting. Around 1951 the revolution hit full force in the form of Muddy Waters's classic band, which included Little Walter Jacobs (harp), Otis Spann (piano), Big Crawford (bass), Jimmy Rogers (second guitar), and Freddy Below (drums). Their classic Chess records virtually define **Chicago blues,** documents of musicians at the height of their considerable abilities. The passion and creativity evident on "Forty Days and Forty Nights," "Standing Around Crying," "Hootchie Coochie Man," and "Mannish Boy" are among the landmarks in black American vernacular music. The Chicago style emphasizes the highly dramatic lead voices of amplified guitars and harmonicas supported by the basic rhythm section of bass guitar, piano, and drums. The music was meant to be heard in clubs on the city's predominately black South and West sides, neighborhood bars where locals came to drink and dance. Bars featuring these bands were the up-North equivalent of the juke joint, and they proved quite popular. This music was popular on records, too. Small labels such as Chess, Cobra, JOB, and others launched (and perhaps ultimately crashed) their businesses based on the marketability of Chicago blues. The popularity of this music continued through the middle 1950s.

Other electric blues musicians—B. B. King, Bobby "Blue" Bland, Little Milton—groomed their performing and recording skills in Memphis before moving north and continuing their skills. Their music is not cut in the classic Chicago mode but rather is influenced by R and B and the gospel sounds of the 1940s and 1950s. Horn sections predominated, and this music profoundly influenced soul music and the "Stax sound" that emanated from Memphis during the middle to late 1960s.

Final Thoughts

Black American secular folk music has a complicated history. Older styles of music, particularly blues, still persist, and they represent some of the most interesting examples of regional American folk music. In some general ways, string band music and balladry overlap with their Anglo-American counterparts, but their distinctive characteristics have been outlined here. These secular traditions, often in tandem with religious music, have also strongly influenced popular music. The folk roots of contemporary popular music are fully explored in the final chapter.

Key Figures and Terms

African American ballad
Chicago blues
coon songs
field holler
fife and drum bands
folk blues
"John Henry"
Scott Joplin
juba
juke joints
Leadbelly
Charley Patton
ragtime
songster
string bands
track laying
Muddy Waters
work songs

Audio

Ain't Gonna Rain No More. Rounder 2016 (LP). This anthology presents a variety of finger-picked guitar styles as well as fiddle and banjo music from Piedmont North Carolina.

The Blues Came Down from Memphis. Charly 67 (CD). An anthology of mid-South/Delta blues recorded by "Doctor" Ross, Joe Hill Louis, Willie Nix, and others for Sun Records in the early 1950s.

Blues in the Mississippi Night. Rycodisk 90155 (CASS/CD). A fascinating set of exceptionally candid interviews and music recorded in the late 1940s by Sonny Boy Williamson, Big Bill Broonzy, and Memphis Slim.

Great Blues Men. Vanguard 25/26 (CD/CASS). This samples both country and city blues by Otis Spann and Fred McDowell, among others.

Great Jug Bands. Origin Jazz Library 4 (LP). An anthology of the best jug band recordings from the 1920s.

Jackson, John. *Blues and Country Dance Tunes From Virginia.* Arhoolie 1025 (LP). A nice selection of tunes by this northern Virginia songster.

Johnson, Robert. *The Complete Recordings.* Columbia C2K 46222 (CASS/CD). Forty-one selections by this pivotal figure who recorded these influential recordings in the late 1930s.

Leadbelly. *Sings Folk Songs.* Smithsonian/Folkways 40001 (all formats). This is but one of many fine recordings by Huddie "Leadbelly" Ledbetter available on Smithsonian/Folkways.

Lipscomb, Mance. *Texas Songster.* Arhoolie 306 (CASS/CD). Recordings from the 1960s and 1970s by this talented singer/guitarist.

Martin, Bogan and The Armstrongs. *Let's Give a Party.* Flying Fish 003 (LP). Contemporary recordings by a black string band that toured extensively in the 1970s.

Non-Blues Secular Black Music in Virginia. BRI-001 (LP). A cross section of black protest songs, fiddle and banjo tunes, native American ballads, and country dance instrumentals.

The Roots of Robert Johnson. Yazoo 1073 (CASS/CD). A selection of classic Mississippi Delta blues recordings in the 1920s and 1930s.

Skiffle Bands. Folkways 2610 (CASS). An anthology of small-group performances recorded in the South during the middle 1950s.

Traveling through the Jungle. Testament 2223 (LP). A collection of fife and drum band and other related selections recorded in the Mississippi Delta between 1941 and the 1970s.

Virginia Work Songs. BRI 007 (LP). A compilation of work song traditions found across the state, including ship caulking, oyster shucking, track lining, etc.

Williamson, Sonny Boy. *King Biscuit Time.* Arhoolie 310 (CASS/CD). Classic small-group, down-home blues recordings from the early 1950s.

Books

Berlin, Edward. 1980. *Ragtime: A Musical and Cultural History.* Los Angeles: University of California Press. Of the ragtime studies available, this remains the best concise history.

Epstein, Dena. 1977. *Sinful Tunes and Spirituals.* Urbana: University of Illinois Press. The author surveys primary and secondary written sources for information about black folk music prior to Reconstruction.

Evans, David. 1988. *Big Road Blues.* New York: Da Capo Press. An often fascinating, very scholarly study of musical creativity and the transmission of blues in central Mississippi.

Jackson, Bruce. 1972. *Wake Up Dead Man: Afro-American Worksongs from Texas.* Cambridge, Mass. Harvard University Press. This is an ethnography of the Texas prison system and work songs, written in the late 1960s.

Oliver, Paul. 1984. *Songsters and Saints: Vocal Traditions on Race Records.* Cambridge: Cambridge University Press. This noted scholar examines the secular and sacred musical traditions found on records prior to World War II.

Scarborough, Dorothy. 1925. *On the Trail of Negro Folksongs.* Cambridge, Mass.: Harvard University Press. An important early twentieth-century collection of black folk music from the Deep South.

Southern, Eileen. 1983. *The Music of Black Americans.* 2d ed. New York: W. W. Norton. More than a history of folk music, this is the best survey of four hundred years of black American musical development.

Video

Blues Like Showers of Rain. Rhapsody Films Video V-4. 30 minutes. An anthology of country blues history featuring historical photographs and performances by Speckled Red, Blind James Brewer, and others.

Chicago Blues. Harley Cokliss Films. 60 minutes. A documentary that focuses on the modern Chicago blues and includes Muddy Waters, J. B. Hutto, Buddy Guy, and Junior Wells, among others.

Deep Blues. Robert Mugge Films. 91 minutes. This interesting documentary looks at blues in the Mississippi Delta and was shot in 1990.

Gravel Springs Fife and Drum Bands. Center for Southern Folklore. 18 minutes. A brief film that documents the social context for this music in the mid-South.

Louie Bluie. Pacific Arts Home Video. 60 minutes. A documentary that examines the fascinating life of Howard Armstrong: string band musician, artist, and storyteller.

Mance Lipscomb: Well Spent Life. Flower Films. 44 minutes. A gentle and loving portrait of a Texas songster who spent his entire life in south-central Texas.

8

Ethnic and Native American Traditions

Until relatively recently, most enthusiasts thought of American folk music almost exclusively in terms of Anglo-American and African American traditions. It remains true that blues, gospel, and other types of well-known folk music come from people who, in the twentieth century at least, speak English. But the importance of the traditional music of non-English-speaking Americans, particularly French and Spanish, is becoming increasingly apparent. And the most noteworthy examples, such as Cajun music, are truly original American art forms, not simply traditional music imported to the United States.

Making the distinction between music in America and American music is critical to understanding this chapter. Because the United States remains the destination for so many immigrants seeking a better life, virtually every country, region, and ethnic group on earth is represented within our population. People bring their cultural baggage with them—foodways, marriage customs, language, and music—most of which gradually assimilate with the already established cultures of the United States. A book that tries to cover all of the ethnic traditions found within our borders would be creating a veritable United Nations of music!

Quite simply, our real interest lies with folk music that developed in the United States as a hybrid of old-world and new world traditions. This creolization usually requires decades of contact, although popular culture is transmitted more quickly. Some of the recent Southeast Asian refugees, for instance, have been making videos of their American-inspired popular music since the middle 1980s. The tens of thousands of refugees from Afghanistan who have arrived in the United States since the Russian invasion in 1980 have not been here long enough for their music to blend with ours. Other groups, such as the Cambodian Hmong and Vietnamese, who have large settlements in California and the Northeast, face the added burden of a musical culture that sounds quite alien to the ears of most Americans. While significant Afghan, Hmong, and Vietnamese communities exist in the United States, their traditional music remains directly tied to their homeland.

The distinction between ''ethnic'' and ''folk'' is equally vital because they are related but not necessarily interchangeable. Folk has already been discussed and defined; ethnic refers to an identity that is created by one's place of origin, language, religion, and common history. Within this identity, one mixes the levels of culture in which we participate—folk, popular, and elite. In order to illustrate some of these distinctions, let's look more closely at German Americans, one of the most long-standing and important European immigrant groups.

In German American musical culture, choral societies known as ''Liederkranz'' or ''Männerchor'' have been popular since the nineteenth century. They engage in active interregional competition, and in major cities they sometimes function as the basis of the chorus for opera companies. German Americans have also predominated in other spheres of elite music. The study of historical musicology was basically founded by Germans in the 1870s.

German Americans have been very well represented in our classical orchestras and in their repertoires. The Chicago Symphony Orchestra was founded by a German-born conductor. Moravian church music has also had a strong impact upon various forms of American sacred music.

Although German Americans have been quite involved in our musical culture, their offerings have little to do with folk music. Most, though not all, of their musical contributions are primarily directed towards elite culture. German American folk music consists almost entirely of German traditional music transported to the United States. One notable exception is the nineteenth-century "singing schools" found in the Shenandoah Valley of Virginia, which were discussed earlier. The German American polka bands of south-central Minnesota, led by concertina players such as **"Whoopee John" Wilfahrt,** represent another twentieth-century manifestation of folk music. The "New Ulm" or "old-time" sound incorporated German dance tunes with an Americanized rhythm section to create an eclectic, distinctly regional sound. Groups like the Jolly Germans, the Six Fat Dutchmen ("dutchman" is a local term for people of German descent), and Eddie Whilfart's Concertina Band brought this blend of folk/ethnic music to audiences throughout the northern Midwest.

Religious and secular organizations play important roles in providing solidarity within ethnic enclaves. Various groups such as the Czechoslovak Sokol, Polish American clubs or Garrison Keillor's mythical "Sons of Knute" (a Norwegian American club made famous on his "Prairie Home Companion" radio broadcasts of the 1970s and 1980s) provide a support network for newly arrived immigrants. Most immigrant groups have used music as one means of maintaining cultural identity. They have imported their native folk and popular music, often performing it for special events, such as Christmas or weddings, that are also celebrated in the "old way." Music becomes one of the critical ways to keep ties to the old country.

Traditions that have been all but lost or forgotten can later be **revitalized**. Several types of grass roots music that are clearly related to the folk music of non-English speaking Americans have enjoyed a renaissance over the past few decades. **Klezmer,** for instance, has undergone a renaissance in the Jewish community since the middle 1970s. Brought to the United States by professional musicians from eastern Europe, klezmer refers to the instrumental dance music played by chamber ensembles of various instruments. It combines elements of folk and popular music into a delightful blend that features improvised solos. Commercial recordings of klezmer bands led by Dave Tarras, Abe Schwartz, and others were popular until the 1930s when its popular appeal diminished. By the 1980s, klezmer was revitalized by younger musicians such as Henry Sapoznik and Andy Statman, who also sparked a renewed interest in the secular dances.

Native American music also contains examples of **revitalization** and **revival,** which refers to traditions that have been totally lost for several generations. The Pima tribe of central Arizona inhabit the sparsely populated and stark desert country along the Gila River. The majority of the Pima were

''Christianized'' by strict fundamentalist missionaries. They lost most of their traditional dances and songs by the dawn of the twentieth century. However, in the 1960s and 1970s, a select number of traditional songs and dances were reintroduced to younger members of the Pima tribe. Specifically, the Round Dance songs, which are usually named for birds like swallows, robins, and orioles, were revived. The Pima's musical revival came about as part of a larger effort to shore up their traditional ways of life in light of Western domination. In addition to the music, some of the younger women were introduced to the almost lost art of making traditional dresses and yucca baskets.

Rather than a cursory survey of the entire non-English-speaking world in the United States, this chapter focuses upon Native American, Hawaiian, Franco-American (Cajun, zydeco), Latino (Tex-Mex), and Scandinavian American folk music. These creolized styles have evolved into dynamic, visible traditions. They are among the most influential and widespread types of folk music created by non-English-speaking Americans. As more primary research is undertaken in ethnic American music, other groups might be added to these ranks in the future.

Native Americans

Long before the Europeans and their captive Africans reached our shores, the United States was populated by a wide assortment of tribes that we now call Native Americans. They actually migrated here from Asia by way of Alaska, eventually settling in the United States thousands of years before Christopher Columbus arrived in the New World. Because of their disparate geographical patterns, among other factors, these groups developed at least seven major distinctive cultural areas: Northwest Coast, Southwest, Great Basin, Plateau, Plains, Northeast, and Southeast. Indians within these cultural areas were further divided into about one thousand smaller units called tribes. Names of some of these tribes are permanently etched into the American past, especially during the European and Anglo-American conquests of the western United States: Sioux, Cheyenne, Cherokee, and Blackfoot. Today the people of these diverse tribes are most often referred to as Native Americans, rather than Indians, and most have been culturally decimated, greatly reduced in number, and resettled onto ''reservations.''

This tragic cultural transformation has greatly affected the music of Native Americans. We know a great deal about twentieth-century Indian music, but relatively little about their earlier periods. Unfortunately, our knowledge of twentieth-century Native American music often does not truly reflect their past. This is due to several critical facts. First, Native Americans did not notate their music. Second, the forced migration of tribes permanently altered their musical traditions. Finally, the impact of European and African American music greatly affected Indian music.

It is safe to say that music has been a very important, perhaps even vital, component of Native American culture. We can make this sweeping observation regarding the music of Native Americans: their music is closely tied to

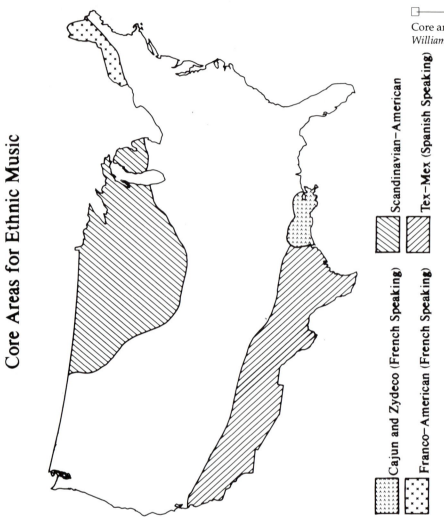

Core Areas for Ethnic Music

Cajun and Zydeco (French Speaking)

Franco–American (French Speaking)

Scandinavian–American

Tex–Mex (Spanish Speaking)

Chesley Goseyun Wilson, a White Mountain Apache living in Tucson, Arizona, playing one of his one-stringed Apache violins. *1989 Jim Griffith photo, courtesy of the Southwest Folklore Center.*

myth and religion and is fundamentally similar across the United States. This is true despite the inherent regional and tribal differences that inevitably occur, not to mention, for example, the influence of Mexican music upon Southwestern tribes. Despite these variations, contemporary Indian music continues to play a unique role in helping to define Native American identity.

Our understanding of Indian music from the twentieth century is traceable to two female researchers who began their work late in the nineteenth century. Alice Fletcher worked with Native American music from the 1880s until her death in 1923, during which time she published many monographs and books. The most notable are *A Study of Omaha Indian Music* (Baltimore, 1893) and *Indian Story and Song from North America* (Boston, 1900). Trained as an anthropologist, Fletcher wrote extensively about the relationship between music and religious ceremonies. Many of these ceremonies had truly cosmic significance; others were designed to heal or assign powers of the occult. Fletcher's pioneering work holds observations that pertain to contemporary Native American music.

Frances Densmore, born some thirty years after Fletcher, came from a background in performance and composition. She became interested in Indian music after hearing live performances at the Chicago World's Columbian Exposition, though she did not actually begin her own fieldwork with the Chippewa until 1905. Concerned primarily with tribes in the Plains-Pueblo area, Densmore gathered healing songs, songs taken from dreams, ceremonial songs, and others for nearly fifty years. Her most comprehensive collection, *Chippewa Music,* was published between 1910–13.

The "modern era" of our knowledge of Native American music begins about the same time as Fletcher and Densmore were working. This period is tied to Jesse Walter Fewkes's recording of Hopi Indian songs in 1889. Sound recordings enabled this music to be preserved in such a way that it could be disseminated and dissected. Tragically, by the 1930s, when sound technology had advanced to the point where the equipment was more portable and the results more palatable, much of Native American music had been radically transformed. Over the past fifty years, the music studied by Alan Merriam, Bruno Nettl, David McAllester, Willard Rhodes, and the other significant scholars of middle-to-late twentieth-century Indian music is significantly different than that first heard by Densmore in 1893.

Although such sweeping generalizations are dangerous, much of contemporary Native American music results from the **pan-Indian movement** that first developed in the 1920s. This movement has tended to greatly homogenize Indian music because of the propensity to gather in large **powwows** that encompass many tribes, sometimes from different parts of the United States. Large powwows evolved from a search for an identity for all Native Americans, irrespective of tribal or regional affiliations. Tribal identity and regional variation have submerged themselves in favor of their identity as an ''Indian'' in present-day American society.

Music and Ceremony

This observation is not universally true because tribal differences do remain. For example, the ghost dance and **peyote** cult that spread from Mexico to Southwestern tribes had become popular among Plains Indians by the 1890s. David McAllester has written most extensively about this phenomenon among Southwestern tribes in the 1940s. Based upon Indian religious practices, the ghost dance also touches upon Native American beliefs regarding the power and significance of dreams and their relationship to healing. The interaction between song and ceremony, which occurs after the ingestion of the peyote, is described by McAllester:

> During the ceremony a drum and rattle, both of special design, are passed, with other paraphernalia, clockwise among the circle of participants. When a member receives the rattle he is expected to sing a number of songs, usually four, after which he passes the rattle on to the next man. The rattle goes ahead of the drum so that, immediately after his turn to sing, each man is the drummer for the man on his left. Four times during the course of the ceremony the leader interrupts the procession to sing special songs which are always used at these times. At other times a participant sings whatever songs he chooses from the repertory at his command, or even extemporize on the spur of the moment (McAllester, 89).

For nearly sixty years, peyote use remained regionalized among Southwestern Indians. But in the late 1950s, its general popularity increased throughout the United States due to greater pan-Indian activity. Even non–Native Americans began using peyote during the psychedelic years of the middle 1960s. Nonetheless, the ghost dance and peyote religion remains central to Navaho culture. In 1989 the United States Supreme Court heard a case about the use of peyote as part of Navaho religious ceremonies. The lawyers representing the Native Americans argued for the legalization of small amounts of peyote for use in such ceremonies, but the Navaho lost the case.

Nonetheless, the instance of the ghost dance and peyote cult underscores that some regional/tribal ties remain in Native American music and the links between music and ceremony. The relationship between music and all types of

---

M u s i c a l   E x a m p l e

This brief performance is of the initial song heard in the First Song Cycle of the Washo Indians, which occurs during the night-long meeting of the peyote cult. It was recorded by the noted ethnomusicologist Willard Rhodes in the late 1940s as part of a larger project documenting the varieties of Native American music of the Southwest. Rhodes captured the beginning of the ecstatic trance, just as the peyote was being ingested. [Folkways 4401]

Title ''Peyote Song''
Performers Washo Indians
Instruments drum and voice
Length 2:19
Notable Features

1. It has a steady rhythm with a rapid tempo.
2. The vocal is moderately ornamented.
3. Its AB form is repeated several times.
4. The somewhat tense voice is in the middle range.

---

social, religious, and even quasi-religious events remains critical. Even in the current pan-Indian movement, nearly all musical events are tied to dancing and some religious ceremony.

Significantly, strong connections remain between the spiritual world and music. The people who sing and dance receive this music from the supernatural, as opposed to creating it themselves. These impulses come from dreams or some other induced state that permits the singers to touch either their distant past or ancestors. In the far Southwest, Pima Indians believe that songs preexist and that they are ''untangled'' in dreams. Thus, some Native American performers are viewed not as creative artists but as special vessels who are closely in touch with the past. Because of this unique relationship, the ability to recreate a performance is critical, though the importance to recreate these songs precisely varies from tribe to tribe.

A minority of tribes, however, do not make these direct connections between spirit and song. They believe that they can compose new songs based on traditional themes and musical motifs. Plains tribes such as the Cheyenne routinely borrow songs from other tribes with whom they have contact. Pueblo Indians, in an attempt to keep their culture ''pure,'' zealously guard their music from outside sources, both Native American and Western.

Nor does Native American music adhere to Western thoughts related to notation and theory, which is anathema to its generally ethereal premise. Indians may not refer to scales, but they are able to distinguish among hundreds of songs that sound similar to untrained ears. Most Native American music is performed by nonprofessionals, who tend to learn through traditional means. The majority of these performers are male, who also have some connection with religious practices. Though we are slowly learning that women sometimes take leadership positions in Native American musical activity, male domination reflects the larger world in which men generally take a leadership position in religious ceremonies. Younger musicians, and would-be musicians, take part in these ceremonies and generally learn through their active participation.

Musical Characteristics

It would be fair to observe that Indian music uses less complex harmony than most other forms of American folk music. In fact, the texture of most Native American music is monophonic; if more than one vocalist is present, they join together in unison or sing in octaves. **Vocables** constitute an unusual aspect of Native American singing that is widespread across the entire United States. These sound like mere nonsense syllables, but actually refer to nonlexical syllables, which serve to fill in or properly space out the lines in a song. They consist of short syllables like ''he,'' ''wi,'' or ''yo,'' which are low-sounding vowels that are usually sung in a nasal voice with glides. While these might sound like gibberish to outsiders, vocables serve also as aesthetic communication that helps to solidify Native Americans' sense of social unity. They impart a special meaning to the singers that transcends the function they serve. Since vocables are most often heard as a chorus, all of the participants know when these syllables will occur. Vocables are akin both in function and form to the ''tra-la-la'' choruses that close some British ballads.

Of course, Native American music is not monolithic and regional variations are still important. Among Native Americans, tribal differences are also quite important. Our knowledge about the different styles of Indian music is limited by the research conducted over the past one hundred years—the music of only about 10 percent of the one thousand Native American tribes has been studied. Furthermore, research undertaken during the 1940s is difficult to compare with research from the turn of the century because of the major cultural changes that have taken place over the intervening time. As a general rule, the musical styles reflect cultural boundaries, and the Western tribes display greater variations than their Eastern counterparts.

Bruno Nettl suggests that the music of Native Americans can be divided into six broad regional groups, each of which uses some kind of drum and rattle accompaniment:

Plains (Blackfoot, Crow, Dakota, etc., of the upper West and Midwest). Their music is marked by descending melodic lines using pentatonic scales. Rattles and shakers produce slight variations among the otherwise repetitive rhythmic patterns. The vocal style tends to utilize low, long tones and is very harsh and pulsating. Plains Indians make extensive use of vocables.

East Coast (Iroquois, Mohawk, Penobscot, etc., from New England through the Great Lakes). These singers favor a more relaxed vocal style. Song forms tend to be more complex, often using a series of contrasting forms such as *aababa*. These phrases within the songs are fairly predictable, which helps to promote antiphonal singing. This important feature is unusual in Native American music.

Southwest and California (Yuman, Hopi, Apache, etc., from central California through New Mexico). A wide variety of scales are found among these tribes. Their voices tend to be lighter or towards the middle range, with a nasal quality. The melodic lines often are broad and sweeping. Flutes are an important instrument and are often played in accompaniment to singing. The songs are set to intricate strophic texts. Native American music in this section is among the most complex in the United States.

Great Basin (Shoshone, Paiute, Havasupsai, etc., from Utah, Nevada, and northern California). Their music generally consists of short songs with very small melodic range and repetition of phrases with little variation. The singing is relaxed and tends to be in the middle register. Great Basin Indians often use pentatonic or tetratonic scales.

Northwest Coast (Nootka, Salish, Tlingit, etc., of western Washington and Oregon). This style is generally complex. It makes use of small intervals and highly ornamented, varied rhythmic accompaniment. The musical forms are complicated and are built from short, repetitive phrases.

North (Eskimo and Inuit in Alaska). Their music is characterized by varied melodies of three or four notes, although pentatonic scales are not unknown. The songs are accompanied by complex percussion patterns, even dotted rhythms. The forms are nonstrophic, and the singing is usually guttural and strained.

Instruments

The instruments used by Native Americans are almost all percussive, which helps to underscore the rhythmic drive heard in much of this music. Aside from the flute, nearly all of them are either rattles or drums. Rattles vibrate when they are struck, plucked, or shaken. Nearly all Native American tribes have used some kind of contained rattle that varies in its construction. Gourds, turtle shells, and woven baskets have all been used to contain small rocks or seeds. Small boxes struck by sticks are among the other types of rattles used by Indians to accompany their religious ceremonies.

Single-headed drums, which are held in one hand and struck by the other, are the most common type. They are found nearly everywhere except California, where they are curiously absent. Double-headed drums are quite rare and may be a nineteenth-century innovation. Small kettledrums, sometimes filled with water to achieve a unique sound, have also been used by Indians in the East and Great Plains.

The bull-roarer is an instrument found across the world, but its presence in the United States is unique to Native Americans. Bull-roarers are widely found in the West but are almost unknown east of the Mississippi River. It produces

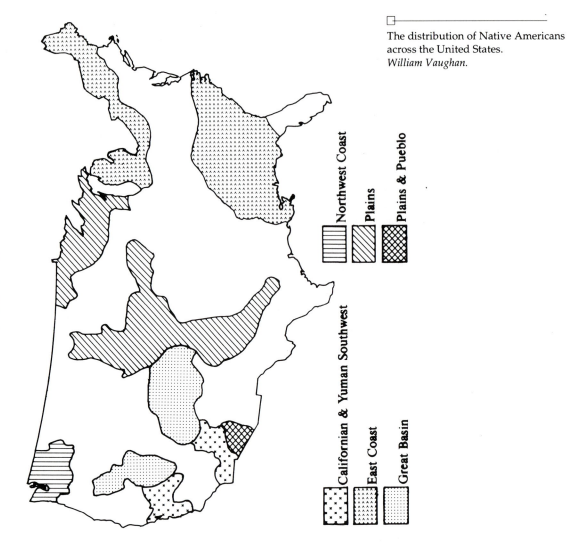

Native American

The distribution of Native Americans
across the United States.
William Vaughan.

Northwest Coast

Plains

Plains & Pueblo

Californian & Yuman Southwest

East Coast

Great Basin

a non-melodic sonority that is controlled by its size and construction. The most common bull-roarer is made of a flat piece of bone or wood with a serrated edge that is attached to string or rawhide and whirled through the air.

Native American music today is increasingly Westernized and quite different than it was prior to colonization. Many younger Native American musicians are turning towards commercial country and rock for their inspiration. Significantly, of the one thousand tribes that once existed, scores have disappeared and most others have been culturally decimated. The push to Christianize Native Americans has changed many of the traditional modes of worship. Westernization has also radically altered the social and economic structures of Native American tribes, further disrupting the ways in which music has been used among Indians. Music is now used to entertain tourists in addition to the closed sacred ceremonies. Many Native Americans maintain a balance between tradition and cultural change in a constant mediation between the white man's world and an Indian heritage.

Powwows

Due to increased electronic communication and the enforced movement of different tribes onto reservations, some Native Americans have unified into a Pan-Indian movement that has provided a stronger sense of solidarity. The singing is dominated by males who usually sing in unison to the accompaniment of a single drum. Contemporary powwows are social and economic as well as religious events. In addition to music, all manner of fund-raising is carried out. Arts and crafts are also sold. Regional and specialized tribal dances are sometimes held in addition to the commonly practiced round dances. Over the past twenty years, there has been a movement to increase unique tribal customs within pan-Indian powwows because of the clear danger of homogenization. This is part of a larger trend within the United States to celebrate our regional and ethnic identities.

Despite such trends, the folk music of Native Americans has been radically altered by the forces of time and the rude intrusion of Anglo-American culture. A small but growing number of Indian rock 'n' roll groups play at

Members of the Tohono O'odham (Waila) Band play on stage at the annual "Tucson Meet Yourself Festival."
1989 David Burkhalter photo, courtesy of the Southwest Folklore Center.

M u s i c a l   E x a m p l e

This selection was recorded in the early 1970s at an outdoor powwow in a small village at the Leach Lake Reservation in north-central Minnesota. This lovely area of the state remains quite wild, and many of the Native Americans continue to spend much of their time hunting and fishing. Unlike many powwows, this one drew almost exclusively from members of the Chippewa (a.k.a. Ojibwa), a tribe that populate the upper Midwest and south-central Canada. Most of the participants are males between the ages of twenty and forty. [Folkways 4392]

Title ''Song from an Outdoor Powwow''
Performers Ojibwa Indians
Instruments drums, rattle, and voices
Length 1:06
Notable Features

1. A deliberate quarter-note rhythm is produced by the drums.
2. The tempo increases slightly during the performance.
3. The voices tend to be in the upper register and are tense.
4. A pentatonic scale is used by the singers.

---

powwows, replacing the more traditional music that has been part of these ceremonies. Commercial country and western music has also been embraced by many Native Americans. During the 1970s, Jim Pepper emerged as one of the few Indians playing modern jazz.

One interesting style of acculturated Native American music, **chicken scratch,** demands a brief discussion and closes this section. This genre developed among the Pima and Papago tribes of south-central Arizona and blends Hispanic, Anglo-American, and Native American styles. Also known as ''waila,'' this music was first heard in the 1860s. Played by small string ensembles, its repertoire was heavily Hispanic-influenced and featured polkas and waltzes. Accordions were heard in chicken scratch bands as early as the 1890s, and by the 1920s new instruments, especially reeds like saxophones and clarinets, were introduced. Contemporary waila bands feature vocals in Spanish and Papago, electric basses, and a repertoire that mixes traditional polkas with contemporary popular songs.

Hawaiian

Because of its multifaceted heritage and its recent (1959) statehood, Hawaii's folk music is both exotic and far removed from that found in the rest of the United States. The population consists of those residents who are descended from early Polynesian Hawaiians, Asians, Caucasians, and others who have migrated from nearby islands over the past several hundred years. A notable revitalization of traditional chant and dance that began in the late 1960s has moved these folk arts into a valued place among contemporary Hawaiians. This movement to recognize local traditions has been called the "Hawaiian Renaissance," and it called attention to "Gabby" Pahinui. He is a slack-key guitarist who almost single-handedly kept the tradition going from the late 1930s until the renaissance began.

The traditional music of the Islands was predominately vocal and tied to the concept of "mana" (cosmic energy), a belief in a sacred life force that fostered a reverence for creativity. Several types of vocal music could be heard in Hawaii, but the "mele" (chant) proved to be the most important. Soloists predominate in traditional Hawaiian chanting. Those who could please their listeners with a sustained, unbroken performance were most sought after. Secondarily, a chanter should excel at prolonging and controlling vowel fluctuation and changing tone through manipulation of the chest muscles. Mele are usually narratives commenting upon religion, historical events, or societal issues.

The well-known **hula** actually refers to a dance that interprets a mele. The older style of hula that interprets animal life has almost disappeared from the Hawaiian repertoire. Hulas can be done sitting down or standing up. But in either case, the complicated gestures are keyed to words or phrases in the mele. Hula mele are formalized into contrasting sections, often *abcbcbcd,* to make them easier to follow. Seated hulas are often accompanied by body percussion or some sort of instrument, while standing hulas are generally augmented by at least one percussionist-chanter. At least two mele, oli and kepakepa, are strictly chanted traditions that are never interpreted by a hula.

Most of Hawaii's folk instruments are percussive, and the majority of them are affiliated with hula mele. For example, the "pahu hula" is a wooden drum made from a hollow log, and its use is limited to accompany the "hula pahu" (hula dance). Other drums are made from indigenous material such as coconut shells ("pūniu"). Rattles made of various indigenous gourds constitute the other important form of Hawaiian percussive instrument. Even beating wooden sticks against one another (kāla'au) can accompany this dancing.

Western music began to be heard in the Islands almost as soon as Captain Cook landed there in 1778. By the early nineteenth century, the influence of Western secular and sacred music began to be felt. The early missionaries brought hymnals, and the French introduced classical music and the necessary instruments to play it. Asian immigrants also brought their own folk and popular music. Ukulele-like instruments made their way to Hawaii in the early 1880s, brought over by Portuguese travelers.

Slack-key (open-tuned) **guitar** techniques brought over by Mexican and other Hispanic immigrants in the 1830s proved to be the most significant import. By the late 1880s, many of the Hawaiian guitarists were tuning their guitars to a major triad, a C-E-G in a C-major chord, and playing a style with a

---

M u s i c a l   E x a m p l e

This mele hula was recorded during a performance on April 8, 1980, at the Bishop Museum in Honolulu. According to the performer, it was initiated by the goddess, Hi'iaka, younger sister of Pele, the volcano goddess. Ko'olau is the lush windward side of the island of Oahu, which is steep and ripe like a rain forest. The rustling of the shell wreaths that embellish the dancers is the sound you hear in the background. [Smithsonian/Folkways 40015]

Title ''A Ko'olau Au' Ika I Ka Ua''
Performer Hoakalei Kamau'u and Kawaiokawaawaa Akim (caller)
Instruments drum and voice
Length 1:35
Notable Features

1. There is basically a duple-meter feel with some minor rhythmic embellishments.
2. A steady, moderate tempo, which increases slightly, is quickly established.
3. The voice is in a fairly high register and has some vibrato.
4. A modified call and reponse is used.

A Ko'olau au 'ike i ka ua
E kokolo a lepo mai ana e ka ua
E ka'i ku ana [ka'i] mai ana i ka us
A'e nu mai ana i ka ua i ke kuakiwi
E po'i [ho'i] mai ana i ka ua me he nalu
E puka, e puka, mai ana e ka ua

From Ko'olau, I watch the rain
The rain that pours on the earth
The rain passes by in columns
It rumbles as it falls in the mountains
The rain rises like the waves of the sea
Lo, the rain comes, it comes

---

slide that produced a unique sound. **Joseph Kekuku** is alleged to be the man who innovated this style when he slid a comb across the strings of his guitar, which was placed across his knees. The sound of a slide guitar may have appealed to Hawaiians because its sustained tones reflected the elongated vowels sung by mele chanters. As the twentieth century dawned on the shores of Waikiki Beach, slack-key guitar was firmly entrenched as part of Hawaii's vernacular music.

This style became influential on the mainland, when a fad for Hawaiian music began in 1915. George E. K. Awai's Royal Hawaiian Quartet, along with other local musicians and dancers, evoked a sensational response at the Panama-Pacific International Exposition in San Francisco. Almost immediately, the Victor company moved to exploit the situation. Their November 1915 catalogue states: "Victor recently announced a fine list of favorite Hawaiian numbers, rendered by the now famous Hawaiian Quintette, who have made such a success in the 'Bird of Paradise' Company; the gifted Toots Paka Troupe, and the Irene West Royal Hawaiians, who have appeared in vaudeville. Although these fine records were intended mainly for customers in the Hawaiian Islands, they have been largely acquired by those Victor customers who like quaint and fascinating music such as this."

The shock waves hit Tin Pan Alley with great force, and songwriters began churning out pseudo-Hawaiian songs for a mass market. As other Hawaiian musicians toured the United States, they brought along other songs, but they also performed the Tin Pan Alley material that their audiences requested. Hulas became caught in this craze, too. Vaudeville stages and circus shows were considered incomplete if they didn't include a "cootch" dancer, who was almost never Hawaiian but generally quite provocative. By the 1920s, many American musicians were singing songs in English with Hawaiian themes, called "hapa haloe." This craze culminated in 1937 when the hapa haloe "Sweet Leilani" garnered an Oscar for best song.

Anglo- and African American folk musicians heard this music and embraced the basic concept of playing an open-tuned guitar with a slide. Some black musicians were already using a similar style, but the Hawaiian fad served to reinforce its popularity. The slurring of the slide upon the strings mirrored the ability of harmonica players to move between the whole and half steps of Western scales. Many of the hillbilly musicians who pioneered the recording of country music were familiar with this style, too. A few musicians, such as the Dixon Brothers, enjoyed extensive recording careers using Hawaiian-style accompaniment. Jimmie Rodgers made several successful records in 1930 using Lani McIntire's Hawaiians to back up his patented blue yodeling and singing. Even Maybelle Carter used the slide technique on a 1929 session, though her influence probably came more directly from African American musicians. Certainly the pedal steel guitar, which developed in the late 1930s and flourished in country music during the 1940s, owes a great deal to the slack-key and Hawaiian fad.

Contemporary Hawaiian folk music involves a synthesis of older traditions and Western influences. It is largely performed for the booming tourist trade, not its informal traditional context. Hulas accompanied by chanting are available to any tourist on a daily basis. The revitalization has continued not only because of the recognition of its past but also because of a vested economic interest in the tourists who wish to see things uniquely Hawaiian.

A hula being performed at the 1989 Festival of American Folklife. *Smithsonian Institution.*

Franco-American
Cajun Country

Despite the state line that divides Texas and Louisiana, **"Cajun** country" constitutes a distinctive folk region that is clearly distinguished by its language, customs, foodways, and music. This small section of the Deep South is one of the United States' most easily identifiable culture areas and one whose mystique has gained wide attention since the early 1980s. While the rich sauces and tangy spices of Cajun food has attracted enthusiastic multitudes, the indigenous Cajun and zydeco music also continue to grow in popularity.

This intriguing part of the country is made unique because of its blend of settlers. In the middle 1700s, the English deported large numbers of French colonists from Nova Scotia, then known as Acadia. They were dispersed across the world, but many of them moved south, eventually resettling in the southeastern part of Louisiana. The new settlers eventually intermingled with local residents, resulting in a cultural mixture known as "Cajun." Cajuns speak a brand of French different from its Parisian counterpart. This is partially because most of the Acadian people originally came from the maritime Breton and Norman sections of France, far from Paris. Moreover, the Cajun language is actually a "creolized" blend that mixes French with English and the slave languages imported from Africa and filtered through the French West Indies.

This uniquely creolized section of the United States is itself fragmented by region. Along the bayous of south-central Louisiana, many of the residents still live in relative isolation. Boats remain a principal mode of transportation, and there is a continuing emphasis upon traditional ways of fishing and upon self-sufficiency. Towards the west, closer to the Texas border, the land is grassy and prairielike. In the middle 1800s, this was the frontier, something like our conception of life and lifestyles on the wild Western frontier. That spirit is found today in the wildcatting oil towns of Lafayette and Mamou, where the economies still ride the waves of boom or bust.

Musical Development Cajun music evolved with the language and the rest of its culture. The early settlers brought with them their older French songs and dance music played on fiddles. They eventually picked up the keening, high-pitched vocal style of the indigenous Native Americans, which has become a trademark of the music. The African American residents contributed a slightly syncopated rhythmic sense and the concept of improvisational singing. Hispanic settlers introduced the guitar to the Cajuns, while Anglo-Americans provided them with new tunes. By the 1850s, most of the basic elements of this highly creolized music were in place.

In the nineteenth century, dances were usually held in homes on weekends, with fiddles, sometimes in pairs, providing most of the music. The diatonic accordion, so well known in Cajun music today, was not introduced into the area until after the War Between the States by German settlers who came to Texas in the 1840s and 1850s. The fiddles and accordions were soon joined together because they could be heard over the loud and raucous dancing. By early in the twentieth century, small dance bands consisting of an accordion, fiddle, some percussion instrument (spoons, washboard, or triangle), and a guitar were found in dance halls all across Cajun country. They played a mixture of polkas, waltzes, two-steps, and other European-derived dance tunes for appreciative audiences. Cajun dances were often held on weekend nights in small, rural dance halls lined with wooden benches under which children slept while their parents danced the night away.

About the same time, a wave of Anglo-Americans invaded southwestern Louisiana and southeastern Texas. The discovery of oil brought them into the area by the thousands. Their arrival, followed by the 1916 ban of creolized French in the schools, signaled an important change for Cajun culture. The modern era of the twentieth century was invading their part of the world. This trend was exacerbated by the socialization fostered by World War I, a slowly expanding transportation system, and the explosion of the mass media. Each of these factors helped to force this unique culture into a secondary position as Cajuns quickly moved to become ''true Americans.'' Cajun music fell victim to this general trend. While some of the musicians stubbornly clung to the traditional songs and tunes, many others absorbed the contemporary trends.

Documenting Cajun Music Fortunately, a handful of them made commercial recordings in the late 1920s. Most notable were the fiddle duets of Dennis McGee and Sady Courville, which still sound hauntingly archaic. But the first Cajun records, ''Allons á Lafayette'' (''Lafayette'') and ''La Valse Qui Ma Portin De Ma Fose'' (''The Waltz That Carried Me to My Grave'') were made

Musical Example

This "stomp" or dance tune is sung by Rodney Balfa, a member of the highly musical Balfa family. Such medium-tempo dance tunes are quite popular throughout southwest Louisiana, although waltzes are always liberally sprinkled throughout an evening of Cajun dancing. This selection—recorded on August 30, 1975, in Basile, Louisiana—is a typical lament about the ways in which women can break a man's heart. [Smithsonian/Folkways 40006]

Title "Bosco Stomp"
Performers Rodney Balfa—guitar and vocal; Bessyl Duhon—fiddle; Allie Young—accordion
Instruments guitar, fiddle, accordion, and voice
Length 3:01
Notable Features

1. It uses an ab form.
2. The vocalist sings in a fairly high register.
3. Lead instrumental breaks are taken by the fiddle and guitar.
4. Duple meter is enhanced by some syncopation.
5. The song is basically played on its tonic.

Y en a des tites brunes
Oui y en a des tites blonds
Oui ye en a qu'assez noire
Que l'diable veut pas les voir
Ca va t'faire des miseres
Ca va t'faire des accroires
Ca va t'faire les aimer
Puis la ca tourne le dos
Ca qui m'fait du mal a moi

Y en des tites brunes
Oui y en a des tites blonds
Oui y en a qu'assez grosses
Que l'diable veut pas les voir

Ca va t'faire des miseres
Ca va t'faire des accroires
Ca va t'faire les aimer
Puis la ca t'casse le couer
Ca qui 'm du mal tite fille

There are some little brunettes
There are some little blonds
There are some who are dark enough

That the devil doesn't want to see them
They will make you miserable
They will make you believe them
They will make you love them
Then, they turn their back on you
That's what hurts me

There are some little brunettes
There are some little blonds
There are some who are fat enough
That the devil doesn't want to see them
They will make you miserable
They will make you believe them
They will make you love them
Then, they break your heart
That's what hurts me, li'l girl

by Joseph Falcon and his wife, Cleoma Breaux. Falcon remembers that the Columbia record executives in the temporary New Orleans studio were dubious about the entire affair:

> They looked at us . . . they were used to recording with orchestras. "That's not enough music to make a record." they said. So George [Burrow, a jewelry store owner from Rayne who wanted to sell Falcon records] had 250 records paid for before I even went to make them. So George started talking: "We got to run it through because that man there . . . is popular in Rayne; the people are crazy about his music and they want his records." But they said, "We don't know its going to sell." They then turned around and asked him "How much would you buy?" He told them he wanted 500 copies as the first order . . . and he made out a check for five hundred records. They started looking at each other. "Well," they said "you go ahead and play us a tune just for us to hear" (Ethnic Recordings, 15).

By the middle 1930s, the Hackberry Ramblers had synthesized Cajun music with early Western swing and were among the first Cajun musicians to use amplified instruments. Electric steel guitars were soon heard in dance halls across southern Louisiana, as were the current popular tunes by Bob Wills and his Texas Playboys. These songs were now pushed forward by the drums that Cajun groups began using. At the front of this modernization of traditional Cajun music was Harry Choates, whose popularity insured him jobs as far west as Waco, Texas. In fact, many Cajuns were leaving home for oil-related jobs in central Texas and Oklahoma. California became home for many transplanted Cajuns during World War II as they left the bayou for the West Coast defense industries.

The impact of Cajuns on related forms of music cannot go unnoticed. Cajun singers such as Joe Werner of the Riverside Ramblers influenced Webb Pierce, among others. Hank Williams, based in Shreveport, Louisiana, home of the "Louisiana Hayride," also underscored the impact of Cajun culture through his recording of "Jambalaya." Many of the Western swing bands included songs such as "Jole Blonde" or a two-step in their repertoire. From the 1940s until the present, Cajun music has left a small but important mark upon commercial country music.

The internal revitalization of Cajun folk music began slowly in the late 1940s. Led by the accordion-playing Iry LeJune, the older songs once more began popping up at dances and on playlists of the local radio stations. Many of these musicians were born in the 1920s to parents with strong ties to traditional Cajun culture. Musicians such as Joseph Falcon and Nathan Abshire were immersed in the culture, though their language and music were kept more private during the decline of the Cajun culture itself. Spurred on by local record and radio entrepreneurs like Eddie Schuler and George Khoury, who knew they had a limited but faithful commercial audience for Cajun music, the inexorable return of Cajun folk music had begun.

In retrospect, the thirty-year attempt to obliterate Cajun culture was doomed. Cajuns are exceptionally hardy people and they tenaciously cling to their traditions. Since the 1930s, outside researchers, most notably Alan Lomax, have been visiting southwestern Louisiana to document the indigenous music. Interest in Cajun music also increased during the early days of the folk revival. Harry Oster, then an English professor at Louisiana State University, spent considerable energy recording Cajun and other styles of indigenous music in southern Louisiana during the middle to late 1950s. At the suggestion of Ralph Rinzler and Mike Seeger, the 1964 Newport Folk Festival became the first major "event" at which Cajun music was featured outside of its home. Despite some uneasiness, Louisiana's more polished, upper-crust society was ultimately pleased that the music of Gladius Thibodeaux, Louis

Famed Cajun fiddler Dewey Balfa performing for a school class in southwestern Louisiana. *Smithsonian Institution.*

Musical Example

There is no Cajun song better known than this one; in fact, it is often referred to as the Cajun national anthem. You will almost inevitably hear "Jole Blonde" if you attend a Cajun music gathering. It first reached the ears of many people in the late 1940s when Harry Choates's version hit the national charts, which spawned many cover versions and answer songs. Since then it has become a song associated not only with Cajun music but with southwestern Louisiana and southeastern Texas in general. This version was recorded in the mid-1950s. [Folkways 4438]

Title "Jole Blonde"
Performers Tony Allemand—fiddle and vocal; Rufus Allemand—guitar
Instruments fiddle, guitar, voice
Length 2:05
Notable Features

1. It is played in a simple triple meter—3/4.
2. You hear a homophonic texture with the fiddle supplying the melody.
3. The tonality is major.
4. Allemand's voice is pitched in a relatively high register.
5. He uses a slightly ornamented vocal style.

Ah! ma jole blond'.
Gar dez don qu'o c'est qu't as fait.
Tu m'as quitte' pou' t'en aller.
Je n'ai pas ma canne en mains, mais toi t'vas l' voir!

Ah! ma jole blond'.
Moi j'm'en vais-t-a naviguer.
Tu vas pleurer-Zavant longtemps pou't'attaper;
Tu voudras t'en rev'ni avec.ton vieux neg'.

Ah! my beautiful blond.
Look what you've done.
You left me to go away.
I don't have my stick on hand, but you'll get it!

Ah! my beautiful blond.
I am going to sea.
You will cry before long, that'll teach you;
You will want to come back to your old negro.

Lejune, and Dewey Balfa was so well received. Since then, Cajun folk music has been heard all across the United States and the world.

Today traditional Cajun music and foodways are well known to millions because of this revival. Inside of Louisiana itself, the Council for the Development of French in Louisiana (CODFIL) has been active in promoting the culture through its efforts to promote French and Cajun language in the public schools. The University of Southwestern Louisiana, located in the heart of Cajun country and whose sports teams are known as the ''Ragin' Cajuns,'' now maintains a center devoted to Cajun studies. These groups have also helped to coordinate several regional festivals featuring local music, most notably the annual Cajun Music Festival in Lafayette. Today younger musicians such as Zachary Richard, Michael Doucet, Marc Savoy, along with an older generation that includes the Balfa Brothers and D. L. Menard, play music at folk festivals and clubs across America.

Zydeco

Zydeco is a special branch of Cajun music. Simply put, it is creolized African American Cajun music. Traditional zydeco music and its performance contexts are very similar to its white counterparts. Found primarily in venues that stretch west from Lafayette to Houston, zydeco has developed since Reconstruction. Whether the musicians favor the older Cajun sound or prefer the blues or soul-tinged music, it is all propelled forward by a rhythmic drive that betrays its Afro-Caribbean background.

The black Americans of southwestern Louisiana are truly Creoles because they are usually a mixture of African, French, and Spanish descent. They speak a hybrid language that mixes its heritage into a blend that even Cajuns have trouble understanding! Most blacks and mulattos came to Louisiana as slaves for French planters in the late eighteenth century or as ''freed coloreds'' following the Haitian revolution that ended in 1803.

The music they play became known as zydeco, a creolized form of the French word for snap beans. Scholars are not certain exactly how the term ''zydeco'' developed into its present meaning, but among themselves local residents often say that it is derived from an old southwestern Louisiana dance tune known as ''Les Haricots Sont Pas Sales'' (''The Snap Beans are Not Salted''). However, this term also shares its origins with the Afro-Caribbean culture that spices up all of this area. The spelling for this lively dance music is not standardized, and the word sometimes appears as zodico, zordico, or even zologo. Zydeco refers not only to music but to the event where the dancing and music takes place. Thus, one can host a zydeco, which includes not only music but food, dancing, and socializing. Especially popular are zydecos held at a fais-do-do, an informal house party where the music and dancing last far into the night.

Although zydeco and Cajun music are closely related, distinctions can be made. Zydeco tends to be played at a quicker tempo. Its melodies are generally simplified with more emphasis placed on its syncopated rhythms. In a Cajun two-step, the first and third beats are accented, while a zydeco two-step accents the second and fourth beats. The repertoire of zydeco musicians also tends to include more blues and fewer waltzes than Cajun repertoires. Cajun bands usually feature a triangle, while zydeco bands favor a vest-fastened washboard known as a ''frottoir.'' Prior to the contemporary models, nineteenth-century zydeco musicians favored a scrapped animal jaw or a notched stick to provide the rhythmic drive.

Among older zydeco musicians, the Fontenot and Ardoin families are noted for their skill, though for many years they played mostly for neighbors and friends. Local interest in zydeco music has increased over the past twenty years to the point that Alphonse Ardoin observed: ''I have a grandson. . . that I'm trying to teach. He's only three years old, but he's interested already. He doesn't know how to play anything yet, but he takes the accordion and plays with it. . . . To be a musician, you have to be committed to music and have it in your family. It has to be in your blood for you to learn easily'' (Ancelet 1984, 87).

Without a doubt, **Clifton Chenier** was the best-known zydeco musician. Before passing away from kidney disease in 1984, he toured extensively, bringing his modern zydeco music to large concert halls and small dance halls across the country. Chenier transformed zydeco music by using his larger, piano-keyed accordion and incorporating elements of blues and rock 'n' roll. His early recording efforts included some R and B releases for Specialty and Chess. But Chenier's breakthrough came in the late 1960s when he began playing at blues festivals and recording his unique music for Arhoolie Records. His band usually included a sax and full rhythm section in addition to his brother Cleveland's washboard.

The impact of zydeco has grown to international proportions over the past decade. The amplified blues-based bands of Terrance Semien, Queen Ida and the Bon Ton Zydeco Band, and Buckwheat Zydeco have toured Europe as well as the United States. They perform for local dances as well as at international blues festivals. The 1983 Opelousas Zydeco Festival underscores the fact that this music continues to thrive in Louisiana.

Conroy Fontenot and Boisec Ardoin, Elton, LA., April 1966.
Ralph Rinzler.

Over the past decade, the unique music and cuisine of southwestern Louisiana have moved into the consciousness of people around the world. In Washington, D.C., one can now find blackened fish or gumbo on restaurant menus and people dancing the two-step in dance halls. Cajun people are not only survivors, they are wonderful ambassadors for their way of life and folkways. A group of younger musicians born in the 1950s, such as accordionist Zachary Richard and fiddler Michael Doucet, have found a large audience outside of the area of their birth. Cajun and zydeco are mainstays of folk-music festivals, and the recordings of Beausoleil, C. J. Chenier (Clifton's son), and the Balfa Brothers command their own ''Cajun'' section at major audio outlets. Clearly, the trend to ''Americanize'' Cajuns that peaked in the 1920s has failed in a grand manner.

Northeastern States

Though not as well documented or as distinctive, the music of French-speaking residents of the United States needs a brief overview. The northernmost sections of New England and New York state contain a large proportion of Franco-Americans, most of whom are Catholic. Some are descended from the migration of Acadians in the middle eighteenth century; others are more recent migrants from Canada. Most of these Canadian immigrants have crossed the border from Quebec over the past 150 years. Some of their folk songs still recollect France or their ancestors' time in Canada and have been sung by generations of Franco-Americans. Many of these songs are associated with the times of the Canadian explorers or the plight of French Canadian farmers.

There is also a tradition of drinking and bawdy songs, ''gaulois,'' that tend to be dominated by male singers. Much of this singing activity takes place in bars and taverns, rather than at home. ''La Bonnefemme Robert'' (''The Lovely Woman Robert'') remains one of the most popular obscene, anticlerical songs. Some men of Acadian descent also continue the tradition of singing a soulful lament, ''complainte,'' that complains of life's difficulties.

The influence of the Catholic church is felt in other ways, too. For example, well-known Gregorian songs that have been heard in church provide the melody for folk texts. Some of these songs make fun of the church and its activities. There was also a turn-of-the-century movement to transform the vocal traditions into large choral pieces or to incorporate dance tunes into more formal instrumental compositions.

French American dance music continues to be more widespread and common in the late twentieth century. Most noteworthy are the waltzes and two-step quadrilles that are most often played on the harmonica, fiddle, or accordion. These instruments usually provide the basic melody while the harmony is supplied by a piano with the ''tapper du pied,'' a rhythmic clogging of the feet, or the spoons adding rhythmic interest. Most of the dance tunes, such as ''Fisher's Hornpipe'' or ''Le Reel de Sherbrooke,'' are well known on both sides of the U.S. and Canadian border. In northern Vermont, the Beaudoin and Riendeau families are well-respected for maintaining the older instrumental traditions.

Despite the long-standing Hispanic presence in the United States, most of the music from South and Central America, the Caribbean, and Europe is either imported or not folk music. The multifaceted migration patterns of Latinos into the United States further complicates the situation. As in the case of most Asian Americans, the majority of recently emigrated Central or South Americans have arrived too recently to create new forms of distinctly Hispanic American folk music.

This would include hundreds of thousands of refugees who have fled war-torn Central America over the past twenty years. Washington, D.C., for example, has one of the largest Salvadoran populations outside of El Salvador. New York City is home to huge Puerto Rican, Cuban, and Haitian populations that have brought their cultures with them and whose musical traditions have remained largely isolated from the mainstream. Occasionally, some form of Latin popular music will influence American popular music. Starting with the tango, which hit Broadway in 1913, dance-related musical crazes such as the rumba, samba, mambo, bossa nova, and salsa, have hit our shores in nearly ten-year cycles.

These exemplify the trendy native of popular culture and suggest the importance of ethnic identity, but they are largely removed from folk culture. Even the music played on drums for ''bomba,'' a Puerto Rican folk dance, remains largely true to its origins. One syncretic form of religious folk song, ''coritos''—praise songs utilized by Hispanic Pentecostalists—bears the unmistakable stamp of black American music. Its strophic form and occasional use of call and response harken back to Africa but are reinforced by the influence of African Americans. Furthermore, the Puerto Ricans' use of electric guitars, reed instruments, and drums reflect contemporary black American Pentecostal practice.

Latino

Mexican Americans have crossed our often fluid borders for centuries and many still retain their musical ties to the South. From Texas westward, the Mexican American presence along the border is indelibly etched into the United States. Much of their music remains close to its Mexican roots, but some crossover into new territory has occurred in these areas. This music has become known as **Tex-Mex** because so much of it is concentrated on the lengthy border of Texas and Mexico. The Mexican American citizens of this area are known as ''Tejanos,'' and some of these families have been inhabitants since it was a Spanish colony.

For most of the past three hundred years, these citizens of the Southwest have remained more culturally allied with Mexico. Most speak Spanish and eat like their Southern brethren. They have assimilated some parts of Anglo-American life, but they have also developed a distinctive Tejanos culture. ''Música Tejanos'' is the manifestation of this subculture that interests us. It is a unique blend of Spanish, Mexican, French, Caribbean, Anglo- and African American music unlike any other form of American folk music.

Tex-Mex

M u s i c a l   E x a m p l e

This brief instrumental was recorded in south-central New Mexico, on April 22, 1950. Like so many aspects of Tex-Mex music, it represents a musical hybrid. Polkas were introduced to the southwestern United States by Europeans settled on both sides of the border. This field recording was done by an important collector of Southwestern folk songs, J. D. Robb, who worked throughout this area in the 1940s and 1950s. [Folkways 4426]

Title ''Polka''
Peformers Librado Leyba—violin; Eddie Ortez—guitar
Instruments violin and guitar
Length 1:26
Notable Features

1. It is taken at a brisk tempo.
2. The tune uses an *ab* song form, about eight measures of each.
3. The guitar backup sounds flat-picked and is quite accomplished.
4. Leyba plays in a rather ornate style, with some small and interesting rhythmic embellishments of the basic melody.
5. There is a slight increase in the tempo from beginning to end.

Nineteenth-century Tejanos musical culture bears the influence not only of the Spanish and Mexicans but of the French, who ruled Mexico in the 1860s. The French introduced or solidified the popularity of dances such as polkas, waltzes, and mazurkas. Another European influence, Germans who migrated to central Texas beginning in the 1840s, began to be felt about the same time. During Reconstruction, Tejano bands consisting of guitars, violins, and various wind instruments were playing across all of southern Texas.

Early in the twentieth century, the ''guitarreros'' (singing guitarists) began to emerge. Guitarreros—balladeers who related stories, news, and information to simple accompaniment—sang in the places where males came together. This largely remained within male culture because guitarreros were so closely allied with drinking, cavorting, and the telling of off-color stories.

Conjunto Norteño A form of dance music called ''música norteño'' (music of the north) or **''conjunto norteño''** (ensemble for the north) is linked with the regional conjunto ensembles that developed in Mexico in the late nineteenth century. These ensembles featured a diatonic **button accordion,** acoustic bass, and a twelve-string guitar known as a bajo sexto. Its inclusion of the German diatonic button accordion, which also filtered into Cajun music, underscores the impact of German culture upon Texas. It is possible that this influence also came from the south in the form of German immigrants from Monterrey, Mexico, who introduced ''acordeóns'' to Mexicans in the 1880s.

Norteño accordion playing actually started as a solitary pursuit. But as its popularity grew, these musicians gradually replaced the wind instruments and violins in ensembles. By the middle 1920s, the basic lineup for música norteño groups became well established. Since the early 1950s, the norteño musicians have performed a mixture of folk, popular, and dance tunes played in 2/4 time.

Santiago Jiménez (San Antonio) and Narciso Martínez (lower Rio Grande valley) emerged as the premier practitioners of this accordion music. They became the ''Tex-Mex'' equivalents of Gid Tanner or Blind Lemon Jefferson—early folk-music artists whose records and radio broadcasts had a wide and lasting impact within their geographical and cultural communities well into the 1930s. By the 1940s, Jiménez, Martínez, and their peers began usurping the role of the guitarreros through their addition of vocalists to their bands.

M u s i c a l   E x a m p l e

Here's an example of the type of music that you could hear in San Antonio, Texas, if you went out dancing at a small bar. Bands playing this type of music are quite common, and they underscore the sometimes close musical relationship between the German and Mexican settlers in Texas. This particular piece seems to have entered the local Tex-Mex repertoire through Patricio Jimenez, who heard German or Bohemian settlers performing it at the turn of the century. Its name in English is ''Put Your Little Foot Out'' and it's a quaint schottische. A schottische has the feel of a waltz but is a four-count dance that requires the couple to hold the third beat one extra count. [Folkways 6527]

Title ''Pan de Maiz''
Performers Ben King
Instruments button accordion, guitar, percussion
Length 1:21
Notable Features

1. A stately compound triple meter (6/8) is heard throughout.
2. The form is simple *ab*.
3. The tempo is moderate and unwavering.
4. No ''lead'' is taken; the accordion simply restates the melody without embellishment.
5. Its rhythm is straightforward with just a hint of syncopation.

By the 1950s, the contemporary música norteño style was set. The bands amplified their instruments, and musicians such as Tony de la Rosa (Kingsville, Texas) began touring across the United States. They played for Tejanos who had migrated north and west in search of better employment. This movement from south Texas has helped to disseminate this Mexican American folk to the conclaves of Tejanos.

Finally, corridos are another type of Mexican-based folk song that has been appropriated by Texas musicians. A corrido is a ballad that is sung to un-adorned guitar, bajo sexto, or accordion accompaniment in 3/4 or 6/8 time. Although there are corridos that do not adhere to the ballad form, most tell structured tales. Many of the pre–World War II Mexican American corridos tell of the conflicts along the border, but the most recent ones describe heroes such as John F. Kennedy or César Chávez. Corridos are generally the domain of male singers. One exception is **Lydia Mendoza** (''The Lark of the Border-lands''), whose guitarrero career has included the recording of many corridos.

Mendoza's gender makes her unusual for a guitarrero, but her early back-ground is hardly unique. Her family as far back as her grandmother played music and she had relatives on both sides of the Texas-Mexico border. Born in 1916, Mendoza came into a family that eventually grew to eight brothers and

Lydia Mendoza of Houston, Texas (1982), began singing with her family group in the 1930s.
Library of Congress, Case Fleischauer.

sisters. In a long interview, Lydia Mendoza recalls the circumstances of her youth:

> I believe I've had a vocation for music almost from the time I was born. I remember clearly that I began to feel drawn towards music when I was four. You must realize that my mother played guitar, and at home after dinner, after she and my dad had rested up, she would pick up the guitar and begin to play and sing. . . . I liked music so much that even then I wanted to play guitar, and I told my mother that I wanted to play like her, and she told me that when my hands got big enough she'd teach me—and that's the way it happened. . . . When I was about eight or nine, I could play perfectly well.
>
> I was the prime mover of music in the household. I liked it, so I wanted my brothers and sisters to play, too. . . . And I guess they liked it, because they all learned to play instruments, and we got a group together. Mother played the guitar, I played violin, one of my sisters the mandolin, a brother played the triangle, and father played tambourine. So we got up a musical group, and then we dedicated our lives to music on a full-time basis. We started off all over the lower Rio Grande Valley, and later on we got as far as Detroit, Michigan, always with our music. We lived one year in the Lower Rio Grande Valley—McAllen, Weslaco, Edinburg, and Kingsville. We would stay a while in one little town. . . [and] play in restaurants and barbershops. Dad would go in and ask permission to play—mostly on Saturdays, when there would be lots of people—and then if folks were there we'd side down and sing, and people would give us tips (*Ethnic Recordings,* 119–20).

Mendoza later settled in San Antonio, Texas, where she married and specialized in guitar playing. She became popular through her radio appearances and her early recordings for the Bluebird Record Company (1934–40). She recorded a variety of material but is best known for her corridos. Whatever form it takes, her brand of music has always appealed to working-class residents on the Texas-Mexico border.

Scandinavian American

Norwegians, Swedes, Finns, and Danes began settling in the United States during the early eighteenth century. The largest wave of Scandinavian immigration took place over a seventy-year period beginning in 1850, when they flooded the upper Midwest from Michigan to North Dakota. Most groups still tend to think of themselves as Danish American, Finnish American, Norwegian American, or Swedish American. There is also a sense of a general pan-Scandinavian culture, but that is subservient to individual nationalistic identities. And, of course, many people rally around the Lutheran church, still its single most important religious institution. Today Scandinavian Americans can be found throughout our country, but the highest concentration still live in the upper Midwest.

Ballads Early in the twentieth century, ballads formed a small but important part of Scandinavian American folk music. These new immigrants brought with them a proud tradition of epic, often mythic, storytelling and ballad singing. Eventually, these traditions, such as the mythical Finnish Kalevala epics, found a new, distinctly American voice. Ballads were sometimes sung to the tunes of well-known Lutheran hymns. By the late nineteenth century, nearly half of all of the Norwegian broadside ballads were being set to such hymns. Most importantly, they were transformed into emigrant ballads during the nineteenth century. Transmitted both orally and by way of printed broadsides, emigrant ballads informed the listeners of the tribulations and the joys of life in the New World. This excerpt from such a ballad sends a warning back to potential emigrants:

> Things certainly were fine over there, to hear him tell about it.
> They didn't have to work like slaves for a living,
> and instead of hardtack they ate fine white bread.
> No taxes and no foreclosures,
> gold to be had for the digging,
> and crops that grew of themselves.
> That's what they said, and lied like the devil (Blegan 1979, 208–9).

Instrumental Music   Like so many other groups, Scandinavian American instrumental music is linked to dancing. A combination of polkas, waltzes, and other related tunes can be heard in dances throughout the upper Midwest. Even some of the older Swedish polkas can be heard today, most of which come from the musical activity of Edwin Johnson and his descendents. Younger revivalist bands such as Wiscandia and Bob and Becky Wernerehl play some of Johnson's tunes. The revitalization of older styles gained momentum during the late 1970s, resulting in the occasional use of plucked zithers—the Finnish kantele, for instance. Like their German American counterparts—youthful polka bands such as the Ridgeland Dutchmen, the New Jolly Swiss Boys, and the Mississippi Valley Dutchmen—younger Norwegian Americans such as Leroy Larson have stirred a renewed interest in local folk music.

A nationalistic spirit has kept the traditions closely identified with specific countries or regions. As early as 1926, fiddler-vocalist Erik Kivi recorded ''Merimiehen Valssi'' and ''Porin Poika,'' which were released on Victor's 78000 series. These were the first commercial recordings of Finnish American folk music recorded in the United States. The record only sold about one thousand copies, but the market was deemed large enough that more than eight hundred Finnish American records were eventually issued during the 1920s and 1930s. Columbia thought enough of this market to issue an entire printed catalogue of Finnish American material that appeared on its 3000–F series. Not all of them were folk music, of course, but traditional music was well represented. Many types of Scandinavian American music were documented on commercial recordings, but the industry's interest in the music waned during the 1940s. So did the community support for the music.

The first Norwegians came to the United States in 1825. They soon migrated westward from New York into the Midwest, reaching Wisconsin within fifteen years. By the 1850s, they had moved as far west as southeastern Minnesota, and within twenty years the Red River Valley had become the region with Minnesota's highest percentage of Norwegians. Like many recent immigrants, these newly minted Norwegian Americans stuck together, often settling in the same county and township. Wisconsin in the 1840s was a land of hardy pioneers, and "sticking together" could mean a few miles to your nearest neighbor.

A rural lifestyle helped to promote a sense of community within Norwegian American enclaves. Summertime work exchanges helped to raise barns and establish local quilting circles. During the winter, which lasts from November into April, these same families gathered weekly. Except for the small, pious Haugean sect, which discouraged dancing, fiddle music, and other related activities, they met for weekly dance parties. Each week a different family hosted the dance, clearing out the parlor and opening the house to all of the neighbors. Neighbors provided the music and some of the food. The dancing often lasted until well into the night.

But by the turn of the century, Norwegian immigrants rarely sailed across the Atlantic Ocean as family units. Males typically came first, worked on farms, and later sent for their families. Farm work often exposed them to other cultures, thus contributing to the mixing of ethnic music traditions. They also came from different regions in Norway, resulting in a more heterogeneous population. The formation of **bygdelags** social and cultural societies consisting of people from the same region of Norway, was the response to this fragmentation as well as to the physical isolation of rural farm life. Bygdelags helped to perpetuate not only the language but regional dialects, customs, and music. Norwegian food such as "lefse," an unleavened bread, and sweet krumkakes were found on the tables at the close of formal meetings. They brought people together in order to celebrate Norwegian Constitution Day on May 17th (Syttende Mai). By the 1920s, there were scores of bygdelags throughout Minnesota and Wisconsin.

"Julebukker" is an old Norwegian custom that occurred in some communities. It can be translated as "Christmas fooling" or "Christmas ghosting." In twentieth-century Wisconsin, it has evolved into a masquerading event featuring cross-dressing and other masking devices. The disguised visitors enter a neighbor's house, while the occupants try to guess their true identity. The teasing usually ends in a dance with fiddles, accordions, and guitars providing the music for waltzes, polkas, and "Yankee dances" (a square dance).

The **Hardanger fiddle** emerged in the late 1800s and early 1900s as the most unique type of violin used to accompany the regional dances brought over by Norwegians. This occurred in part through the bygdelags and in part through the localized concentration of immigrants from western and southern Norway. Named for the rural section of Norway from which it originated,

Norwegian American Folk Music

Norwegian American dance band
(The ''Big Four'' or Nyen Family
band), Blair area (west-central
Wisconsin), early 1900s.
Courtesy Wisconsin Folk Museum.
Photographer unknown.

these distinctive fiddles are ornately decorated. A Hardanger fiddle is also a
little bit shorter and narrower than other fiddles and features a fingerboard that
is virtually flat. The layout of the fingerboard encourages the musician to play
more than one string at a time. Strung underneath the fingerboard and attached
to the bridge are four or five strings, which sound sympathetically. This gives
the Hardanger a fuller sound and an unusual timbre. Hardanger fiddles were
important enough to spawn the Hardanger Violinist Association of America in
the early twentieth century. Further evidence of revitalization is the contemporary revival of this organization in Wisconsin and Minnesota.

The distinctive, localized styles of rural dance and music imported from
the old country inevitably evolved into Norwegian American styles. The older
couple dances—springar, polska, and springeleik—gave way to the more generalized European forms of polkas and waltzes. Although the use of the Hardanger fiddle declined during the twentieth century, conventional fiddles
remained the lead melodic instrument. They were slowly augmented by both
button and piano accordions. Greater contact with other Scandinavian Americans, particularly Swedes, and ''Americans'' lead to a broader repertoire. A
study of Norwegian American instrumental music conducted by ethnomusicologist Leroy Larson in the early 1970s concluded that approximately 10 percent was of Norwegian origin and another 10 percent from Sweden. Even
Norwegian Americans were not immune to the process of regional adaptation,
which accounts for the ability of musicians to perform music for specific ethnic groups or a more general Scandinavian American audience.

Norwegian Swing   Turn-of-the-century Norwegian American folk music was still heard at informal public events such as a barn raising or in homes. But dance halls slowly emerged as the location of choice for this music, and a semiprofessional circuit of musicians and "barn dance" halls developed during the 1920s. Thorstein Skarning and his Norwegian Hillbillies were among the bands that played for dances in barns that no longer held cattle but were specifically engaged for such events. They worked the same circuit as other Scandinavian American bands such as the Viking Accordion Band and Ted Johnson and his Scandinavian Orchestra. These small ensembles of between five and ten pieces often included not only fiddle and accordions but a variety of reed and brass instruments, used to perform arrangements of older folk dance tunes.

By the late 1930s, such "ethnic" bands had paralleled a trend in American country music by groups like the Hoosier Hotshots to "professionalize." Both styles moved to increase the size of their ensembles by adding reed and brass players to augment the basic ensemble of stringed instruments. In this respect, they became more like the small swing bands of Benny Goodman or Glenn Miller. Their core repertoire of old-time instrumentals did not change, but it was augmented by popular dance tunes and novelty songs in order to appeal to a wider audience. Informal attire was replaced by either matching suits or "hayseed" costumes consisting of overalls, plaid shirts, and straw hats, which helped to solidify their rural, down-home image.

These tactics worked for a while; they transformed Norwegian American folk music into a format that was more palatable for a larger audience. However, by the close of World War II, this music faced a sharp decline and most of the bands retired. A cadre of musicians playing more traditional styles of Norwegian American music remained, though they rarely performed in public. Such musicians have become more apparent during the revitalization of old-time music that began in the middle 1970s.

Contemporary Norwegian American Folk Music   Today Norwegian American folk music, which is largely instrumental, can be heard at monthly dances held at community centers or in the homes of older musicians. It is also one of the drawing cards for the annual Norwegian festivals held in Detroit Lakes, Fergus Falls, and other small communities in central Minnesota. The "Nordic Fest" at Decorah, Iowa, hosts an annual three-day old-time music program, while in Mt. Horeb, Wisconsin, there is a smaller Scandinavian musical festival. Perhaps the largest such event is the fiddle contest at Yankton, South Dakota. Because the crowds can sometimes grow quite large, it is not uncommon for these bands to use amplifiers or amplified instruments. The music is presented as an important manifestation of Norwegian culture, and people often ask for the "old tunes," waltzes, polkas, and reinlanders (a Norwegian variant of the schottische) that they heard forty or fifty years ago.

Accordions and fiddles have moved back to the front of the band, and they are often backed up by guitars, pianos, or a bass guitar. The musicians

Norwegian American musicians on
porch, 1928, west-central Wisconsin
(Westby, WI, area).
Courtesy Wisconsin Folk Museum.
Photographer unknown.

themselves tend to be in their sixties and seventies with a sprinkling of
younger folks learning the repertoire. Their repertoire tends to be eclectic,
mixing some older Norwegian American tunes such as "Tutlut's Waltz" with
pieces learned from contemporary visiting Norwegian musicians or from tapes
of Norwegian folk music. Distinctly Bohemian, Irish, and Swedish American
tunes learned from other Minnesota, North Dakota, and Wisconsin residents
form another part of the repertoire. The music tends to be played in simple or
compound duple or triple meter with contrasting *ab* sections. The texture is not
very dense, and the dynamic range falls into the middle and is rather narrow.
The overall feeling is one of very clearly articulated and melodic playing underpinned by a steady rhythm meant for dancing. Yet there is enough subtle
rhythmic interest to keep even the most demanding listeners tapping their toes
in anticipation of the next variation.

Final Thoughts

The study of ethnic folk music in the United States is not nearly as advanced as our knowledge of Anglo-American and African American traditions. The music itself is as varied as the ethnic and racial groups themselves. For Americans who live outside of these ethnic traditions, this music sounds fresh and new. Ethnic music is infused by popular culture more quickly and readily than by folk culture. This results in music, usually urban manifestations such as Puerto Rican salsa or South African high life, that lies outside of our scope. Revitalization movements that began in the late 1960s and early 1970s, approximately ten years after the "folk revival," have helped to place the spotlight on several of the ethnic groups described in this chapter.

Key Figures and Terms

button accordion
bygdelags
Cajun
chicken scratch
Clifton Chenier
conjunto norteño
Hardanger fiddle
hula
Joseph Kekuku
klezmer
Lydia Mendoza
pan-Indian movement
peyote
powwow
revitalization
revival
slack-key guitar
Tex-Mex
vocables
Whoopee John Wilfahrt

zydeco

Audio

Across the Fields—Traditional Norwegian-American Music from Wisconsin. Wisconsin Folk Museum. This cassette-only anthology of "fiddle tunes and button accordion melodies" is a fine survey of the field.

American Indian Music for the Classroom. Canyon Records. A four-record/cassette set that comes with a teacher's guide and booklet.

Cajun Social Music. Smithsonian/Folkways 40006 (CD/CASS). This collection of recent recordings includes performances by Nathan Abshire, Hector Duhon, Marc Savoy, and others.

Chenier, Clifton. *Live at St. Mark's.* Arhoolie 313 (CD/CASS). There are many fine Chenier albums on Arhoolie, but this live performance is particularly compelling.

Chicken Scratch. Canyon 6093 (LP). An anthology of Southwestern styles featuring Elvin Kelly, Los Reyes, and the Molinas.

Conjunto! Texas-Mexican Border Music. 3 records. Rounder 6023/24/30 (CASS/CD). A well-annotated, three-volume sampler featuring some of the masters—Flaco Jiménez, Santiago Jiménez, etc.

Jakie, Jazz 'Em Up—Old Time Klezmer Music 1912–26. Global Village C-101 (CASS). A lively collection of vintage klezmer recordings by Abe Schwartz, Art Shryer's Modern Jewish Orchestra, and others.

Lydia Mendoza. Arhoolie 219 (CD/CASS). A poignant retrospective of this influential singer's career.

Norwegian-American Music from Minnesota: Old-Time and Traditional Favorites. Minnesota Historical Society, St. Paul, Minnesota, 55101. This audio cassette and fourteen-page monograph provides a succinct survey of the field.

Songs of Earth, Fire and Sky: Music of the American Indian. New World 80246–2 (CD). Perhaps the best single overview of the field.

Songs of Indian Territory: Native American Music Traditions of Oklahoma. A first-rate monograph accompanies this cassette, which is available from the Center of the American Indian, Kirkpatrick Center, 2100 N.E. 52nd Street, Oklahoma City, Oklahoma 73105.

Vintage Hawaiian Music: Steel Guitar Masters 1928–34. Rounder 1052 (CASS/CD). *Vintage Hawaiian Music: The Great Singers 1928–34.* Rounder 1053 (CASS/CD). These two packages provide a nice sampling of commercial recordings of folk and folk based Hawaiian music.

Books

Ancelét, Barry. 1984. *The Makers of Cajun Music.* Austin: University of Texas. 1984. A nice overview that features wonderful photographs, plenty of primary data, and interviews.

Blegan, Theodore. 1979. *Norwegian Emigrant Songs and Ballads*. Reprint. New York: Arno Press.

Densmore, Frances. 1926. *The American Indians and Their Music*. New York: Women's Press. This book provides an overview of Densmore's work to the mid-1920s.

Ethnic Recordings in America: A Neglected Tradition. 1982. Washington, D.C.: Library of Congress. Contains seven essays or articles ranging from an autobiography of Lydia Mendoza to ''Commercial Ethnic Recordings in the United States.''

McAllester, David. 1949. *Peyote Music*. New York: Viking Fund Publications in Anthropology, no. 13. This book looks at the use and importance of peyote in the music and culture of Native Americans.

Nettl, Bruno. 1954. *North American Indian Musical Styles*. Philadelphia: American Folklore Society. Nettl provides a useful overview of the important styles of Native American music found throughout the United States.

Paredes, Americo. 1976. *A Texas-Mexican Cancionero: Folksongs of the Lower Border*. Champaign: University of Illinois Press. An interesting book covering old and new corridos that are found in both Mexico and Texas.

Pena, Manuel. 1985. *The Texas-Mexican Conjunto: History of a Working-Class Music*. Austin: University of Texas Press. The finest book to date on the subject. It is both a musical and historical exploration of this accordion-based music.

Robb, John. 1980. *Hispanic Folk Music of New Mexico and the Southwest: A Self-Portrait of a People*. Norman: University of Oklahoma Press. An important summary of Robb's many years of collecting and studying this music.

Roberts, Helen. 1977. *Ancient Hawaiian Music*. Reprint. New York: Dover Press. A scholarly examination of traditional dance and music that includes extensive musical discussions.

Savoy, Ann. 1984. *Cajun Music: A Reflection of a People*. Vol.1. Gretna, La: Bluebird Press. Although this is primarily a songbook, it includes interviews, background information, and photographs.

Video

Del Mero Corazon (Straight from Their Heart): Love Songs of the Southwest. Flower Films. 28 minutes. Norteño music and culture is the focus of this documentary.

Hawaiian Rainbow. Sony Video Software. 85 minutes. The rich and varied traditions of Hawaiian music, including slack-key guitar and hula chants, are explored here.

Hot Pepper: The Life and Music of Clifton Chenier. Flower Films. 54 minutes. A portrait of the late, undisputed ''King of Zydeco.''

J'ai Ete au Bal. (I Went to the Dance). Arhoolie ARH-V103. 84 minutes. A wonderful documentary about Cajun and zydeco music featuring such masterful musicians as the Balfa Brothers, Queen Ida, and Dennis McGee.

A Jumpin' Night at the Garden of Eden. First Run Features. 75 minutes. A substantial documentary about the history of klezmer from the teens through its revitalization in the 1970s.

Keep Your Heart Strong: Life along the Pow-Wow Trail. 54 minutes. Intermedia Arts Minnesota. This film explores the phenomenon of contemporary Native American powwows.

A Kingdom of Fiddlers. Wisconsin Folk Museum, 100 South 2nd Street, Mt. Horeb, Wisconsin 53572. 18 minutes. This program explores the development of old-time fiddle music in rural Wisconsin communities.

Kuma Hula: Keepers of a Culture. Rhapsody Films. 85 minutes. A detailed study of hula music and dancers, which was shot in the late 1980s by Robert Mugge.

Spend It All. Flower Films. 30 minutes. This is a lusty look at Cajun culture, which highlights the music of Marc Savoy, Nathan Abshire, and others.

Tex-Mex: The Music of the Texas-Mexico Borderlands. SHAN-V1206. 60 minutes. A tour of the cantinas, clubs, festivals, and even prisons where Flaco Jiménez, Lydia Mendoza, and others perform.

The Folk Revivals

A "folk **revival**" refers to the interest of younger singers and musicians from outside of a regional or ethnic group in perpetuating its music. And it also stimulates a renewed commercial and popular interest in traditional music. There have been successive waves of folk revivals in each generation as at least some members discover and reinterpret the past. These waves vary in size, intensity, and focus. During strong revivals, our population of guitar pickers and banjo players with ties to traditional music increases. During the twentieth century, early string bands, Appalachian folk songs, and blues have been the object of this curiosity on the part of the general public.

In the 1990s, however, the term also has a more concrete meaning for many people born shortly before or during the "baby boom." For them the folk revival began slowly in the late 1950s and peaked with the 1964 **Newport Folk Festival** when **Bob Dylan** first appeared in public with an electric guitar. This specific revival evokes a certain nostalgia for aging baby boomers: simpler times before the Vietnam War fully exploded, their own misspent youth, civil rights struggles, sing-alongs at hootenannies, and "Puff the Magic Dragon." Much of this chapter focuses on the folk revival that lasted from the late 1950s through the middle 1960s.

The musicians who are associated with this folk revival belong to two related, but separate, groups. Let's look at them in order to help reinforce the earlier distinctions between folk music and folk based music. In one group are folk musicians such as Mississippi John Hurt (blues) and Bill Monroe (bluegrass). Their music was "bred in the bone." Both of these influential musicians grew up within the musical culture, not to mention the racial and regional communities, that spawned blues and bluegrass.

The other group of musicians consists of those who interpret folk music. Eric von Schmidt, for instance, generally performs blues. He was born and raised in Westport, Connecticut, and studied art on a Fulbright scholarship in Florence, Italy, in the early 1950s. During the late 1950s and early 1960s, von Schmidt played blues around New England, particularly in the greater Boston area. Despite his love and respect for Sleepy John Estes and Leadbelly, Eric von Schmidt grew up within the white middle class, far from the direct ties to African American culture and music. Von Schmidt later consciously chose to step outside of his own background and identify with the very expressive language of black American blues. Traditional music also inspired Bob Dylan, Joan Baez, and Tom Rush, who began their careers by singing their own interpretations of folk songs but who have evolved into highly respected singer/songwriters. Such musicians play folk music or folk based music, rather than being folk musicians themselves.

Red Roots

Many of the musicians who cut their teeth during the folk revival were inspired not only by traditional music but by an older generation of traditional or folk based musicians. The early sixties folk revival was simply another retrospective; one of the periodic, popular excursions into our unique American roots. This was not the first twentieth-century reevaluation that resulted in commercial viability. During the late teens, Henry Ford tried to revitalize American folk dance in the Midwest with his ''old-time'' bands that featured hammered dulcimers.

Traditional music cast in a more politicized form crept into the American consciousness beginning in the middle 1930s, spurred on by the Depression and left-wing activists who viewed it as the ''voice of the people.'' The veterans of this movement largely served as role models for the early 1960s folk revival.

M u s i c a l   E x a m p l e

Woody Guthrie contributed many great songs to our contemporary musical culture: ''Vigilante Man,'' ''Pastures of Plenty,'' ''This Land Is Your Land,'' and many others. ''Do, Re, Mi'' is a fine example of the socialist protest songs that he began performing in the late 1930s. A committed popularist and socialist, Guthrie lived through the Depression and felt a great deal of animosity towards the capitalist system that seemed to offer much but deliver little. Guthrie lost a long battle to Huntington's Chorea (a slowly debilitating neurological disease) in 1967 that began affecting him some fifteen years before. [Folkways 2481]

Title ''Do, Re, Mi''
Performer Woody Guthrie
Instruments guitar and vocal
Length 2:29
Notable Features

1. It is performed in a major tonality.
2. The simple finger-picked guitar accompaniment to his laconic vocal forms a homophonic texture.
3. The song is structured in an *ab* form.
4. The melody is relatively conjunctive and uncomplicated.
5. Guthrie's nasal, relaxed vocal falls into the middle register.

Lots of folks back east they say,
Leavin' home every day,
Beatin' a hot old dusty way to the California line.
'Cross the desert sands they roll
Gettin' out of that old dust bowl.
Think they're a coming' to a sugar bowl,
But here's what they find:
Oh, the police at the port of entry say,
''You're number 14,000 for today!'' Oh!

Refrain:

If you ain't got that do, re, mi, folks,
If you ain't got that do, re, mi,
Why you'd better go back to beautiful Texas,
Oklahoma, Kansas, Georgia, Tennessee;
California's a garden of Eden,
A paradise to live in or see;
But, believe it or not,
You won't find it so hot
If you ain't got the do, re, mi!

If you want to buy a home or farm,
That can't do nobody harm,
Or take your vacation by the mountains or sea,
Don't swap your old cow for a car,
You'd better stay right where you are,
You'd better take this little tip from me.
'Cause I look through the want ads every day,
But the headlines in the paper always say.

Refrain:

Not all of the folk based music from this period was overtly political. Another group viewed folk music as a bucolic escape from the pressures of the modern world and a return to traditional American values. Some, such as Richard Chase, spent much of their energy collecting folktales and songs, performing only occasionally. Others, like John Jacob Niles, used it as an apolitical springboard to further themselves. Trained as an opera singer, Niles parlayed his Kentucky heritage into a new career. He also displayed a modest ability to play his own unique, homemade instrument which he called a dulcimer but which is only distantly related to the standard plucked Appalachian dulcimer. Niles brought his unique interpretations of this music, an uneasy mix of formal ''old world'' sensibilities with Southern American folk, to audiences across the country and made some commercially successful recordings for Victor.

Meanwhile **Pete Seeger,** the **Almanac Singers, Moses Asch,** Woody Guthrie, the Weavers, **Alan Lomax,** and Leadbelly established themselves as integral parts of the politicized folk song movement. Dr. Charles Seeger, an eminent academic musicologist and patriarch of the famed musical family, served as a de facto cultural commissar of this movement. The ''folk camps''

Folk song collector Richard
Chase performing in the late
1930s.
Library of Congress.

(Pineville, Kentucky), craft schools (Penland, North Carolina), and experimental colleges (Black Mountain College) began in the 1930s to explore the possibilities music holds as an agent for social change and to reexamine America's "identity." Union organizing and workers rights were also major issues, as was the role of the Communist party in helping to reshape the United States. The Communist newspaper the *People's World* once described this music as "the songs of people, of farmers, of workers, of laborers, and they come from the directed contact with their work, whatever it is. . ." (Denisoff 1971, 59).

This was a time for protest songs that decried the social and economic condition of many Americans. The capitalist system was carefully scrutinized and criticized by singers, many of whom belonged to or sympathized with the American Communist party. Struggles for the recognition of unions, especially in the Appalachian coalfields, were one central theme. Several of the New York City–based activists, notably Seeger and Lomax, helped to bring recognition for the battles fought by their Kentucky brothers and sisters. During the late 1930s, Aunt Molly Jackson, Sarah Ogan, and Jim Garland often sung at union rallies held in the Northeast to raise money for Kentucky union members. They sang the decidedly pro-union "Which Side Are You On?" which opens like an old British broadside:

> Come all of you good workers
> Good news to you I'll tell
> Of how the good old union
> has come in here to dwell.

For these protest singers, folk music was the people's music and it served a political end. The period at the beginning of World War II marked a renaissance, a sort of "folk music revival" that emphasized our underrepresented working class. Folk music came into vogue and could be heard in a variety of informal contexts. These musicians, most of them white, performed at parties, Communist party fund-raisers, and pro-union rallies. In New York City, the Almanac Singers stood at the core of this movement. They were formed in

1941 and originally consisted of Pete Seeger, Lee Hays, Millard Lampell, and John Peter Hawes. Shortly thereafter, Woody Guthrie joined the group, which was dedicated to writing and singing topical ''folk'' songs favoring the left wing. Their ranks also included black blues singer Josh White, who had moved to New York City from South Carolina in search of a new audience. For this collective, the worker, folk, and people meant the same thing. They lived together in a communal house in Greenwich Village and everyone contributed to the expenses. The Almanac Singers represent the quintessence of the left-wing urban folk song movement of the late 1930s and early 1940s.

The outbreak of World War II slowed down their activity as both Pete Seeger and Woody Guthrie served overseas. But the message rang back clearly following Japan's surrender in 1945. Most of these folks remained active into the 1950s, making the occasional commercial foray into mainstream America. This segment of American culture stood poised and ready to gain their greatest commercial viability when Peter, Paul, and Mary began to hit the big time.

Mass Media and Popular Culture

One obvious question is what caused this particular revival? As traditional music became more widely exposed through the mass electronic media, their base of commercial support moved far beyond the communities that spawned them. Music lovers eventually consumed greater amounts of music by way of their radios and phonograph records and, eventually, television. Urban in-migration, modernization, and the development of suburban tract homes placed more Americans even further from their rural roots. Although major record companies never stopped selling traditional music, their interest in it stumbled three separate times: following the Depression's devastation; the middle 1950s, as rock 'n' roll was suddenly catapulted into the commercial spotlight; and the years that began with the ''**British Invasion**'' music. Such changes do not occur overnight, of course, but the banishment of blues, gospel, and types of folk music from the powerful mass media that touch hundreds of millions of American citizens was swift and undeniable.

The radio was one of the media that reacted most quickly to the changing forces in American popular and folk culture. Outside of urban centers, the early morning farm reports and live fifteen-minute country music shows continued hand in hand well into the 1950s. In upstate New York, for example, the vestiges of this era remained for many years. The last early morning farm market report that I recall hearing on Schenectady's 50,000-watt giant WGY occurred around 1966. As television gradually lured more of the audience and the personalities away from radio, both media have become mired in a blur of network programs. The style and content of programming in both radio and television are very similar no matter where you travel in the United States.

Record companies followed a similar path. The eclectic, local, traditional performers that were documented prior to 1930—including such delights as Six Cylinder Smith, Carter Brothers and Sons, and Emery Glenn—were now considered anachronistic and noncommercial. Major companies stuck with proven sellers, most of whom were not folk musicians. A handful of small companies, such as Timely and Asch (New York City), emerged in the late 1930s. They stepped in to help fulfill this need, but they only issued a handful of records before Word War II virtually ground their business to a halt.

Hundreds of small, short-lived companies sprang up across the United States following World War II: Macys in Houston; Mutual in Bassett, Virginia; J. V. B. in Detroit; and RPM in Los Angeles. The majority of the **independent record companies** suffered from undercapitalization and went bankrupt because of the cash-flow drain. However, they were more willing to gamble on untried talent of all descriptions, and they fundamentally replaced the major companies in marketing folk music and records with regional appeal, including polka music, blues, and white gospel music.

As the interest of large, corporate entities in American roots traditions declined, there was a concurrent rise in the number and popularity of interpreters of vernacular music. Doris Day, Patti Page, and Tennessee Ernie Ford moved out of their usual pop music territory during the 1950s to provide record companies with their own versions of traditional material. Groups like the Weavers, which helped propel Pete Seeger's performing career, proved immensely successful in the early 1950s. Between 1950 and 1952, this group sold over four million copies of records for Decca with their interpretations of Leadbelly's "Goodnight, Irene"; Woody Guthrie's "So Long, It's Been Good to Know You"; two African-inspired tunes, "Tzena, Tzena" and "Wimoweh"; as well as "Kisses Sweeter Than Wine." The lush orchestrations of noted arranger Gordon Jenkins adorned most of the Weavers' records, a far cry from the music's roots but symptomatic of its blanching. Such an aesthetic compromise appeared to be necessary in order to make the music palatable to the widest possible audience. For better or for worse, Pete Seeger had become a viable commercial entity, and he found it difficult to negotiate this exceptionally treacherous path.

The early 1950s can now be seen as a dark, ominous period in American politics that affected our entire society. Joseph McCarthy led the Communist witch-hunt, resulting in a muted creative period in all of the arts. The blacklisting of television and radio writers for left-wing sympathies resonated with the "red taint" of the late 1930s and disrupted the careers of many authors and actors. In 1954 Elvis Presley burst into American popular culture, helping to dispel some of the gloom with his brazen, timeless message of teenage angst and sensual lust. Elvis and his Sun Record cohorts—Jerry Lee Lewis, Carl Perkins, Johnny Cash, and Roy Orbison—pioneered rock 'n' roll, moving grass-roots music further away from the American culture that nurtured it and into a commercial purgatory.

Field Research

Of course, the scholarly interest in vernacular music never totally dissipated. A few dedicated researchers continued scouting the countryside, particularly in the South, for undiscovered talent. Harold Courlander, for instance, spent a

Alan Lomax and his sister, Bess Lomax Hawes, performing in the late 1970s.
Smithsonian Institution.

considerable amount of time in Alabama recording black folk musicians in the early-to-mid 1950s. He stayed in one community for an extended period of time, concentrating on every expression of folk music that he could locate within a limited geographic boundary. The Guggenheim Foundation sponsored Courlander's field research, which resulted in a well-respected book, *Negro Folk Music U.S.A.,* and several long-playing phonograph records on Folkways that serve as an important model for the presentation of field research.

Alan Lomax returned from his self-imposed European exile in 1956 and soon resumed his American fieldwork. In 1958 and 1959, Lomax reprised his Library of Congress style that began on the trips with his father in 1933–34. These sweeping trips carried Lomax across the entire South, resulting in the ''Southern Folk Heritage'' series on Atlantic and Prestige's ''Southern Journey'' set of records. These recordings brought important singers like Mississippi bluesman Fred McDowell to the attention of the general public just as the folk revival was beginning.

Motivated by an interest in early New Orleans jazz, **Samuel Charters** moved to New Orleans in 1950 and slowly involved himself in researching blues music. One of the pioneers in the field, Charters recalls these heady days as a young white man in the South looking for the lost blues legends that had appeared on race records some thirty years before:

It is impossible to imagine how much that seemed like a lost world—it was like Atlantis! We had no idea what this world was like, what it represented, and if we would find people from it. When I suddenly began finding that these men were relatively young and that many of them were still alive, I was stunned. The first book that I wrote, *The Country Blues* [1959], I wrote in a very exaggerated, purposefully over-romanticized style. I did it on purpose to emphasize the romance of finding old blues singers. At that point in the '50s I had the South to myself. Nobody else was doing this. I didn't have any money. I didn't have any university affiliation. I was simply on the road in battered old cars that I borrowed. . . '' (Charters, interview with the author, Dec. 12, 1988).

These men simply reconfirmed what is now abundantly clear: regional folk music had not expired, it merely disappeared from the commercial marketplace. Contradances in Vermont never stopped, not all of Montana's cowboy singers had ridden into their final sunset, nor had the all-day African American ''shape-note'' singings in the Deep South entirely ceased. And although they have been staples of regional American culture, many years would pass before Tex-Mex cuisine, blackened fish, and Cajun two-step dancing would became chic in New York City. Such traditions are submerged from the view of most Americans, who remain largely ignorant of the regional traditions across the United States outside of their immediate view or own experience.

The 1960s Folk Revival

The corporate interest in the folk revival really began in 1958 when the Kingston Trio recorded ''Tom Dooley,'' a murder ballad that Frank Warner had collected in western North Carolina from banjo player and singer Frank Proffitt. Their version was a million-seller, and its success motivated others to reexamine folk music in a more commercial light. Such trends led to an upswing in folk music gatherings and the development of groups such as the Brothers Four, the Limeliters, and other neo-folkies. By the early 1960s, the revival was in full swing, and the more enterprising people once more began marketing this music to a mass audience. This was even true on college campuses as it gradually became fashionable to once again study the printed legacy of James Francis Child and John Lomax's early work with cowboy singers.

Traditional music suddenly found itself back in demand. Younger people exposed to this music for the first time picked up a guitar or banjo and learned their rudiments in order to become a folk singer. The music was called ''folk'' because of its Southern background, its roots in traditional forms, the fact that it was largely played on acoustic instruments, and for lack of any other convenient term. To be a folk singer was in vogue and trendy.

Subscriptions to magazines such as *Sing Out!* (founded in 1952) increased. *Broadside,* which featured topical and left-wing protest songs, and the more clean-cut *Hootenanny* became new additions to newsstands. Not all of the performers caught up in this movement were white-bread, clean-cut college students singing and playing in their local coffeehouses. In addition to the authentic folk musicians, other singers fit into the mold of *Hard Hitting Songs for Hard Hit People,* a collection of American protest songs from the 1930s to the 1950s. This was the new generation of protest singers in the tradition of Woody Guthrie, Cisco Houston, and Pete Seeger, who looked at music as a vehicle for social change.

The civil rights movement and the slowly expanding Vietnam War provided the perfect fodder for these topical performers. Mark Spoelstra, Peter LaFarge, Buffy Sainte-Marie, Joan Baez, Phil Ochs, and Tom Paxton were among the most visible members of this clique. Suddenly, musicians with acoustical instruments and songs about troubling themes attracted record contracts, some with major companies like Columbia. While the large companies wanted a slice of the folk music pie, they remained skeptical of the movement's political implications. The McCarthy era had begun less than one decade before, and major American corporations are inherently conservative. In the late 1950s, independent companies such as Electra and **Folkways** struggled to fill this void.

Folkways actually began in 1939 when Moses Asch, a Polish-born immigrant who arrived in the United States at the end of World War I, started the Asch Record Company. It all but shut down in 1941 due to the shellac shortage caused by World War II. When the war abated, Asch countered first with the Disc Record Company of America and then Folkways in 1947. His purpose was to record all types of oral material, including jazz, poetry, ethnic

---

M u s i c a l   E x a m p l e

When the Harvesters (Ethal Raim, Joyce Gluck, Walter Raim, and Ronnie Gluck) recorded this selection in 1959, they had just arrived in Hollywood after a long drive from New York City. They were a prototypical ''folk group''; Ethal Raim worked for *Sing Out!* and taught at the Neighborhood Music School, while Walter had been an assistant conductor of the [Harry] Belafonte Folksingers. The Glucks worked at other full-time jobs and played music on the side. The Jewish Young Folksingers Chorus served as an important, common bond, and one of their aims was performing songs from around the world in Yiddish, Spanish, and Hebrew. This selection, however, is one of Woody Guthrie's best-known songs and speaks of his dream for a truly United States of America. [Folkways 2406]

Title ''This Land Is Your Land''
Performers The Harvesters
Instruments banjo, bass, guitar, four voices
Length 2:16
Notable Features

1. It is performed in a major tonality.
2. Loose harmony singing can be heard on the chorus.
3. The voices fit into middle registers.
4. A simple duple (2/4) meter is heard throughout.
5. It uses a verse-chorus form.
6. A pleasantly rich homophonic texture is established by the mixture of the voice and instruments.
7. The lead singers alternate throughout the song.

Refrain:

This land is your land, this land is my land,
From California to the New York island;
From the Redwood forest to the Gulfstream waters,
This land is made for you and me.

As I went walking that ribbon of highway,
I saw above me that endless skyway,
I saw below me that golden valley,
This land is made for you and me.

Refrain:

I roamed and rambled, and I followed my footsteps,
To the sparkling sands of her diamond deserts,
And all around me, a voice was sounding,
This land was made for you and me.

Refrain:

When the sun came shining, then I was strolling,
And the wheat fields waving, and the dust clouds rolling,
This land was made for you and me.

Refrain:

traditions, the sounds of insects, and grass roots music. Asch himself muses about his work:

> To do a record is to create art, content, and package. I had to do something that would work visually. I issued folk music, which was the bastardized pop of the day, to an audience who would appreciate it even though the guy who sang it was an old black country musician. I had to show this had value and content.

The cover of one of Folkways' most political albums, issued in 1960. *Folkways Archive/Smithsonian Institution.*

> Woody Guthrie came to New York City. He came to me and said, ''This is my home and I want to express myself here.'' We understood each other. Woody was a true hippie, illustrative of Walt Whitman. . . . He had a frame and he used the music of American folk song as the base for his words. Woody would fit it into what he wanted to say'' (Asch, interview with Mike Shwartz, 1971, in Folkways Archives).

By the height of the revival, Moses Asch had already issued over a score of records by Pete Seeger, Woody Guthrie, and the **New Lost City Ramblers.** His stable also included several multi-record sets that surveyed American folk music and history in songs. Albums by blues performers such as Brownie McGhee and Leadbelly and country music pioneer Ernest Stoneman dotted the growing catalogue. Asch himself estimated that Pete Seeger's Folkways records annually sold between thirty and forty thousand during the early 1960s. Seeger performed regularly at hootenannies, clubs, and churches. His peripatetic lifestyle brought him across the entire country and much of the world. Moe Asch also gave voice to newer and younger folk based singers like singer/guitarist **Dave Van Ronk,** who was caught up at the vortex of the revival.

Dave Van Ronk, too, was attracted to American vernacular music, but early jazz emerged as his first love. He recalls that

> what molded me musically, were the 'moldy-fig' wars of the late 1940s. . .the traditionalists, who I call the Platonists, felt there was an original form that was pure. They felt the original form had degenerated, so here we have Preservation Hall [New Orleans's famous jazz club] as Plato's Cave. The modernists were aesthetic Darwinists and I think they were every bit as stupid. What is newer and more 'developed' is not necessarily better. You can't apply either yardstick to aesthetics. . . . Being an adolescent at the time, I was an absolutist and I had to jump one way or the other. As soon as I was aware that this titanic tempest-in-a-teapot was going down. . . I stopped listening to my Dizzy Gillespie records for about seven years. I got over it. I'm happy that I have a huge collection of Gillespie and Parker!'' (This and all other quotes from Van Ronk are taken from an interview with the author on January 21, 1991.)

For about five or six years, Van Ronk stuck with traditional jazz. A high school dropout, Van Ronk was determined to make his living through musical performance. So he moved to Manhattan and promptly lost forty pounds that first year away from home. He not only played guitar, he usually took over the vocal chores because he didn't mind and could sing loudly. However, by the middle 1950s, the ''steam had just totally gone out of the traditional jazz revival'' to the point that he'd often ''play for Union scale and have to slip them back something under the table. You were lucky to get two gigs in a week, more often you'd get one gig in two weeks.''

Although Van Ronk loved this music, his future as a performer of traditional jazz seemed bleak. Van Ronk, along with others interested in old 78-RPM records from the 1920s and 1930s, used to haunt the Jazz Record Center at 47th Street where the blues and jazz records were often mixed together. This is where he got a taste for Southern blues singers such as King Solomon Hill, Blind Lemon Jefferson, and Furry Lewis. He gradually gained a greater taste and appreciation for folk music, especially blues, and decided to make a switch from jazz to folk. After all, he already had both the basic guitar technique and a powerful, gruff voice.

Van Ronk views this move as ''technically retrogressive and partly lateral.'' It was also a sound, and not surprising, aesthetic decision because of his ongoing interest in the grass roots of twentieth-century American music. Just as the Russians were becoming the first to get into the space age by putting up Sputnik, Dave Van Ronk was making the more earthy transition to folk music. It was not that difficult because he moved into a compatible circle of ''neo-ethnics.''

In New York City, these folks tended to congregate in Washington Square. This gathering point not far from New York University at the edge of Greenwich Village became the weekly meeting and training grounds for folk music. People came to swap songs, look over banjos and guitars, talk about upcoming gigs, and see their friends. Barry Kornfeld, a thoughtful veteran of the scene, wrote in the August/September 1959 issue of *Caravan* magazine: ''At 2 PM every Sunday, from the first balmy days of April to the last of the fair October weather, large numbers of instrumentalists and singers gather, from whose ranks there will emerge some fine professionals and some equally fine, or at least equally intense, amateurs who will follow in the footsteps of their predecessors. [We] presupposed the existence of Washington Square gatherings as we had presupposed the existence of grass, trees, and, of course, park departments.''

The Washington Square scene really began in the middle 1940s, about the time that World War II drew to a close. Musicians such as George Magolin, who today is as obscure to most folk music lovers as the Six Foot Dilly, would play his guitar in the afternoons. More famous ''folkies'' also made their way to Washington Square during the immediate postwar years. Fiddler Allan Block, Tom Paley (later of the New Lost City Ramblers), Harry Belafonte, progressive banjo wizard Roger Sprung, and Pete Seeger could be heard there on a good day. This assembly point was a true institution by the time that Dave Van Ronk himself became a regular there in the middle 1950s.

These Washington Square hootenannies were rather informal affairs, mostly for fun. Van Ronk often performed by himself, but for awhile he teamed with Roy Berkeley and they played as the "Traveling Trotskyite Troubadours." Perhaps as an antidote to Bobby Darin, Frank Sinatra, and other contemporary popular singers, it was also a multiethnic group eager for new musical experiences. Live music and musical interaction were the key. Van Ronk recalls that "the people that I was hanging around with were into all kinds of stuff; everything from bluegrass to African cabaret music. All across the boards. I was a sponge . . . picked up everything that I heard. Everything was going into the same meat-grinder. All of us were sort of like that. People specialized in old-time music would all of a sudden launch into a country blues. It was much more eclectic."

And it became more serious, too, as people decided to try and make a living from playing folk music. The Folk Singers Guild was one response to this new interest in traditional music. Though not an all-encompassing organization, the Folk Singers Guild nonetheless affected the New York City folk scene. The hundred or so members were mostly, but not all, musicians. Washington Square served as the primary venue for most Guild members; however, it also organized a few small concerts in local halls. Van Ronk recalls that "we used to go over to the Sullivan Street Playhouse. . . in the days before *The Fantasticks* moved in. It was on Sunday nights when they were 'dark.' We would have three, four or five people doing maybe twenty minutes or a half hour. That was really the only playing experience that most of us got. There wasn't anything else; there were no clubs. . . . Gerdes [Folk City] didn't start until about '61.''

Paul Clayton, one of the most active New York folksingers in the late 1950s, refused to join the Folk Singers Guild. He used to attend meetings but would never join because he was a professional who made his living singing and recording. By 1960 Clayton had made at least a dozen albums and had served as Van Ronk's principal mentor. Black guitarist Rev. Gary Davis became another of his heroes, and he learned much from the older man's highly influential finger-picking style. Van Ronk views Davis as a peer, albeit "older, more experienced, . . . and more talented." They worked many of the same clubs and Van Ronk became most intimately acquainted with the Reverend Davis in the late 1950s. In 1961 he was booking acts for one of the coffeehouses on McDougal and remembers, "I had Gary there every possible time I could. Unless it was an absolute full house, then I would be sitting in front of the stage watching those fingers. That's the only way you can really learn. I'd ask him, 'How do you do this?' He'd be only too happy to show me [and] then he'd cackle when I got it wrong, which was usually. It was that kind of thing that Gary and I had in common."

McDougal Street was home to Van Ronk at this time. Izzy Young's Folklore Center, which served as the informal headquarters for New York City's folksingers, sat just a few doors down from Van Ronk's apartment. This long, narrow store was crammed full of books, records, and posters announcing folk and jazz events. A friendly, rambling establishment, the Folklore Center became the crossroads and switchboard for local folksingers as well as visitors. Young presented some of the first concerts by the New Lost City Ramblers and Peggy Seeger and Ewan MacColl. He later served as the booker for Gerdes's Folk City when it was still called the Fifth Fret. "If somebody came into town and wanted to get a hold of someone or wanted it to be known that they were there . . . they went to the Center and Izzy would broadcast it; whether you wanted him to or not!"

Some singers, including Van Ronk, virtually lived at the Folklore Center. Folksingers, instrument makers, entrepreneurs, and budding academic folklorists could be found there. College programs in folklore were new, and several Washington Square/Folklore Center regulars were attracted to the scholarly life. But in the late 1950s, Roger Abrahams, Ellen Steckert, and Kenny Goldstein, each of whom eventually earned a Ph.D. in folklore and taught in universities, hung out there. Abrahams and Steckert went on to record for Folkways, while Goldstein eventually produced scores of folk music records for a variety of labels.

M u s i c a l   E x a m p l e

A longtime resident of the Northeast, Sandy Ives has for many years taught English and folklore at the University of Maine. In 1959 Ives included this song on a collection that he recorded for Moses Asch. Most of the songs were collected directly from older singers in Maine, often from men working at lumbering camps or fishermen, and they often sang about their life and work. This one he learned from Charles Sibley of Argyle, Maine, and its title refers to the small log buildings in which the lumbermen lived. Notice that it starts with the formulaic greeting so common in native American ballads. [Folkways 5323]

Title "The Shanty Boys"
Performer Edward "Sandy" Ives
Instruments guitar and voice
Length 2:25
Notable Features

1. The song is set in a major tonality.
2. Ives sings in the middle register with a very relaxed voice.
3. You hear a spare, homophonic texture.
4. Its musical form is strophic.

Come all ye good jolly fellows, come listen to my song.
It's about the shanty boys and they get along.
We're all good, jolly fellows as you will ever find
To wear away the winter months a-whaling down the pine.

The chopper and the sawyer, they lay the timber low.
The swamper and the teamster, they haul it to and fro.
You ought to hear our foreman soon after the break of day.
"Load up your team two thousand feet—to the river you'll steer away."

Crack! Snap! goes my whip, I whistle and I sing.
I sit upon my timber load as happy as a king.
My horses they are ready and I am never sad.
There's no one now so happy as the jolly shanty lad.

Noon will soon be over, to us the foreman will say,
"Put down you saws and ax, my boys, for here's your pork and beans."
Arriving at the shanty, 'tis then the fun begins.
A-dippelin' in the water pail and dinglin' of the tin.

And then to us the cook will say, "Come fella, come fly, come Joe.
Come pass around the water pail as far as the water goes."
As soon as lunch is over, to us the foreman will say,
"Put on your coat and cap, my boys, to the woods we'll bear away."

We all go out with a cheerful heart and a well-contented mind,
The days don't seem so long among the way pine.
You ought to hear our foreman, soon after the sun goes down,
"Put down your saws and ax, my boys, to the shanty we are bound."

Arriving at the shanty with wet and damp, cold feet,
We all put off our larrigans, our suppers for to eat.
We all play cards 'til nine o'clock, then into our bunks we climb,
To wear away the winter months a-whaling down the pine.

Goldstein, in fact, recorded and initially notated Van Ronk's Folkways recordings. Intent on getting a recording out to the public in order to promote his folksinging career, Van Ronk bothered everyone he could think of in the business. Dave finally got both Electra and Lyrichord interested in him, but in 1959 he convinced Moe Asch that he was actually ready to record. And Kenny Goldstein served as the A and R (artist and repertoire) man and the basic link between Van Ronk and Moe Asch. Van Ronk recalls: "Kenny came to pick me up; he drove me out to Long Island, where he was living at the time. He had a little studio in his basement. I think I did it in one session, certainly no more than two. I'll say this for him, [Kenny] got a better quality recording in his basement than Moe did in the more formal studio set-up. . . . He let me call the shots pretty much. I'd worked out the arrangements and these things were pretty much standards in my repertoire. They were worked out carefully; I'd been honing them for some time.''

The selections that Van Ronk recorded for Folkways and other smaller companies draw largely from African American music. They reflect a clear, long-standing interest in his heroes; among them are Bessie Smith, Jelly Roll Morton, Jimmy Yancey, and Louis Armstrong. Van Ronk always admired keyboard players and approached the guitar pianistically, which is one reason why he never played with a slide or bottleneck. Within a few years after making these recordings, Van Ronk's repertoire and approach to music had radically changed. He still loved the early recordings by Scrapper Blackwell, Blind Boy Fuller, Snooks Eaglin, but his own persona began to emerge: ''I was developing an approach and a style that was really quite different from that of my models. A few years down the line, I simply had no interest at all in [merely] emulating my models.''

The movement away from mere emulation described by Van Ronk typifies many in the folk revival. Traditional music first caught the attention of **Judy Collins** and Bob Dylan, but after several years they moved on to more creative pursuits. First they began writing their own material; albums and live performances mixed folk music with original songs. Slowly they moved into the popular mainstream by adding electric instruments and even lush string orchestrations. This process was repeated many times and once again highlights the symbiotic interchange among corporate America, popular culture, and our own grass roots. Professional performers like Buffy Sainte-Marie, Pete Seeger, Tom Paxton, and Joan Baez inarguably helped to ignite a minor musical revolution based on the earlier blues, gospel, and country artists they so admired. However, their careers also intertwined with the cultural upheaval of the 1960s, and they soon moved exclusively into folk based music.

Another independent company, Vanguard Records, began as a classical label but quickly signed Eric Anderson, Buffy Sainte-Marie, Joan Baez, and other folk based artists when their commercial stock rose. These artists did so well that by mid-decade, Vanguard's roster expanded to include Doc Watson, Mississippi John Hurt, and Skip James. The blues sessions were produced by Samuel Charters, who obtained carte blanche in order to build Vanguard's blues roster. Charters also explored the Chicago blues scene, producing an influential three-record set, *The Chicago Blues Today!* The Lawrence Welk Group presently owns the Vanguard catalogue, and Sam Charters has repackaged much of his own material into a new CD-only ''Mid-Line'' series designed to reach a new generation of listeners in the 1990s.

Most of the strong commercial interest focused on younger, city-bred performers. Bob Dylan emerged as the one performer that the major companies could not ignore. After shifting his home from Hibbing, Minnesota, to New York City in 1959, Dylan's personality and music gradually impacted upon

Willard Watson and Doc Watson,
Deep Gap, N.C., 1976.
Ralph Rinzler.

this burgeoning scene. *Broadside* published his songs "Masters of War," "Blowin' in the Wind," and "It's All Right," and he appeared on the cover of *Sing Out!* in October 1962. Dylan himself was dismissed as a performer early in his career. "Can't sing and can't play" was the rap against him. However, he caught not only the attention of commercial folk music enthusiasts but the ear of Columbia Records executive John Hammond, who had previously committed Count Basie and Billie Holiday to contracts. In 1964 Bob Dylan became a Columbia Records artist. One decade later, Hammond's aural facilities for spotting talent once again proved correct when he signed rocker Bruce Springsteen to Columbia Records.

Bob Dylan has profoundly affected American popular music and culture. Except for his early recording (on harmonica) with Mississippi bluesman Big Joe Williams, Dylan's music had few direct connections with authentic American folk music. He was inspired by Woody Guthrie, Pete Seeger, and others, and he continues to acknowledge his debt to the genre. The blues also struck Dylan as powerful music, particularly the message of a song such as Skip James's evocative and poetic "Hard Time Killin' Floor Blues," which he initially recorded in 1931:

> "Hard time here, everywhere you go.
> Times is harder, than ever been before.
> Well the people are drifting from door to door.
> Can't find no heaven, I don't care where you go."

Joan Baez at the Newport
Folk Festival in 1967.
Ralph Rinzler.

But his most significant contribution lies with topical songs and more personal messages aimed at a general audience. Dylan's music is a perfect example of folk based music reaching a mainstream, popular audience. The importance of this distinction becomes clearer in light of Dylan's audiences in 1963 and thereafter.

The famous August 28, 1963, march on Washington, D.C., during which Martin Luther King, Jr., delivered his renowned "I Have a Dream" speech, was attended by Joan Baez, Bob Dylan, and many other city billy commercial folksingers. Dylan lent support to the voting rights and civil rights movements in an event that drew international attention. And he was not the only one to sing out about social injustice and problems. Their course had been charted many years before by the Almanac Singers, among others. Tom Paxton, Peter Krug, Phil Ochs, and countless others felt it their duty to comment upon topical issues of the day, but they also wrote songs based on their own personal discontent, malaise, and social injustice. This trait set them apart from their earlier models and established clear precedents for the careers of popular singer/songwriters such as Joni Mitchell, Tom Rush, Cat Stevens, and Neil Young. Each of these performers was caught up in the "folk boom" and included their own interpretations of traditional material in their repertoires before gaining fame for their own writing.

Although television shows like ABC's "Hootenanny" were broadcast to audiences nationwide, the apex of this revival came with the 1963 Newport Folk Festival. This gathering of protest singers, topical songwriters, commercial folk groups, and traditional musicians such as Doc Watson, Frank Proffitt, and Clarence Ashley drew an unprecedented, huge crowd of thirty-seven thousand people and made a major media splash. Music festivals are nothing new—fiddle contests had been held in the South for decades, and Newport itself had been home to jazz festivals since the 1950s. The 1963 Newport Folk Festival stood as the largest such conclave and a raving success, both in the popular press and the folk community's own publications. Its $70,000 profit also underscored the commercial viability of this music.

The folk revival was not confined to New York City and New England. Coffeehouses and small clubs offered folk entertainment in cities and college campuses across the entire country. In Minneapolis, the white blues trio of Kerner, Glover, and Ray played in churches that turned over their meeting space to a coffeehouse for friends, and eventually at larger folk clubs like the Extrordinaire. Paul Nelson began a small folk music magazine, *The Little Sandy Review,* in 1959. The North Beach of San Francisco was home to many clubs featuring both jazz and folk music. Lou Curtiss started selling instruments and hosting concerts in San Diego in the early 1960s and is still going in the 1990s.

A few musicians caught up in this movement branched out in a new direction. Erik Darling, Frank Hamilton, and Billy Faier all began their careers by learning to play old-time or bluegrass. But within a few years, they began bringing in elements of jazz and influences from non-Western music into their playing. These experimenters from the early 1960s found only a small audience for their hybrids and were about thirty years ahead of their time—by the early 1990s, they seemed to be much closer to the mainstream.

Nineteen sixty-four marked a dramatic change in commercial folk music. After three halcyon years of success, commercial exposure, and a wave of recordings, two major events rocked the relatively small world of American folk music. The summer brought the next Newport Folk Festival with Bob Dylan as one of its principal attractions. Dylan now possessed a public persona that had begun to conflict with the event's self-perception. His motorcycle jacket and electric guitar brought Dylan immediate disfavor. He violated a well-established perception that folk music can't be played on anything that needs to be plugged in—never mind that many country blues players had been using electric guitars for more than a decade. Moreover, his repertoire reflected the undercurrents that flavored his new Columbia issue, *Another Side of Bob Dylan.* Dylan had transcended his role as a ''folksinger'' but was not entirely clear about being an American artist. The moralizing tone of his previous songs was tempered by uncertainty and the feeling that he might not have all of the answers. This new persona, so quickly and unexpectedly revealed at Newport, had serious repercussions within the community of commercial folksingers. Over cups of coffee and in the folk press, the debate raged over this turn of events: had Dylan sold out, where was folk music headed, is folk music becoming too commercial? This angst only fueled the winds of change blown in by the new ''Mercy-Beat'' records.

During the folk revival, rock 'n' roll and black rhythm and blues had entered a near-moribund phase. Elvis had joined the army, Chuck Berry was in jail, Jerry Lee Lewis became a *persona non grata* after marrying his thirteen-year-old cousin, and then Buddy Holly died in a plane crash. Furthermore, no new cult heroes emerged in the popular music scene. Black pop music remained equally quiet, though the Motown Sound was about to emerge from Berry Gordy's Detroit studio. In fact, there was precious little new to prick the ears and libidos of white and black teenagers. Folk songs offered adults a brief respite from the hybrid, African American–inspired music of rockabilly and rock 'n' roll. This bucolic era lasted until the ''British Invasion'' of 1964 brought the equally subversive sounds of the Beatles, the Rolling Stones, the Dave Clark Five, and others into homes across the United States.

The revival sagged by the late 1960s, at least from a purely commercial perspective. It helped to create some hybrids, such as the **folk rock** of the Byrds and the Flying Burrito Brothers, who reached across the United States with their blend brewed at clubs like the Ash Grove in Los Angeles. Post-1965 Bob Dylan can also be considered a folk rocker. His records with The Band are particularly fine examples of folk based rock music. Simon and Garfunkel, Tim Hardin, and Leonard Cohen are also products of this movement. On the West Coast, folk-rock was smoothed out yet more and popularized by the Lovin' Spoonful, the Mamas and the Papas, and Sonny and Cher. The peak of commercial success for folk-inspired rock and pop music was 1965 and 1966.

Inevitably, the rise of Haight-Ashbury and *Sgt. Pepper's Lonely Hearts Club Band* heralded another shift in American popular culture, one that expanded people's minds away from folk music into other realms. By 1970 Americans had lived through acid rock, the 1968 Democratic Convention, massive music festivals at Woodstock and Monterey, Richard Nixon's election, the ''Summer of Love,'' as well as the deaths of Janis Joplin, Jimi Hendrix, and the folk revival. Meantime, the Vietnam War staggered on into the 1970s.

But this grass roots movement continues today, and the interest in folk culture remains very eclectic. Individual coffeehouses can be found across the United States, but now folk music associations abound. The combined Washington, D.C., and Baltimore metropolitan areas alone contain the Middle Maryland Folklore Association, the Folklore Society of Greater Washington, the Western Maryland Folklore Society, the Baltimore Folklore Society, and several other smaller organizations. These groups are supported by thousands of members, and each one publishes a monthly newsletter that lists musical events at local clubs, informal shape-note sings, and workshops for learning to write folk songs. They also include schedules for English morris dancing, swing dance events, New England contradancing, square dances, Swedish couple dancing, and other events related to ethnic and folk dancing.

A British Invasion

Shortly after Dylan's Newport appearance, the number of records by British musicians became a full-fledged onslaught. Their music began to appear on the American charts, supplanting Motown artists, pop vocalists, and the commercial folk balladeers. The Beatles, Beau Brummels, Herman's Hermits, Rolling Stones, Dave Clark Five, and the Animals became fixtures on American Top 40 radio. By late 1964 these groups, and others, had begun to tour the United States. The early appearances by the Beatles represented a phenomenon in American popular culture that surpassed the mania displayed for Elvis Presley when his career was launched in 1955.

Significantly, most of these British groups displayed a strong propensity towards American vernacular culture and music. Led by the Beatles, the Rolling Stones, and the Who, British groups assaulted our popular culture with their unique hybrid of electric guitars, working-class English sensibilities, and a distinctive love for black American music. Many of these musicians had been attracted to this music during the ''skiffle-band'' (a British version of folk music mixed with rockabilly) era of the middle-to-late 1950s. This led many British youths to discover the imported recordings of Howlin' Wolf, Chuck Berry, Robert Johnson, Muddy Waters, Memphis Minnie, and Leadbelly. The middle 1960s saw ''cover'' versions of American blues music by English rock groups appearing on radios and records in homes across the United States. American youth raved over the Rolling Stones' version of Howlin' Wolf's ''Little Red Rooster,'' Cream's cover of ''Outside Woman Blues'' (Blind Willie Reynolds), Sonny Boy Williamson's ''Eyesight to the Blind'' by the Who, and Led Zeppelin's rendition of ''You Shook Me'' (Willie Dixon). No doubt only the most hip American listeners understood the arcane British allusions to blues culture, such as the fact that the Moody Blues are named for a song performed by Louisiana harp blower Slim Harpo in 1963.

American blues musicians such as Big Bill and Muddy Waters began touring England and Europe in the middle 1950s. By 1963 packaged ''folk blues'' tours became annual overseas events, and the Yardbirds (featuring Jimmy Page and Eric Clapton) began recording with touring stars like Sonny Boy Williamson and Memphis Slim. The combination of touring American blues heroes and the easy availability of early and current blues records only helped to reinforce the popularity of blues in England. So did its lyrics about fun, sexuality, and alienation, three themes that appealed to aspiring, adolescent musicians.

Some of the early blues reissue records also had profound impact upon future rock megastars. Eric Clapton liked the electric blues, but the country blues was his first, true passion. Mississippi Delta blues singer Robert Johnson was his hero: ''I was around fifteen or sixteen, and it came as something of a shock to me that there could be anything that powerful. . . . If you didn't know who Robert Johnson was I wouldn't talk to you. . . . It was as if I had been prepared to receive Robert Johnson, almost like a religious experience. . . . His music remains the most powerful cry that I think that you can find in the human voice, really'' (from the booklet accompanying *Robert Johnson: The Complete Recordings,* pp. 22–23).

The Blues Boom

This lionization of the African American blues tradition by Europeans led not only to increased record sales and tours overseas but to a renewed interest in this country. The swift change in popular tastes and the general interest in blues truly surprised Sam Charters, who recalls that

I wrote *The Country Blues* and it came out in 1959, and I went to Europe for one year. . . . I had gone simply to get myself away from what I had been doing steadily for ten years. I wanted to get on with my own creative work, I'd always thought of myself as a writer, not as a researcher. I came back in 1961 and the whole world was searching for their local blues singer. They had a copy of *The Country Blues* in one pocket and a tape recorder in hand! To go with the book I did the first RBF album, which sold and sold and sold. Virtually every song on it was picked-up, like ''Statesboro Blues'' and ''Walk Right In,'' of course. I think that record did as much as anything to introduce the blues. It was the first time that anyone had really heard this. RBF [a reissue record company owned by Folkway's Moe Asch] was set up to be my window to the world. I did 24 or 25 of them rather quickly. At about the same time I did the Lightnin' Hopkins recording, which caused an enormous stir. So suddenly it was obvious that there was something out there'' (Charters, interview with the author, Dec. 12, 1988).

Significantly, the consciousness-raising occurred primarily among young whites. Worn copies of race records began appearing on tapes that circulated within a small circle of dedicated fans, and in 1964 OJL (Origin Jazz Library) became the first record company devoted to reissuing this music on long-playing records. The interest on the part of younger whites also resulted in the rediscovery of older blues musicians who had recorded in the 1920s and 1930s. Using clues gleaned from race records, Dick Spottswood, Nick Perls, John Fahey, and others traveled across the Deep South locating Robert Wilkins, Skip James, Eddie ''Son'' House, Mississippi John Hurt, and Bukka White. These men launched new, albeit brief, musical careers complete with concert tours and recordings. Due to declining health or shifts in interests, other surviving musicians from this era—Gus Cannon, Memphis Minnie, Peg Leg Howell, or Kokomo Arnold, for example—only marginally benefited from the revival.

The impulse to relocate black blues singers was not unique to the middle 1960s. Alan Lomax was scouring northern Mississippi for the late Robert Johnson when he located Muddy Waters on Stovall's plantation in 1941. Samuel Charters traveled to Memphis as early as 1954 in order to speak with Furry Lewis, Will Shade, Milton Robie, and other veterans. The primary differences were the development of a younger (nearly entirely white) audience for blues, making concert tours and the sales of albums possible. Their way was paved by the ''folk revival'' of the early sixties, followed by the ''blues boom'' of the middle 1960s.

From a cultural point of view, these shifts also underscore important changes in the consumption of this vital form of American folk music. The blues boom existed through the support of white audiences, not under the aegis of black listeners. Folk blues singers in the 1960s often played in coffeehouses and concert halls, though in the rural South, musicians such as R. L. Burnside continued to labor in the juke joints and rough clubs of northeastern Mississippi. While the blues boom affirmed that not all of the older blues singers had died with the advent of rock 'n' roll and soul music, it also reaffirmed that this

M u s i c a l   E x a m p l e

Dave Van Ronk was intimately involved with the blues boom both as a performer and one who booked blues musicians into clubs. This piece is a convincing and interesting example of the interpretation of blues by a white performer. Van Ronk has adopted a text first sung by the vaudeville artist Bessie Smith in the 1920s and set it to a guitar arrangement based on Scrapper Blackwell's ''Down South Blues'' (1928) to create a unique blend. [Smithsonian/Folkways 40041]

Title ''Black Mountain Blues''
Performer Dave Van Ronk
Instruments guitar and voice
Length 3:59
Notable Features

1. Van Ronk sets this in the classic twelve-bar blues form.
2. It is performed in a major tonality.
3. The guitar's sharp timbre contrasts with Van Ronk's deep, gruff voice, setting up an effective tension.
4. Its meter is duple with a very regular rhythm.
5. The singer uses slight vocal ornaments at the end of the first line of each stanza.

Well, on Black Mountain, well, a child will spit in your face. (repeat)
All the babies cry for whiskey, all the birds sing bass.

Well, on Black Mountain they're as mean as they can be,
I say, on Black Mountain they're as mean as they can be,
You know they uses gunpowder just to sweeten their tea.

Well, on Black Mountain, well, you just can't keep a man in jail,
I say, on Black Mountain, well, you can't keep a man in jail,
Well, if the jury finds him guilty, the judge will go his bail.

I had a gal on Black Mountain, the sweetest gal in town. (repeat)
Met a sweetback man and she threw me down.

I'm going back to Black Mountain, me and my razor and my gun. (repeat)
I'm gonna cut her if she stands, shoot her if she runs.

tenacious music still enjoyed some grass roots support. Not only was R. L. Burnside still playing blues in Mississippi, but other "unknowns" such as Baby Tate, Mance Lipscomb, Bill Williams, Elizabeth Cotten, Elester Anderson, and Jack Owens had kept the tradition going.

Back to the Mountains

Not surprisingly, parallel activity was occurring in white folk music as younger scholars and collectors returned once more to the source. The talented multi-instrumentalist Mike Seeger—of the Seeger family, which included Pete, Charles (an eminent musicologist), Ruth (a composer), Peggy (another musician), and Tony (an ethnomusicologist)—became interested in bluegrass and old-time music in the middle 1950s. By the late 1950s, he and two other city billy musicians, John Cohen and Tom Paley, formed the New Lost City Ramblers, the first of the truly conscious "revival" string bands to explore the many avenues of their roots. The New Lost City Ramblers performed many types of American folk music, though most of it emanated from the South. Many younger people were first exposed to string band music through the ensemble work of the Ramblers. They learned their music directly from folk musicians, older records, and field recordings.

A keen collector with an inquisitive mind, Mike Seeger was also interested in learning the fate of the older musicians that he had heard on Harry Smith's pioneering three-record set for Folkways, *Anthology of American Folk Music*. Seeger, Bob Pinson, Joe Bussard, Malcolm Blackard, Donald Lee Nelson, Dave Freeman, and others scoured the South, particularly the Southeastern mountains, locating the early recording artists: Dock Boggs in Wise County, Virginia; the daughters of Fiddlin' Powers in neighboring Coeburn; Clarence Ashley of Mountain City, Tennessee; and Dorsey Dixon in Rockingham, North Carolina.

Not only did they rediscover the first generation of recording artists, these new collectors found a thriving group of musicians who had never left the South and whose work had not been preserved on records. Important "new" traditional singers such as Roscoe Holcomb in eastern Kentucky and ballad singer Dillard Chandler, who lived near Asheville, North Carolina, made field recordings that were eventually released on Folkways. In addition, John Cohen introduced a new medium to the folk revival, the ethnographic documentary film, that resulted in short films devoted to Holcomb and Chandler. He has continued to produce films and his most important statement on the subject at hand is *Musical Holdouts,* which addresses regional genres of American music. Once more technology impacts upon folk music in the United States, this time in a conscious effort to visually preserve and interpret.

The renewed interest in American folk music inevitably resulted in a new generation of interpreters, whose backgrounds were usually antithetical to the roots and upbringing of the musicians whom they idolized. Many of the revivalists were younger Northern musicians attracted to the wide variety of roots music they heard on Folkways or Vanguard records or saw at folk festivals

The Highwoods String Band performing at the Smithsonian Festival of American Folklife in the 1970s.
Smithsonian Institution.

from Berkeley to Philadelphia. Unlike groups such as the Limeliters or the Kingston Trio, most of these musicians tended to learn this music directly from the masters and faithfully reproduce it. They viewed themselves as carriers of the torch passed from one generation to the other, often fearing that younger members of the community had passed over this music in favor of more contemporary forms: bluegrass, soul, Nashville country, or rhythm and blues.

Mac Benford of the Highwoods String Band recalls his own musical experiences that began in the early 1960s:

> The dominant role models for the whole scene were the New Lost City Ramblers, who combined expertise as musicians and folklorists. Their performance style was based on their extensive knowledge for old-time music recorded in the '20s and '30s. In addition to their own performances, the concerts, films, and records that they produced of older musicians still stand as shining examples. . . . Many amateur folklorists now began enrolling in academic programs to earn credentials for what they had already been doing for love. As the folk boom of the '60s gathered momentum, the campuses of colleges and universities across the country became meeting grounds for the academic world and old-time musicians. This was the situation when my most notable musical venture. . . first got rolling. The timing couldn't have been better. . . . The support we received was so active that in just three years after Highwoods had teamed up to try our luck at the southern fiddler's conventions in the summer of 1972, we had been chosen to become part of the Smithsonian's Touring Performance Service; we were picked to represent old-time music on a U.S. State Department tour of Latin America; and we had become a favorite group at most of the major folk festivals'' (Mac Benford, *Old Time Herald,* Fall 1989, p. 23).

This trend resulted in new performance venues and avenues for both traditional musicians and those who have revived and interpreted earlier styles. A circuit of festivals, coffeehouses, and small concert halls catering to folk-music devotees developed across the country. This circuit supported musical programs by a wide range of artists, ranging from a semi-retired blues performer like Sleepy John Estes to an ensemble that has revived the contradance music heard at a town hall in southern New Hampshire or a string band that learned at the feet of Wade Ward in Galax, Virginia.

Hundreds of thousands of music fans have been exposed to a wide range of music by these means and to performers with increasingly eclectic repertoires. They hear groups with tongue-in-cheek names such as ''The Mighty Possums,'' ''Mice in the Attic,'' and ''Moose Chowder.'' Many of these bands unblinkingly mix Irish tunes, Western swing, British ballads, rockabilly, and Southern fiddle tunes. Revival bands of all descriptions have become the staple ensemble for many young white instrumentalists interested in alternatives to popular music groups.

As the years go by, this diversity becomes more pronounced and institutionalized. For example, at the 1991 ''Dance Augusta'' workshops in the hills of West Virginia, the first session was ''Cajun week.'' This workshop attracted enthusiastic dancers primarily from the Middle Atlantic states who came for instruction in ''couples dance styles of southwest Louisiana. . . in the two-step, jitterbug, waltz, Cajun blues dancing and zydeco.'' The flyer also

---

M u s i c a l   E x a m p l e

One of the most talented and long-lasting of these eclectic string bands is the Red Clay Ramblers, who are based in and around Chapel Hill, North Carolina. Founded originally in the early 1970s as an informal group, within a few years the band members had quit their teaching, library, and other day jobs in order to devote themselves to music. Since then they have toured throughout the United States and parts of Europe, recording numerous times for independent labels and working with several off-Broadway shows. ''Tell It to Me'' was derived from a 1920s recording by the Tenneva (a diminutive for Tennesse and Virginia) Ramblers. In addition to the old-time tunes, the Ramblers now feature a refreshing mixture of original material, sacred songs, and Irish instrumental tunes. [Folkways 31039]

Title ''Tell It to Me''
Performers The Red Clay Ramblers (Mike Craver, Tom Carter, Bill Hicks, Al McCanless, Tommy Thompson, Laurel Urton, and Jim Watson)
Instrument banjo, fiddles, guitar, washtub bass
Length 2:29
Notable Features

1. A rich and varied homophonic texture is heard.
2. There is harmony singing in the lead vocals and on the chorus.
3. It is performed in duple (2/4) meter at a rapid tempo.
4. There are several instrumental leads by the fiddle and banjo.
5. The song maintains a steady, high dynamic level.

Going up Cripple Creek, coming down Main
Trying to make a living for to buy cocaine
Cocaine's gonna kill my honey dear

Refrain:

Tell it to me, tell it to me
Drink corn liquor, let the cocaine be
Cocaine gonna kill my honey dear

Sniff cocaine, blow it at night
Sniff cocaine if it takes my life
Cocaine's gonna kill my honey dear

Refrain:

Sniff cocaine, sniff it in the wind
Doctor said it'll kill but wouldn't say when
Cocaine gonna kill my honey dear

Refrain:

All you rounders think you're tough
Feed your women on brandy and snuff
Cocaine gonna kill my honey dear

Refrain (repeat)

advertised that attendees would experience ''Cajun culture, dance parties, snacks, and more.'' The musicians included not only southwest Louisiana natives Dewey Balfa, Boisec Ardoin, and Canray Fontenot, but also Tracy Schwarz (one of the New Lost City Ramblers' founders), Matt Honey, and Bob Smakula.

New Entrepreneurs and Frontiers

A new breed of entrepreneurs also entered the record business. Moe Asch started Folkways back in the 1940s, but virtually no one else came into the business during the 1950s because of a perceived audience shortage. This changed, of course, beginning with the folk song revival, and any number of small record companies moved in to fill the void. Chris Strachwitz, for instance, began **Arhoolie Records** (Berkeley, California) in 1961 with an album by the Texas songster Mance Lipscomb. Over the years, Strachwitz has branched out into other areas, including ethnic music, avant-garde jazz, reissues, and norteño, and now possesses a catalogue with over 250 titles.

Rounder Records of Cambridge, Massachusetts, has followed a similar path from its stance as an antiprofit ''collective'' in 1971 to a major independent company with hundreds of titles in its catalogue. Most other companies—Flying Fish, Folk Legacy, Shanachie—have sprung forth from similar roots but have issued a similarly eclectic mixture of regional, revivalist, folk based, and older traditional music.

Another aspect of the folk music revival is a renewed interest in ethnic traditions. Earlier in this book, I briefly discussed the interaction between commercial record companies and ethnic musicians during the teens and twenties. Ethnic traditions always existed in their communities; like blues and hillbilly music, they never ''died.'' Unlike the other two genres, ethnic traditions never really moved beyond their grass roots audiences to become part of popular culture. This is partly the result of language differences, making the words sung in Yiddish, Swedish, Ukrainian, or Spanish unintelligible to those whose tongue is English.

The ghettoization of ethnic music is also related to the relative inaccessibility of the mass media, particularly radio and record companies. Except for those serving a major urban center or smaller community dominated by members of a certain cultural/language group, most radio stations do not serve the musical needs of ethnic groups. Similarly, record companies generally do not sell enough discs to warrant paying much attention to foreign-language records. In this case there simply is not the demand to make such ventures profitable enough to make them attractive. Moreover, the longer the period of time that ethnic groups reside in this country, the more acculturated they generally become. This also creates a weaker demand for the tangible products of their musical culture.

The 1970s and 1980s witnessed a strong movement towards multicultural perspectives in the arts, education, and the humanities—a reawakened awareness that the United States is not a monolithic society. One minor result of this new assessment is the understanding that ethnic music plays some part in our cultural fabric. Since 1970 we have witnessed **revitalization** movements in klezmer, Native American, Hawaiian, and Norwegian American, among others. This music was merely submerged by the commercial forces that shape our daily consciousness, bubbling along within the confines of their communities.

The Folklife Center of the Library of Congress sponsored a conference and a book about ethnic traditional music in the United States. Both Pekka Gronaw and Richard K. Spottswood have undertaken the most basic and extensive discographical work related to ethnic music in the United States. Spottswood's seven-volume discography, *Ethnic Music on Records,* is the standard reference book on ethnic recordings up to 1943. Despite the increased emphasis on ethnicity, the focus of the most recent folk revival has been upon American folk music as opposed to traditions imported to this country.

A promotional photograph from the 1975 Festival of American Folklife, which featured these mariachi musicians.
Smithsonian Institution.

Folkways has always included ethnic American releases in its catalogue, while Arhoolie's Chris Strachwitz's fondness for Spanish American and the creolized forms from Louisiana and east Texas assured their places in his company. The bulk of the recording of ethnic music, however, was undertaken by small companies dedicated to meeting the needs of their targeted narrow audiences. As they usually do in our capitalist society, commercial companies sprang up to fill the void left by major companies. In New York City, for example, the influx of Caribbean immigrants has created a thriving business for entrepreneurs hustling concerts and dances in addition to records and tapes. Canyon Records in New Mexico has been serving the Native American communities, albeit mostly Southwestern tribes, since the early 1960s. The documentation and marketing of the popular and folk music of ethnic enclaves remains, even today, largely unknown outside of the communities themselves.

Calypso, reggae, and styles from Haiti, Cuba, and other countries along the Caribbean Rim have influenced music in the United States for many years. This has occurred several times during the twentieth century alone, especially with jazz. From its roots in the Deep South, and New Orleans in particular, Cuban polyrhythms affected jazz. Jelly Roll Morton noted the "Spanish tinge" in his own music, perhaps as the result of his own partially Hispanic background. In the late 1940s, the craze for instruments such as bongos and conga drums swept through jazz, resulting in tunes such as "Cubana-Be-Cubana-Bop" and "Manteca."

Yet the folk revival has left permanent marks upon our musical awareness. In the early 1990s, some very popular singer-songwriters—most notably, Suzanne Vega, Michelle Shocked, Tracy Chapman, Indigo Girls, and R.E.M.—all clearly bear the heritage of American folk music in their own work. The popular press continues to trace and help create new musical trends; the 1970s and 1980s brought alternative journals and magazines devoted to American vernacular music. Folk music publications such as *Living Blues, The Old-Time Herald,* and other more ephemeral magazines have chronicled the history and development of vernacular music. Most of the noncommercial college and National Public Radio stations devote some of their weekly programming to folk music. In short, a small but formidable network of resources devoted to the preservation and dissemination of folk music exists.

Europeans still retain a strong hand in documenting our musical heritage. All of the major discographies of blues, gospel, and early country music have been compiled by Englishmen and were first published overseas. This ironic situation remains as true today as it did in the late 1930s when Hughes Panaisse wrote a pioneering scholarly book on jazz and assembled its first discography. If only American scholarly interest had been so strong fifty years ago! Several of the major collections of race and hillbilly records are in the hands of European collectors, while record companies such as Interstate (England) and Heritage (Austria) issue more records of black blues than any American company. The European-based *Old-Time Music, Blues Unlimited,* and *Soul Bag* have printed hundreds of issues devoted to American folk music.

Final Thoughts

All of this attention, American or otherwise, simply highlights the fact that our grass roots culture continues to fascinate and affect us. Even after more than sixty years of intervention, technology remains a strong force in shaping folk music. The most remote sections of America are dotted with satellite dishes, just as the same houses contained primitive radios in 1927. Despite all of these ''advances,'' the VFW in Fairview, Virginia, still holds its bimonthly square dances with old-time string band music. KPLK in New Ulm, Minnesota, is no longer the ''Polka Station of the Nation,'' but it continues to play an hour's worth each day. Just because Bob Wills is dead, Western swing and two-step dancing have not disappeared from Texas dance halls. In east Texas and Louisiana, Buckwheat Zydeco and Queen Ida remain in demand for dances where zydeco and creolized Cajun music rule the weekly dance halls. Regional folk music in the United States is not dead; it remains lurking just below the consciousness of popular culture.

Key Figures and Terms

Almanac Singers
Arhoolie Records
Moses Asch
British Invasion
Samuel Charters
Judy Collins
Bob Dylan
folk rock
Folkways Record Company
Woody Guthrie
independent record companies
Alan Lomax
New Lost City Ramblers
Newport Folk Festival
revitalization
revival
Pete Seeger
Dave Van Ronk

Audio

Dylan, Bob. *John Wesley Harding*. Columbia KCS 9825 (LP). Original material that portrays Dylan's folk roots.

Flying Burrito Brothers. *Gilded Palace of Sin*. Edsel CD-191 (CASS/LP). A classic recording that illustrates the folk rock movement.

Folk Song America: A 20th Century Revival. Smithsonian Collection of Recordings RD 046 A4 21489 (CASS/CD). This elaborate, multivolume set includes an excellent monograph by Norm Cohen and is a sterling example of how to reissue American music.

Greatest Folksingers of the Sixties. Vanguard 17/18 (CASS/CD). A sampler that includes strong performances by Joan Baez, Phil Ochs, Tom Paxton, and others.

Guthrie, Woody. *Dust Bowl Ballads*. Rounder 1040 (CASS/CD). These topical songs and ballads from the late 1930s are arguably Guthrie's best recordings; many other fine records are available on Smithsonian/Folkways.

Johnson, Robert. *The Complete Recordings*. Columbia C2K 46222 (CASS/CD). Forty-one selections by this pivotal figure who recorded these influential recordings in the late 1930s. The accompanying booklet contains essays by Stephen C. LaVere, Keith Richards, and Eric Clapton.

New Lost City Ramblers. Smithsonian/Folkways 40036 (CASS/CD). A repackaging of some of their best work.

Seeger, Mike. *Old-Time Country Music*. Folkways 2325 (LP). Mike's fine interpretations of songs and instrumentals from the Upland South.

Seeger, Pete. *The Essential*. Vanguard 97/98 (CASS/CD). A stirring sampler of Seeger's most popular work from the early 1960s; there are also fine records on Smithsonian/Folkways.

Weavers. *Reunion at Carnegie Hall, 1963*. Vanguard 15/16 (CASS/CD). A triumphant reprise of the group some thirteen years after they first made headlines with ''Goodnight, Irene.''

Books

Denisoff, Serge. 1971. *Great Day Coming*. Urbana: University of Illinois Press. Discusses the relationship between the left-wing political movement and grass roots music.

Dunaway, David King. 1981. *How Can I Keep from Singing: Pete Seeger*. New York: McGraw-Hill. A biography of Pete Seeger up to the late 1970s.

Klein, Joe. 1980. *Woody Guthrie: A Life*. New York: Knopf. The definitive biography of this important figure.

Lieberman, Ronnie. 1988. *My Song Is My Weapon*. Urbana: University of Illinois Press. A personalized view of the folk revivals and left-wing politics.

Von Schmidt, Eric, and Jim Rooney. 1979. *''Baby, Let Me Follow You Down'': The Illustrated History of the Cambridge Folk Years*. Garden City, N.Y.: Anchor Books. This is an entertaining, insider's view of the folk revival in Boston.

Video

Folk City 25th Anniversary Concert. Rhino-VHS 1977. 83 minutes. A celebration of Gerde's club in New York City, with Arlo Guthrie, Tom Paxton, Joan Baez, and others.

Judy Collins. Rainbow Quest 212–1106. 52 minutes. Part of the Pete Seeger-hosted series, this highlights Collins early in her career.

Musical Holdouts. John Cohen Films. 60 minutes. A fascinating view of traditional and regional folk based music shot mostly in the early 1970s by John Cohen.

Peter, Paul and Mary: 25th Anniversary Concert. Rhino-VHS 1950. 88 minutes. Taken from a live performance in Nashville that was originally broadcast over PBS.

The Folk Roots of Contemporary Popular Music

10

All of the significant forms of American popular music that have emerged since World War II have strong roots in African American folk music. Our focus is on the swiftly changing, ephemeral pop music scene that spawned rockabilly, Motown, rap, and other related forms. Records by Frank Sinatra, Dinah Shore, and Tony Bennett have sold millions of copies since the 1950s, but they are closely related to the swing era and American popular composers such as Cole Porter, the Gershwins, and Jimmy Van Heusen. Songs from the musical theater since World War II—*South Pacific, A Chorus Line,* or *West Side Story*—have also been renowned; however, they too come from a similar popular music aesthetic. Disaffected white youths tend to look towards other rebels or ''outsiders'' such as Robert Johnson, Little Richard, Aretha Franklin, or Run DMC for inspiration and change in their musical culture.

Black Codes from the Underground

Popular black music, with its strong roots in the community and in the streets, has witnessed the emergence and spread of rhythm and blues, Motown, soul, funk, and rap since the close of World War II. The late twentieth century represents a new era in black music. By way of records, tapes, live performances, radio, and television broadcasts, dynamic black American music has influenced music across the world, most notably in Africa and Europe. During the late Reconstruction era, ''jubilee'' religious groups regularly visited the nations across the ocean; one hundred years later James Brown drew hundreds of thousands almost worshipful listeners to his Ghana concerts. The popular ''highlife'' sounds of southern Africa that developed during the 1930s are highly charged with American jazz. By the mid-1980s, respected electric blues performer Johnny Copeland had recorded an album in Africa accompanied by native musicians, following the leads of jazz artists Ornette Coleman and Yusef Lateef. Twentieth-century products of this African American creative spirit (blues, gospel, and jazz) doubtless rank among our most vital and important contributions to the musical world. Black American music gives clear voice to a culture that cherishes improvisation in its everyday life and whose spirit has deeply influenced musicians not only in our own country but across the entire globe.

Aside from the popular forms that have gained widespread exposure through the mass media, the diversity of vernacular music largely remains a series of black codes from the underground. People across the world know the Motown ''soul'' music of the Four Tops and the Jackson Five, or the ''rap'' sounds of Public Enemy, 2 Live Crew, and Ton-Loc. Far fewer people, however, listen to early twentieth-century blues and gospel artists; they remain blissfully ignorant of the roots of our own contemporary popular music. These singers have descended from a rich, varied legacy buried in the obscurity of everyday life or, more often, simply in the past. Because their music is almost entirely unheralded in our schools and shunned from today's commercial marketplace, the names, lives, and music of most older black musicians largely remain unknown to the general public.

Improvisation in Black Music

African American folk performers are always trying to make "their own sound" or utilize something to make them sound unique. **Improvisation** in black folk music is a valued skill and takes many forms. Instrumental and vocal improvisations represent the basic ways musicians seek individuality in a performance. Most black folksingers view their ability to replicate musical styles as a gift. Inherent aptitude is undeniably part of this process, but many folk musicians (black and white) also go through an apprenticeship with a master musician. This learning process is one aspect of folk music that bears closer scrutiny, but it clearly involves a long period if the younger musician is striving for mastery. The nuances of performance (vocal inflections, interplay between the voice and the instrument, tuning of the instrument, even posture and facial expressions) are part of learning music.

Showmanship or **clowning** is part of black folk performance practice, too. Older blues singers speak in awe of the tricks that musicians such as Charley Patton and Tommy Johnson performed in the 1920s: playing the guitar while holding it above their heads, behind their backs, or picking it with their teeth! I have seen the late South Carolina medicine show performer, Peg Leg Sam, perform spellbinding visual tricks with his harmonica, a legacy of his years on the road. Sacred musicians are not beyond pulling a trick or two. Memphis gospel performers sometimes "worked" a crowd by walking among them or by leaping onto church pews while singing with microphone in tow. These performance practices might be shunned by many other audiences, but in front of an understanding black crowd, they are quite acceptable, even expected.

Clothing provides musicians with another chance to improvise. Fashion trends are sometimes set by musicians. The late 1980s **B-Boy** fashion sense—characterized by high-top, multicolored, untied sneakers; sweat suits; and bright hats—swept across the nation from its hearth area in hard-core urban areas. These fashions have cut across racial and ethnic lines, informing other African Americans as well as Asian Americans and white folks in the heartland of Iowa. What began as a folk expression of urban black males was picked up by popular culture and quickly transported throughout the United States. The widespread dissemination of rap followed a similar pattern and helped to reinforce a "homeboy" attitude.

The voice is quite a versatile tool, and black singers often use a variety of techniques—growls and slurs—in order to create an original sound. Mississippi blues singers like Howlin' Wolf or Robert Johnson often employed a falsetto and a vocal leap of an octave for dramatic effect. Bobby McFerrin, who emerged as a solo and jazz singer in the early 1980s, calls upon an arsenal of similar vocal effects that reflects his African American heritage. Improvisation is at the core of McFerrin's performances, and he freely draws upon "false" voices (falsetto and bass ranges), whoops, vocal trills, and other techniques in

Musical Example

Sonny Terry was born just after the turn of the century in the Piedmont of North Carolina. Totally blind since childhood, Terry earned his livelihood by way of music. The harmonica was his chosen instrument, and he became a virtuoso instrumentalist by the time that he was in his twenties. His early repertoire included country dance tunes, religious songs, and blues. Terry also learned to play many of the standard ''novelty'' pieces, such as ''Lost John'' and ''Fox Chase.'' This exceptional train imitation was recorded in the middle 1950s. [Folkways 32035]

Title ''Locomotive Blues''
Performer Sonny Terry
Instruments harmonica and voice
Length 3:25
Notable Features

1. Terry cleverly mixes his instrument and vocal effects into a seamless whole.
2. There are numerous changes in tempo that reflect the story line.
3. Note the many ''effects''—slurring, whooping, etc.—that Terry obtains from his small instrument.

Spoken: Well, ladies and gentlemen, this that old local train leaving out from Washington, D.C., heading south. The old fireman got up and rung his bell; he rung it like this, you know. Whoosh!

Well, you know that old fireman sat down and the old engineer got on up and blowed his whistle, blowed so lonesome; sorta like this.
Then the old engineer sat down, said, ''Oh, well, leaving here.'' Just reached down and grabbed the starter, pulled it off and start off easy; like this.

They got way on down the curve, when that old fireman rung the bell, something like this again. Ssshh!

And then old fireman sat down and the engineer said, ''Blow your whistle 'cause we're going a little fast here. Maybe a cow be on the rail and we can slow up on it.'' Blow his whistle lonesome, you know.

They got on down, pulling that little grade, you know, the train got to slowing down, got to doing like this.
Got over that grade, balling the jack, way on down the road. Getting on close down towards Richmond, Virginia.
He's blowing for Richmond, Virginia, now.
Pulling up in the yard now, fixing to stop. Whoosh!

Golden Gate Quartet, circa 1948.
Kip Lornell.

his performances. Another essentially solo artist, the lone worker in the field, sang freely improvised arhoolies. These singers frequently utilized not only free meter but vocal techniques such as yodels or halftone slides in order to regain the proper pitch.

Gospel quartet singers like Wilmer Broadnax (''Little Ax'') of the Spirit of Memphis or Ira Tucker of the Dixie Hummingbirds are highly regarded for their battery of vocal tricks. In fact, the church has been the training ground for innumerable secular singers. Many of the popular black singers from the soul era to the present arrived from backgrounds in religious music. Sam Cooke, Aretha Franklin, Dinah Washington, and Lou Rawls are just four of the performers who came up through the gospel ranks to reach stardom in midcentury. The church is where many of them learned to reiterate words or phrases for dramatic effect (''Lord, lord, lord''), toss out words in a call and response with their audience (''Let me hear an Amen!''), or add a wordless moan for emotional emphasis. In one guise or another, most live performances of black popular music in the 1990s contain many of these same elements.

In order to capture a more distinctive sound, black folk performers sometimes imitate sounds heard in nature or in the real world. The Golden Gate Quartet, for instance, rose to national prominence in the late 1930s partly on the strength of their uncanny train imitation, ''Gospel Train,'' an early, striking example of the jubilee quartet sound. Daniel Womack, a contemporary blind musician from Virginia, highly prizes his vocal ability to imitate animals. In both black and white tradition, the harmonica is used to imitate a fox chase or a train chugging down the track. Fiddles have been heard to simulate birds on ''Listen to the Mockingbird,'' which remains a standard tune at fiddle contests.

Lyrical improvisation is another way in which black musicians ''make their own songs.'' This is most often accomplished through the use of oral formulas involving the substitution of phrases or words to create a new work. It is often found in strophic forms of black folk music: blues, work songs, and spirituals that utilize a verse-and-refrain format. Formulas can help to extend the length of a song. The spiritual ''Our Meeting Is Over'' expands through the simple substitution of names:

> Father, now our meeting is over, father we must part. If I never see you anymore, I have loved you from the start.
>
> Mother, now our meeting is over, mother we must part. If I never see you anymore, I have loved you from the start.
>
> Brother, now our meeting is over, brother we must part. If I never see you anymore, I have loved you from the start.

Blues singers often make even greater use of more complex oral formulas. Such formulas are partly based on the memorization of specific lines, verses, and songs. More importantly, this memorization helps the singer to maintain patterns in which stanzas appear to be created spontaneously. Using this format as a building block, blues singers can render long, intricate performances. Some blues musicians are more inventive than others, of course, and make better and more extensive use of these oral building blocks. Others rarely vary their performances from one instance to another, almost as though a song is complete once it is composed and sung. Most singers rely upon these formulas to some degree, jauntily creating a new image by substitutes: ''My jet black gal won't give me but one thin dime.'' This line becomes ''That woman of mine keeps all my spending change.'' By the same token, ''House lady, house lady, what in the world is wrong with you?'' uses a few key substitutions to become ''Good gal, good gal, how come you do me like you do?''

Scholars have observed that the blues is an example of improvisation in everyday life; blues singers like Sleepy John Estes, Robert Pete Williams, and Big Joe Williams are among the most interesting and powerful poets in the field. Their language is both colorful and inventive. Their images are often both powerful and arresting, as in Robert Pete Williams's line, ''I've grown so ugly, I don't even know myself.'' Blues lyrics sometimes transcend the everyday world into the surreal, such as this line from a blues by Bo Weevil

An integrated blues ''jam session'' at the 1986 Festival of American Folklife.
Smithsonian Institution.

Jackson: ''Heard a mighty rumbling deep down in the ground.... Was the boll weevil and the Devil stealing somebody's brown.''

Visual and physical showmanship, an array of vocal techniques, and lyrical improvisation contrast with the general aesthetics of Anglo-American musical culture. Grass roots black performers strive first to learn or even master the idiom. The next step is to make it their own, to place a unique imprimatur or stamp onto it. This is where the creative aspects of black culture come into greatest relief. In general, these creative aspects of African American folk culture have informed both black and white popular music.

Rhythm and Blues

African American popular music in the postmodern era has not escaped its roots. Nor has it tried. The ''new Negro'' of the 1950s was striving to affect social, economic, and cultural advances, but the historical facts of slavery, disenfranchisement, and segregation proved to be a strong legacy. The folk roots of black music have been confirmed time and again into the present day. Rhythm and blues, a term coined in 1949, emerged as the first black popular music following the close of World War II.

Like so many forms of modern popular music, **R and B** grew out of the blues, especially those rural forms that had migrated to the North. Unlike rural blues, though, R and B is not the province of a solo artist. It is an urban form of black music that first arose in New York City and Los Angeles and that owed a strong debt to swing bands, piano boogie-woogie, and the **Louis Jordan** style of ''jump bands.'' The use of a full rhythm section of piano, bass, and drums helps to set the scene for early rock 'n' roll. Saxophones became an important voice in these ensembles, too. R and B from the late 1940s almost always used the blues form with a simple duple or quadruple meter. Its debts to popular styles are clearest in these regards.

The traditional heritage of R and B is perhaps most evident in the vocals. ''Shouters'' like Roy Milton, Joe Liggins, and Amos Milburn used some of the moans and guttural vocal techniques of the earlier blues singers and gospel stylists. Their voices were also powerfully rich. Many R and B performers also engaged in the call-and-response patterns found in black folk music. Sometimes it was a vocal chorus responding to the lead singer. In other instances, the saxophone section engaged in a dialogue with the vocalists.

In the early 1950s, R and B vocal groups like the Platters, Drifters, Orioles, and Coasters also began gaining attention. Within a few years, they were joined by solo male singers such as Brook Benton and Jackie Wilson, many of whom began their careers with vocal-harmony groups. Such groups soon began adopting song forms other than twelve-bar blues and started using eight- and sixteen-bar songs that reflect the influence of gospel and even Tin Pan Alley composers. R and B gradually blended with other forms. By the middle 1960s, Ray Charles, Sam Cooke, and Aretha Franklin pioneered a style that became known as ''soul.''

But R and B had a profound influence on early rock 'n' roll. Its earliest practitioners mainly appealed to the black community, but by 1953 it was gaining a younger, white audience. They were enthralled by **Little Richard,** an outrageous performer whose piano antics, forceful shouting, and commanding stage presence won him a large multiracial audience. Not only was he moving salaciously on stage, but he also wore makeup! Little Richard was exactly the kind of African American blues performer that caused parents a great deal of worry. But teenagers like Jerry Lee Lewis and **Elvis Presley** appreciated his music and rebellious spirit.

Rockabilly

This dynamic musical hybrid began in **Memphis** with **Sam Phillips** and Elvis Presley as its primary progenitors. Phillips had launched **Sun Records** in 1951 with a roster of local artists: Dr. Isaiah Ross (''The Harmonica Boss''), Rufus Thomas, the Ripley Cotton Choppers, and Hot Shot Love. They were mostly black musicians because Phillips saw a void in the marketplace. The fact that he loved their fierce, hot, energetic music was of great importance, but Phillips knew that he needed a white interpreter of African American music in order to sell lots of records.

Elvis Presley literally walked into his studio in July 1954, and he possessed all of the musical ingredients for which Phillips was searching. Growing up in Tupelo, Mississippi, and Memphis, he admired hillbilly music, particularly the talents of Roy Acuff, Ernest Tubb, and Hank Williams. His family was also immersed in the emotionally expressive Pentecostal Assembly of God. Presley and his backup duo had infused these influences with a 4/4 shuffle beat and the syncopated feeling of ''race'' music. Phillips knew this as soon as he heard Presley dig into his version of Arthur ''Big Boy'' Crudup's ''That's Alright, Mama.'' The spirit of black music was at Presley's core: a slightly accented backbeat, the vocal shading and slides, an energetic defiance, extensive use of the twelve-bar blues form, guitar licks that echoed B. B. King and Lonnie Johnson, and the repertoire.

It wasn't quite country and it wasn't too ''black.'' Sam Phillips was struck by this synthesis, but who would consume this music? Radio was still basically segregated, and most record companies continued to maintain separate race and country series. Still, there had to be a marketplace for this music somewhere. Figuring that somebody would purchase this music, Phillips released it as Sun 209, ''That's All Right'' and ''Blue Moon of Kentucky'' (a Bill Monroe number) by ''Elvis Presley—Scotty and Bill.'' The other musicians referred to were Scotty Moore (guitar) and Bill Black (bass), the members of Presley's trio. The revolution had begun.

Rockabilly is aggressive and uncomplicated. Classic rockabilly is performed by a small ensemble (usually a trio or quartet) using an insistent duple meter to accompany an often frenzied vocal. The entire sound is characterized by an echo created in the studio and by inexpensive amplifiers. In this respect, it mirrors the sound achieved by Chicago blues artists such as Muddy Waters and Howlin' Wolf. Its secular, black folk roots are complemented by a strong dose of religion. Presley openly admired African American gospel singers and sometimes went to hear the Spirit of Memphis Quartet perform in local churches.

Within a year of Presley's initial release, Memphis became a mecca for aspiring rockabilly artists. They came from throughout the Mid-South and were as steeped in black music as their hero. Billy Lee Riley drove across the Mississippi River from Arkansas, while Carl Perkins dropped down almost due south one hundred miles from Tipton, Tennessee. They were followed by Jerry Lee Lewis of Ferriday, Louisiana, who helped to popularize the boogie-woogie and honky-tonk styles of piano. Lewis picked up his wild piano style from listening to local blacks and from his experiences in the Pentecostal church. From Memphis itself, Johnny Burnette, his brother Dorsey, and Paul Burlison stepped forward to form the Rock 'n' Roll Trio. Their classic 1956 recordings for the New York City–based Coral label mark the diffusion of this music from its birthplace to a distribution network outside of the Mid-South.

The early rockabilly artists were wild. They not only sang and played like black men, they sometimes adopted the African American aesthetic of ''clowning.'' Like their black counterparts in contemporary rhythm and blues, singers such as Roy Brown and Wynonie Harris, they put on a good show. Jerry Lee Lewis would play the piano with his feet. Red suits, a red Cadillac, and matching dyed red hair became Sonny Burgess's trademark. Billy Lee Riley and His Little Green Men were famous for ''Flyin' Saucer Rock and Roll,'' a rockabilly song about Mars and music. These young men liked to take chances, and Sam Phillips gave them the room to create. Fast cars and alcohol were two facts of life for most of the rockabilly pioneers. They also liked dirty songs by black artists. In addition to Presley's borrowings, the early covers by white artists included Malcolm Yelvington and Star Rhythm Boys' ''Drinkin' Wine Spodee-O-Dee'' (Sun 211) and several other songs inspired by Roy Brown's ''Good Rockin' Tonight.''

Inevitably, the message, spirit, and influence of rockabilly spread beyond the Mid-South. By 1955 Gene Vincent, Wanda Jackson, and Eddie Cochran were boppin' in the Midwest and on the West Coast. The music slowly became safer and more generic as Buddy Holly, Ricky Nelson, and the Everly Brothers instilled pop sensibility into their music and lifestyle. Rockabilly became more smooth, less raw, and gained acceptance across the country, and by 1960 it had been virtually subsumed by more mainstream rock 'n' roll, which was informed by similar folk and popular roots.

Early Rock 'n' Roll

Ten months after Elvis Presley first stepped into the Sun studio, *Billboard* certified ''Rock Around the Clock'' as a hit. Bill Haley and the Comets appealed to white teenagers, providing an alternative to the even more rebellious image of rockabilly. Both genres shared many of the same musical characteristics: heavily accented backbeats on the second and fourth beats, a solo lead singer

A quintessential rockabilly record
from Memphis.
Kip Lornell.

who was occasionally joined by a vocal chorus, the vocal alternating with an instrumental chorus, and the extensive use of electric guitar as a lead instrument. Unlike rockabilly, it was not uncommon for rock 'n' roll musicians to employ a small horn section, usually featuring an alto or tenor saxophone.

Even Elvis Presley was moving towards rock 'n' roll as a safer alternative to rockabilly. In 1955 he became an RCA Victor artist and within a year was reaching an increasingly large and interracial audience. Records such as "Hound Dog," "Don't Be Cruel," and "Jailhouse Rock" sold well, and he was emerging as a megastar. Once again, at the heart of his music was the blues in a rapidly paced, energetic style. Presley was selling records to black, white, and Hispanic audiences in every corner of the United States within two years of singing with this major label.

This crossover appeal helped to open the door for Little Richard and Chuck Berry. Their style of highly charged rock 'n' roll with lyrics aimed at a teenage audience brought them to the attention of white listeners. Even New Orleans's **Fats Domino** was able to sell his souped-up rhythm and blues to a white audience. **New Orleans** R and B proved to be particularly appealing to white audiences towards the close of legal segregation. This music usually employed the same instruments as rock 'n' roll, but it was saturated with polyrhythms derived from its Afro-Caribbean background. Electric guitars were less prominent and the music was often played at a more leisurely tempo. New Orleans R and B had plenty of energy, but it lacked rockabilly's frenetic edge. Domino was a leading exponent of this music and lead the way to commercial success with hits such as "Blueberry Hill" and "I'm Walking." He was joined by lesser-known artists such as Lloyd Price, Smiley Lewis, and Huey "Piano" Smith. They were best known in the African American community, but each of them enjoyed a bit of success in rock 'n' roll circles.

There was a cultural and parental outcry against rock 'n' roll. It was destructive, antisocial, and crude. A film such as the *The Blackboard Jungle,* which featured "Rock Around the Clock," became the cinematic parallel of rock 'n' roll. Furthermore, it was argued that rock 'n' roll promoted promiscuity, juvenile delinquence, a rebellious nature, and racial unrest. The infusion of

M u s i c a l   E x a m p l e

Early rock 'n' roll and rhythm and blues clearly follow regional trends. New Orleans R and B is similar but not identical to its Los Angeles counterpart. By the late 1950s, when this selection was recorded, these differences were being documented in small studios throughout the United States. This performance is typical of the Deep South and shows a distinct coupling of rock 'n' roll and R and B, with a clear eye towards the popular music market. [Folkways 2865]

Title ''Solid Gold Hat''
Performer Al White and His Highlighters
Length 1:51
Notable Features

1. The tempo is brisk.
2. Some sections are rubato, but most of this performance is in a solid duple meter.
3. Listen for the ''riffing'' horns that provide a ''call and response'' with the vocalist.
4. The harmonic underpinning is the basic blues progression.
5. The lead vocalist is relaxed, more like a pop singer than a true rock 'n' roll or R and B singer.

You've seen them in the beaches, playing in the sand,
Sitting on the boardwalk to get a tan.
You've seen 'em in the movies, on the TV screen.

Refrain: But you ain't seen nothing, until you've seen. . .
My baby, my baby in the solid gold hat.
Well, won't you take them up to town, she's my baby,
She's my baby in the solid gold hat.

You've seen them in the country, you see them in the town.
You see them every time that you look around.
You've seen 'em looking chunky and you've seen 'em lean.

Refrain:

You've seen them on the dance floor, in their evening clothes
Looking like a princess from head to toe.
You've seen 'em wearing purple, yellow, red, and green.

Refrain:

African American musical culture into white music underlined the entire problem. Atlantic Records was at the vanguard of this movement; it was one of the important forces in selling black American culture to white youths. It also helped to promote similar musical tastes among black and white youths, who bought many of the same records and who wanted to attend integrated concerts! Such social changes proved to be very problematic for a legally segregated society.

Fortunately for America's parents and our cultural stability, the impact of rock 'n' roll diminished within a few years. Just as the folk revival was gaining steam in the late 1950s, rock 'n' roll began taking a more innocuous stance. Electric guitars, emotional vocals, energy, and the defiance was slowly giving way to slicker musicians. The blues and its musical compatriots were moving over to accommodate the Tin Pan Alley school of songwriting. Bobby Darin, Paul Anka, and Pat Boone made romantic love hip again, while Danny and the Juniors' and the Crew-Cuts' sentimentalized and overproduced versions of the black vocal group style sold in large numbers. They were followed in short order by the California surf music of the Beach Boys, Jan and Dean, and others. By the early 1960s, rock 'n' roll had ceased to be a viable vehicle for rebellious expression.

Motown and Soul

Soul emerged as the next wave of urban popular music, and **Motown** Records in Detroit served as its Northern headquarters. Founded in 1960 by Berry Gordy, Jr., Motown preceded the soul revolution by several years. However, by the end of the decade, Motown had grown into one of the largest black-owned-and-operated corporations in the United States, as well as a force in popular music. Mary Wells, Diana Ross and the Supremes, the Four Tops, Stevie Wonder, and the Jackson Five were among its top acts. It specialized in pop soul and emphasized sophisticated, sometimes innovative, string arrangements played by studio orchestras. Motown records tended to have strong appeal throughout the black community, with crossover appeal to a white audience, too. In fact, it used the color-blind slogan ''The sound of young Americans'' in an effort to reach white listeners.

Elsewhere—especially in the Stax studios in Memphis and the Atlantic Records studio in Muscle Shoals, Alabama—a different brand of soul music was being documented. This was the ''deep'' Southern soul of Wilson Pickett, Aretha Franklin, and **Otis Redding,** which was much closer to its black musical heritage than its Detroit counterpart. With more direct links to blues and gospel, Southern soul tugged at the heart and emotions of its listeners. These often occurred in ''soul ballads,'' slow-tempo songs with heart-wrenching lyrics about the problems between men and women.

Otis Redding stepped forth as the quintessence of male Southern soul singing. Following a career that included stints as a vocalist with various R and B bands, a frustrating career singing imitations of Little Richard, and washing cars, Redding hit it big in 1962. Like Elvis Presley, he got his big break in a Memphis recording studio. But Redding was in the Stax studio, his second home until an airplane crash took his life on December 10, 1967. During this five-year period, Redding recorded hit after hit in the soul idiom. Many of his originals—''Respect,'' ''Sitting on the Dock of the Bay,'' and ''I've Been Loving You Too Long''—became standards. Others came from less likely sources: the Rolling Stones' ''Satisfaction'' and Bing Crosby's ''Try a Little Tenderness.''

Redding's singing is instantly recognizable, unmistakable, and it springs directly from his Southern black ancestry. All soul singers owe debts to blues singers like Bessie Smith, Peetie Wheatstraw, and B. B. King, but Otis Redding was particularly close to the gospel tradition. Like the great gospel soloists, he had great control over the dynamics in his voice and enjoyed playing with subtle rhythmic shifts in order to vary his message. Redding had also mastered other techniques—melisma, rasping, chanted interpolations—heard every Sunday in African American churches.

As mainstream popular black music, soul lasted about eight years longer than Otis Redding. Other Stax artists such as Sam and Dave, Carla Thomas, and Al Green had major hits on both the ''soul'' (black) and ''pop'' (white) *Billboard* charts. Curtis Mayfield, who was involved in the gospel and civil rights movement, emerged as one of the important socially aware black music voices during the late 1960s. In the early 1970s, the Gamble-and-Huff ''soft soul'' sound of the O'Jays, Spinners, and Herald Melvin and the Blue Notes shifted the focus to Philadelphia. However, by mid-decade funk and disco had supplanted soul music as the predominate form of black pop.

Rap

Rap music results from the hybridization of folk and popular trends. It emerged nationwide in the late 1970s and has made extensive use of the technological aspects (twelve-inch singles, scratching, electronic sounds, and dance remixes) that place it solidly within the popular realm. So does its emergence from the urban, black, and largely male culture. The funk style gained popularity in the early and middle 1970s, but rap soon moved in to supplant soul as the next major force in black popular music.

This music was first heard in black clubs and discotheques in New York City in the middle 1970s when disc jockeys began talking and chanting over highly syncopated instrumental tracks by Funkadelic, Chic, Parliament, and other funk artists. Its most immediate musical precedent is the ''toasting'' style pioneered by Jamaican disc jockeys in the 1960s, who recited simple rhymes, political poems, and plain doggerel over a prerecorded track. American blacks were exposed to toasting in the Caribbean clubs of Brooklyn and the South Bronx. By the late 1970s, the Sugar Hill Gang, Grandmaster Flash and the Furious Five, and the Soul Sonic Force were selling their ten-inch ''dance mix'' singles in black and gay clubs throughout New York City. Within a few years, major record companies had stepped in, and even white pop artists such as Blondie got into the act.

Rap then quickly moved into America's cultural mainstream. Break dancing became popular among black and white kids throughout the United States. In 1984 two films, evolving around this urban musical culture, *Breakdance* and *Beat Street,* were released. Local permutations such as **Go-Go,** a mixture of funk and rap, remain popular in Washington, D.C. Go-Go artists like Chuck Brown engage their audience in antiphonal style, much like a Pentecostal church service: ''Do you want to get down?'' ''Let's get down, let's get down!'' Rap artists from across the United States have remained popular and controversial into the 1990s.

Part of the controversy revolves around the political and sexual nature of the lyrics, which are often seen as volatile, lewd, and misogynist. These are traits that tie rap directly to black folk culture. Black protest songs are a part of black oral tradition that goes back to slavery and has continued into the work-song tradition of the twentieth century. They tend to be sung or spoken rather than written about within the black community. Rap is simply the latest voice of protest that has been heard in Mississippi fields and the streets of Harlem for over two hundred years. The obscene lyrics are another part of black tradition that can be heard on blues records from the 1920s and in the toasts that most black males know. Playing ''**the dozens**'' is another insult game heard throughout black America, though predominately among the young. This same aesthetic is basically transferred to rap.

Rap's preoccupation with strongly syncopated accents and body percussion also has a strong, long-standing link to folk culture. Throughout the nineteenth and twentieth centuries, most styles of black music have held rhythmic interest in high esteem. Earlier manifestations include the fife and drum bands, washboards that are used to accompany blues singers and in zydeco bands, and the jawbones that provided an accompaniment to black accordion players. Body percussion is tied to this aesthetic and is still seen today in children who play a game of ''hambone,'' during which they use both hands to slap their body in a pronounced, sometimes syncopated, duple meter, and recite short rhymes. A standard opening line is ''Hambone, hambone, where you been? Around the world and back again.'' This verbal format also emphasizes that call (question) and response (answer) remains vitally important in black culture.

The technological aspects of rap, particularly **sampling,** provide another example of the folk aesthetic at work. Sampling involves selecting a short piece of music, running it through a computer or synthesizer, and then inserting it into your own rap. Sometimes it's a distinctive phrase or a loop that plays over and over again. Contemporary artists usually sample older styles of black music—James Brown is a particular favorite—thus using an oral means of infusing older styles with rap. Part of rap's creativity stems from a synthesis that is based upon the black American musical legacy.

Postmodern television history would have you believe that **MTV** (Music Tele-vision, VH-1, etc.) pioneered the integration of musical themes with visuals, which are known as music videos. These are short films (three to ten minutes long) that illustrate a song. Music videos have exploded in popularity in the last ten years, but the truth is that filming musicians is not new, nor is filming vernacular music of any sort of innovation. The legacy of music videos ex-tends back before the Great Depression.

As early as 1928, shortly after the advent of ''talking pictures,'' American folk musicians were captured on film. These short pieces played at commer-cial theaters, permitting the viewers to watch and hear two to three minutes of contemporary folk music artists. Bela Lam (Stanardsville, Virginia), Whis-tler's Jug Band (Louisville, Kentucky), and the Rust College Jubilee Group from Mississippi were among the groups documented during the first few years of this new wave of technology. The closest parallel to MTV from this period is *St. Louis Blues,* a twelve-minute film starring Bessie Smith that chronicles the love problems that entangle the legendary blues singer. It closes with Smith and a group of singers in a beer joint singing the theme song.

At least two well-known folk artists from the 1920s and 1930s, Leadbelly and Charlie Poole, made trips to Hollywood in order to star in feature-length films that were never completed. Of course some of the singing cowboys of the silver screen, most notably Gene Autry and Roy Rogers, began their ca-reers as folk singers with a distinctly Jimmie Rodgers bent to their playing. But most folk performers were limited to short clips that appeared on movie screens as a prelude to a feature film. In the late 1940s, some juke box opera-tors distributed machines that for a dime would play a two-to-three-minute musical short called a ''soundie.'' The intent of soundies is identical to that of a music video on MTV: a brief, thematic musical short designed to get you to purchase the product.

The Ancestors of MTV

Final Thoughts

Although we live in a postmodern world marked by rapid musical and cultural change, our roots are never entirely obscured. The trends in popular music have become increasingly fleeting and ephemeral as we become a more global society. But the latest musical revolution is always informed by whatever preceded it. Two dynamic, energetic, and emotional forms of black folk music that emerged in the twentieth century, blues and gospel, continue to have a strong impact on popular music. Some of the traits they developed—most importantly, the blues form, syncopated rhythms, and certain vocal techniques—have become so inculcated in late twentieth-century pop music that we forget from where they come. But at one time, they were truly bred in the bone.

Key Figures and Terms

B-Boy
clowning
Fats Domino
the dozens
Go-Go
improvisation
Louis Jordan
MTV
Memphis
Motown

New Orleans
Sam Phillips
Elvis Presley
R and B
Otis Redding
Little Richard
rockabilly
sampling
soul
Sun Records

Audio

Brown, James. *Star Time*. Polydor 849 108–4 (CASS/CD). Five hours of classic R and B/soul by the ''hardest working man in show business.''

The Fifties: R and B Vocal Groups. ACE 212 (CASS/CD). This package hits some of the highlights of the genre by the Jacks and Five Bells, among others.

Get Hot or Go Home: Vintage RCA Rockabilly 1956–59. Country Music Foundation 014 (all formats). A double set that comes with an eight-page booklet.

Our Significant Hits. Specialty 2112 (CASS). A solid sampling of late 1950s black rock 'n' roll by Lloyd Price, Sam Cooke, Little Richard, and others.

Rock and Roll Show. Deluxe 1019 (CD). Classic mid-to-late 1950s selections by Chuck Berry and Screamin' Jay Hawkins, among others.

Street Corner Memories. ACE 205 (LP). A set of vocal groups from the 1950s: the Passions, the Harps, the Elegants, etc.

Sun Rockabilly—The Classic Recordings. Rounder SS-37 (all formats). This set includes strong performances by Billy Lee Reily, Warren Smith, and other Mid-South musicians.

The Top of the Stax. Stax SCD 88005–2 (CD). A multi-CD boxed set that samples the Mid-South soul sound.

We Got a Party—The Best of Ron Records, Vol. 1. Rounder 2076 (CASS/CD). This covers some of the important figures in New Orleans R and B: Professor Longhair, Irma Thomas, Chris Kenner, etc.

Books

George, Nelson. 1988. *The Death of Rhythm and Blues*. New York City: Pantheon Press. This book reviews the changes in black popular music since the 1930s in light of the white dominated music industry.

Guralnick, Peter. 1979. *Lost Highways: Journeys and Arrivals of American Musicians*. Boston: David R. Grodine. A series of thoughtful essays covering blues, country, and rock performers from the 1940s through the 1960s.

Marcus, Greil. 1972. *Mystery Train: Images of America in Rock 'n' Roll Music*. 2d ed. New York City: E. P. Dutton. Marcus writes provocatively and insightfully about the role of The Band, Sly Stone, Randy Newman, and Elvis Presley in American culture.

Miller, Jim, ed. 1980. *Rolling Stone Illustrated History of Rock*. New York City: Random House. A comprehensive history of the first few decades of rock.

Tosches, Nick. 1984. *Unsung Heroes of Rock 'n' Roll*. New York City: Scribners. Poignant and humorous views of some of the lesser-known pioneers of the idiom.

Video

Blue Suede Shoes: A Rockabilly Session. MCA-VHS80425. 60 minutes. Dave Edmunds, Eric Clapton, and others help to recreate the rockabilly music that influenced them in this informal film.

Chuck Berry: Hail! Hail! Rock 'n' Roll. MCA-VHS80465. 121 minutes. This is a detailed, popularized documentary about the grass roots rock 'n' roller, which features wonderful concert footage and lots of Eric Clapton, Keith Richards, and other blues influenced musicians.

James Brown Live in America. Rhino-VHS1904. 60 minutes. Basically a concert performance, this is an exciting program by one of the most influential R and B/soul singers.

Fieldwork in Postmodern America

11

*I*ntroducing *American Folk Music* has described the rich history of traditional music in the United States, an aspect of our culture deserving of far more historical and contemporary research. This work can be undertaken with relative ease because we are quite literally surrounded by, and immersed in, our own musical culture. American folk music touches everyone's lives at some juncture: overhearing the jump-rope game songs of children as we walk down the street, watching B. B. King and Lucille (his guitar) perform a blues number as part of the annual Grammy Awards ceremony, recalling the lullabies sung to us by our mothers, or hearing a string band play an old-time fiddle tune at the local music festival. Despite its reputation as "old-time" or conservative music, innovation within artistic and culturally defined norms has characterized American folk music since its beginnings. After more than two hundred years of development, it remains abundantly clear that our own rich musical world of wonder demands serious attention. And field research is arguably the most important and timely path that one can take in researching these genres.

This final chapter encourages and prepares you to explore the musical world around you with an open, more informed ear and mind. Libraries, **archives,** and private collections contain invaluable, irreplaceable, and rich caches of printed and aural material. There are a number of noteworthy repositories across the United States. The Archive of Folk Culture at the Library of Congress, the University of North Carolina's "Southern Archive," the Wisconsin Folk Museum's Archive, the "Blues Archive" at the University of Mississippi, and the "Archives of Traditional Music" at Indiana University

Ralph Rinzler collecting Cajun music for the Smithsonian Institution in 1964.
Smithsonian Institution.

each contain unique material: manuscripts, field recordings, videotapes, photographs, and interviews. Held in perpetuity, this material will always be available for researchers. Fieldwork, however, is more energizing and capricious. It also adds valuable material to the very archives that people explore for their primary research.

Helping you to accomplish your own original fieldwork is the objective of this chapter. If this sounds like a daunting prospect, it should not be. Fieldwork reflects other aspects of life, for it alternately frustrates, excites, surprises, bores, and disappoints. Any interaction with human beings implies risks, but it can also bring great rewards. The opportunities for fieldwork abound; it can be as simple as stepping out your door in order to speak with some children playing outside. You may venture into a church in order to speak with members of a gospel choir or even interview members of your own family. Your task: to select and document some aspect of a musical community directly tied with American folk or folk based music. Specific research topics within a musical community are suggested later in this chapter.

Communities represent one way to examine musical phenomena. **Musical communities** are generally loose-knit, often eclectic groups of people coalescing around shared, specific musical interests. Such communities can be found in any genre of American music—jazz, blues, classical, or bluegrass. Some are more casual and ephemeral than others. However, the community of black gospel quartet singers in Memphis, Tennessee, has evolved over more than sixty years into a complex, truly extended family through birth, marriage, religious beliefs, proximity, and shared values. The musicians themselves—as well as disc jockeys, record company officials, promoters, and enthusiasts—can be included among the members of such a ''family.''

A *family,* quite possibly your own or that of one of your friends, is one place upon which you might concentrate your research. Our **families** are often the first place that we encounter music. This can occur in many contexts: a record collection, radio, church services, or family musical sessions. Just as most of us have family folklore (when to open Christmas presents, how birthdays are celebrated, or the name for automobiles with one headlight), there is often music that we learned within our family. Many parents sing lullabies to their children; perhaps you sing them to your own. Summer-camp songs are often transmitted within families, among siblings or between parents and their children. Maybe you learn Christmas songs from your parents, reaffirmed each year during the early winter holiday season. Someone in your family may have informally taught you simple instrumental tunes—''Go Tell Aunt Rhody,'' ''Chopsticks,'' or ''Turkey in the Straw''—on the piano, guitar, or another instrument.

Secular *organizations* of all descriptions incorporate some type of musical activity associated with them. Sports teams, for example, often have pep bands or marching bands taking part in each game or match. All of the branches of

Musical Communities and Fieldwork

the U. S. military support ensembles that perform many types of music for a variety of occasions. Educational institutions on all levels sanction many musical groups such as choral singers, wind and jazz ensembles, and orchestras. Fraternal lodges (V.F.W., American Legion, Elks, or Moose) sometimes include bands as part of their organization. Some service groups hold musical competitions as a means of fund-raising or for disseminating scholarship money to promising young musicians.

Many of us are exposed to music through *religious* affiliations. There are many examples of musical communities in the context of religion. Music, of course, is part of nearly every sect's weekly services. The music of the Church of Jesus Christ of Latter Day Saints (Mormons) has a distinctly American tradition that goes back over one hundred years. Methodists prefer the grandeur of hymns written in the eighteenth and nineteenth centuries, often set to the music of masters such as Bach. Those brought up in the Pentecostal faith recognize the camp-meeting songs of the nineteenth century and more recently composed gospel songs, which are often performed by family groups or other ensembles. Similarly, people belonging to African American Baptist churches are familiar with the twentieth-century gospel songs that predominate in the Sunday services and Wednesday evening prayer meetings.

Musical communities also spring up around *commercial* enterprises. Much of the music that we consume on a daily basis—in elevators, on most radio stations, by way of television theme songs, or on our CDs or cassette tapes—is performed by paid professionals. Commercial music frequently bombards our senses through means outside of our control such as in grocery stores, some of which even have their own ''stations'' that praise the quality and goodness of their operation. In other contexts, like concerts or in our own homes or automobiles, we can choose the types of music to which we listen. The commercial music industry in America is enormous, multifaceted, and, for most of us, pervasive.

Accomplishing Fieldwork

Fieldwork is rarely the overwhelming hurdle that some people expect. It is difficult to do well, especially in the beginning. But with a lively interest, careful preparation, and experience, one's timidity decreases while the quality of the results increases. A persistent field-worker who is genuinely interested in a topic and the people whom one meets often uncovers information and documents material that simply does not exist in libraries and archives. Your field research can often be combined with previously published articles or information into an original paper that really adds something new. Fieldwork rarely stands alone; it almost always needs to be placed into the context of our existing knowledge.

The key to successful fieldwork includes these steps:

1. Selecting a subject
2. Focusing on your topic
3. Library and listening preparation
4. Preparing questions for your interview
5. Communicating your intent
6. The interview itself

Topic   Your fieldwork situation should relate to some aspect of American folk music. I suggest that you investigate one of the genres covered in this book. Because you are likely to be neophytes in this arena, or simply shy, readers may wish to select a more familiar musical style. Above all, pick a musical style that truly appeals to you or with which you have had personal experience. Here are seven possible subjects that involve fieldwork: the folk revival in your area, an ethnic music group, members of an occupational group (cowboys, miners, railroad workers, etc.), the organizers of a coffeehouse or folk music festival, a folk instrument maker, traditional songs or elements in the repertoire of a contemporary rock music group, or a blues performer. Many state and some local arts councils have folklorists on their staff, who can sometimes offer suggestions for fieldwork.

Focus   Once you select a topic, be aware that its focus may change as you ask questions and learn more. Focus is an important key to fieldwork. You may begin with a general line of inquiry or interest, such as ''Bohemian American polka music,'' but you need to refine your research to ask a more specific question. ''The development of Bohemian American polka music in central Minnesota'' refines your subject further. With even greater research, you may decide that a focus upon the ''importance of Whoopee John Wilfahrt in the development of Bohemian American polka music in New Ulm, Minnesota'' specifies precisely what you wish to know. Now you have a manageable core topic, arrived at by a refinement process that began with a general interest. Don't be afraid to let the topic lead you into new areas of inquiry about which you knew nothing or for which your background research did not prepare you. The troika of an open mind, library and listening preparation, and the process of refinement leads to the best fieldwork.

Preparation   Successful fieldwork begins with careful preparation before you go into the field. After you select a topic that interests you, check what literature has been written on the subject. Your search may prove futile because so many areas of American music await the scrutiny of intelligent writers. However, if you select the folk revival, blues, cowboy songs, or gospel music, then a wealth of published information is at your disposal. An informed fieldworker needs to be familiar with the important figures in the music, its historical development, and, above all, with the sound of the music itself. Listen to the music! The bibliographies and discographies that close the chapters in this book list the important literature and musical selections in American traditional music. Use them as a stepping-stone for further inquiry, but do not try to read everything on a subject. A library or archive provides you with the background tools necessary for work in the field, but your true mission lies outside their walls.

Questions   Fieldwork involves asking questions . . . of the right people. The identity of "right people" is sometimes obvious from the beginning of a project. If you have decided to study an individual—a dulcimer maker, blues singer, ballad singer, or disc jockey—your focus will almost certainly lead you in the correct direction. But gaining entrees to other communities may not be so easy. Fieldwork can be hindered by the researcher's gender, age, ethnic background, or race. On the other side of the coin, being an "in-group" member often facilitates fieldwork because of the contacts and your immediate acceptability.

Your questions should cover such basic information as the date and location of the interview; full name; date and location of birth; previous places lived. You will probably want to include some of these other general questions:

How long have you been involved in this activity?

From whom did you learn?

Was this tradition within your family?

Who first exposed you to this type of music?

What role have books or the mass media played in learning music?

Who else do you know that I should talk to about this?

Communication   Once you have located someone of interest, a "straight-ahead" approach works best to assuage fears and suspicions or simply as a matter of courtesy to explain your research. You must clearly identify yourself and your own role as a student, then delineate the nature of your project and your interest in the music. This can be done quickly and efficiently, and such candor often places people at ease. Always tell this person who might have sent you or how you came to speak with them. Initial inquiries about a musical community frequently lead one to the head of an organization—barbershop quartet, folk music festival, musician's union, or gospel group. Such contacts may not immediately yield results, but a formal introduction helps to "sanction" or legitimize your work and will probably lead you in the right direction.

Interview   The **interview** itself is a critical part of fieldwork. A written list of questions or topics for discussion is often a good idea, but don't be dogmatic about using this list. They are merely guideposts; let the interview proceed into new or unexpected areas if they seem fruitful or interesting. Remember that your interviewees know more about the subject than do you, which is why you are seeking their knowledge and perspective. You may start with simple factual questions. As the situation relaxes and the questions flow more easily (hopefully they will), then move on to more complex issues. Use your intuition. If a subject appears too difficult or painful to answer, then move on.

A poorly conducted interview may be better than no interview at all, but if it is not going well, do not be afraid to take a break or suggest that you come back at a better time.

Rarely will you want to interview a person as soon as you meet them. It takes a while to ascertain their actual position within the musical community and what might be important to discuss. With an intricate or more detailed research project, you will probably find that a single interview is insufficient; you will often gain new insights or information with multiple interviews. You can also learn much by letting the interviewee lead the way and by your tacit encouragement—simply nodding your head or a quick verbal affirmation. Most people enjoy talking about themselves and providing their viewpoints.

Here are some other tips: Make sure of the correct spellings of names; ask if you are not sure. Clarify dates as precisely as possible; the summer of 1971 is more helpful than in the ''early 1970s.'' Ask for specific locations; Reno, Nevada, is more precise than ''somewhere out West.'' Ask about older photographs or written materials, such as a diary, that might stimulate their thoughts. If undertaken in the right spirit and within a nurturing context, the interview can yield an immense amount of valuable information. Rules, so goes the cliche, are meant to be broken. If you are unable to easily interview someone again, then it may be necessary to push certain issues or topics. You also might need to interview someone the first time you meet them. Use your intuition, good judgment, and you may profit by breaking the generally accepted maxims.

I wish that I had violated them on several instances. In the fall of 1979, while working within the community of black gospel quartet singers in Memphis, I conducted a brief interview with Elijah Jones. I knew only that Jones trained gospel quartets and that he was not in the best of health. Within two months, it became abundantly clear that he was one of the important keys to my entire project, so I called for an appointment. During the intervening eight weeks, Jones had died and his wife had thrown out all of his personal effects related to his fifty-year musical career—hundreds of photographs, placards, contracts, and newspaper clippings! My short initial interview is the only account of Jones's place in musical history. In 1970 I was searching with good success for down home blues singers in Albany, New York. I came across an elderly black man who played the fiddle and used to work with medicine shows, but he didn't interest me because he was not directly part of the blues tradition. Three years later, after I became more aware of African American string band music and had met several medicine show performers, I went back to visit this gentleman. I could not even recall his name, but I remembered the house. He, too, had passed away, another potential treasure of information irrevocably lost. These anecdotes are another way of reminding you of fieldwork's timeliness and that you can add to our knowledge of American music history, too.

Ethics   Much space has been devoted to the **ethics** and the morality of fieldwork in the literature of anthropology, folklore, and ethnomusicology. These questions become more problematic in cultures outside of our own, but American fieldwork is usually much less cloudy. Honesty and clarity of communication are the fundamental keys to confronting these occasionally sticky issues. There are sometimes legal issues regarding the ownership and rights of musical performances captured on tape and stored in an archive, but these are more often overshadowed by the researcher's extralegal responsibilities. Be sure to ask if the interviewee wishes to place restrictions, for whatever reasons, on the material.

Your responsibilities as an active and ethical field worker might some day include keeping folks informed about the release of recordings, giving them copies of your own work (if they desire), arranging for public performances, or gaining newspaper, television, or radio publicity for musicians within the larger community. This list implies a level of activity and commitment that may transcend your initial research project. Nonetheless, such work is often on the agenda of many ethnomusicologists, folklorists, and American music scholars. These scholars are taking an increasingly avocational role in their work, particularly in helping the music reach a larger audience or in underscoring the music's importance within its own community base. Others take a more benign, hands-off role, arguing that objectivity and distance must be maintained in order to preserve scholarly integrity. Each fieldwork situation comes with its own organic problems and rewards. Some lend themselves to public presentation or tend to place the field worker in the role of a social or musical advocate, while this may be wholly inappropriate in other contexts. Fieldwork within a musical community presents new opportunities, challenges, and research possibilities each time you go out. If field research were wholly predictable or too easy, then the thrill is gone.

The famed writer and folklorist Zora Neale Hurston collecting folk songs in Florida, circa 1936.
Library of Congress.

Fieldwork involves technology as well as the human touch. In our modern world, nearly everyone who formally interviews people—be it anthropologist, newspaper reporter, Internal Revenue Service field agent, or ethnomusicologist—takes electronic ''notes'' of the meeting. Field notes used to be handwritten, but tape or video recorders are becoming nearly ubiquitous. The advantages of using recorders nearly always outweigh the problems they present: cost or availability or the hassle of setting up the equipment.

If you are not able to or do not wish to tape-record an interview, then by all means do not rely solely upon your memory. The memories of human beings are often faulty and never 100 percent reliable. A small **notebook** is an invaluable tool, for it allows us to write down factual information, such as a name, address, or phone number, that would require tedious tracking down on the recorder. It can also be useful for quietly recording your own impressions regarding the situation, especially if the session includes or is a performance. These notes often prove to be important later because they can refresh your memory in recalling its ambiance, flavor, or details. In retrospect, trivial events sometimes loom more important as we become more intimately familiar with our subject. Notebooks also gather this information in one place, rather than written things on small slips of paper.

These days properly capturing an interview or a performance often equates to modern technology. In the late twentieth century, **cassette tape recorders** are easy to obtain and simple to use. Most people know how to use one already; if not, their accurate operation does not require an advanced degree. Contemporary cassette tape recorders rarely require more than loading the blank tape (don't forget to bring extra tapes and batteries), simultaneously pressing down the ''record'' and ''play'' buttons, and making certain that the built-in microphone is pointed in the proper direction. Some cassette machines permit the use of an external microphone. The use of an external microphone, particularly for recording music, is desirable because it nearly always yields superior results. Other hints for good results in field recordings: use Type II/High Position/Cr O2 tape, never buy cassette audio tapes longer than ninety minutes, and use the best possible tape recorder and microphone.

Videotape recorders have become more prevalent and decreasingly expensive since their introduction to the general public in the 1970s. For interviews their main value is as a visual record of the person. Videotaping interviews usually result in a static visual documentation with little use beyond archival storage. Musical performances inherently lend themselves more kindly to videotaping. They allow us to review a performance in a format more closely related to its natural context. Videotapes often capture nuances—gestures, posturing, performance styles—that are not always easy to remember, and permit the researcher to transcribe the words of songs, anointed speech, or other oral information.

Still **cameras** are also valuable tools and have been for many decades. They freeze images for us to savor in print, an important detail in itself. A

Nuts and Bolts of Fieldwork

35-mm camera is a versatile tool that can capture a simple, effective portrait of a musician or the broad panorama of a musical performance. They are easy to use, preferable in most fieldwork, and useful in a variety of situations. The results of a still camera can be utilized in a final class report, an exhibit of photographs, on the cover of a phonograph record, or to illustrate a magazine article. The questions what type of camera to use, black and white versus color film, and the merits of slides and print film relate to the specific ends of your project. Choosing the best medium for visual documentation is also part and parcel of your budget.

Written forms can also be useful for obtaining certain information. They facilitate the gathering of repetitive data and are particularly valuable for survey studies that sample many people. A survey form can also document basic factual information, such as names, instruments played, transmission of musical knowledge, and telephone numbers. A survey of musicians within a county, for example, is perhaps best undertaken using a form or questionnaire. Such a form can also supplement a series of more intensive interviews within a specific musical community.

Conducting fieldwork related to folk music is also partially determined by your goals. For a college student using this book as a text, the goal is probably handing in a final project for a class grade. You may wish to innovate and ask your instructor if a carefully edited videotape or audio documentary can be submitted as your class project. You might write a publishable article or mount a photographic exhibition in lieu of a term paper. Or you could simply submit photographs, taped interviews, or video material as an addendum to your written paper.

Those with grander ambitions (college student or otherwise) might want to think about wider dissemination along the lines that I've already suggested. If the musician or musical group is talented enough, there may be commercial interest in the music. You might approach a public radio station about a series of documentary programs related to regional music. The local art museum may be receptive to a series of concerts by the musicians with whom you are involved. The explosion of cable networks and local access channels could lead to the visual presentation of the music you have explored.

Final Thoughts

Fieldwork requires innovation, exploration, and a sense of ''carpe diem'' (seize the day). Students don't always want to be force-fed information, and such musical fieldwork underscores the fact that you are capable of adding to our body of knowledge through original efforts. Such work serves not only as an adjunct to library resources but as a vital pathway to primary resources that are all too often missing from our knowledge of American vernacular music. A well-executed field project is also challenging and fun because it reveals a musical world that has been awaiting discovery.

Key Figures and Terms

archives
cameras
cassette tape recorder
ethics
families
interview
musical communities
notebook
written forms

Books

Ives, Sandy. 1980. *The Tape-Recorded Interview: A Manual for Field Workers in Folklore and Oral History.* Knoxville: University of Tennessee Press. Although Ives does not focus on music, he carefully discusses fieldwork in light of oral histories that are documented with tape recorders, photographs, and field notes.

Jackson, Bruce. 1987. *Fieldwork.* Urbana: University of Illinois Press. A pragmatic and theoretical guide to fieldwork based on the author's own classroom and worldly experience, divided into four parts: ''Human Matters,'' ''Doing It,'' ''Mechanical Matters,'' and ''Ethics.''

Karples, Maude. 1958. *The Collecting of Folk Music and Other Ethnographic Material: A Manual for Field Workers.* London: International Folk Music Council and Royal Anthropological Institute. A somewhat pastoral but still valuable guide by one of the pioneering field collectors of ballads in the Appalachian mountains.

Titon, Jeff, ed. 1985. *Worlds of Music.* New York: Schirmer and Company. An introductory textbook on ethnomusicology that covers music from Africa, Eastern Europe, and the United States. It concludes with a fine chapter, ''Discovering and Documenting a World of Music,'' on musical fieldwork.

Selected Song Index

Index